Handbook of Professional Tour Management

Second Edition

OTHER BOOKS IN THE TRAVEL MANAGEMENT LIBRARY SERIES

GUIDE TO STARTING AND OPERATING A SUCCESSFUL
TRAVEL AGENCY, THIRD EDITION

GROUP TRAVEL OPERATIONS MANUAL

FOREIGN INDEPENDENT TOURS:
PLANNING, PRICING, AND PROCESSING

EFFECTIVE COMMUNICATIONS IN THE TRAVEL INDUSTRY

THE DICTIONARY OF HOSPITALITY, TRAVEL & TOURISM

YOUR CAREER IN TRAVEL, TOURISM, AND HOSPITALITY,
SECOND EDITION

TRAVEL AND TOURISM MARKETING TECHNIQUES,
SECOND EDITION

COMPLETE GUIDE TO TRAVEL AGENCY AUTOMATION,
SECOND EDITION

FINANCIAL MANAGEMENT FOR TRAVEL AGENCIES

TRAVEL AGENCY POLICIES AND PROCEDURES MANUAL

LEGAL ASPECTS OF TRAVEL AGENCY OPERATION,
SECOND EDITION

TRAVEL AGENCY GUIDE TO BUSINESS TRAVEL

LEGAL FORMS FOR TRAVEL AGENTS

BUDGETING FOR PROFIT AND MANAGING BY GOALS

GUIDE TO TRAVEL AGENCY SECURITY

Handbook of Professional Tour Management

Second Edition

Robert T. Reilly

Delmar Publishers Inc.®

Dedication: *To my wife, Jean,*
and the miles we've
shared together

Delmar Staff
Sponsoring Editor: Mark Huth
Developmental Editor: Lisa Reale
Project Editor: Carol Micheli
Production Coordinator: Larry Main
Design Coordinator: Susan Mathews
Art Director: John Lent

Printed in the United States of America
Published simultaneously in Canada
by Nelson Canada,
a division of The Thomson Corporation

10 9 8 7 6 5 4 3 2 1

Library of Congress Cataloging in Publication Data

Reilly, Robert T.
    Handbook of professional tour management / Robert T. Reilly.—
  2nd ed.
       p.   cm.
  Includes index.
  ISBN 0-8273-3525-3
    1. Tour guides (Persons) — Vocational guidance. I. Title.
2G154.7.R45,   1991   90-3555
910.4'068—dc20   CIP

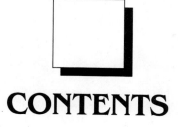

CONTENTS

INTRODUCTION

Tour management is one of the many specialized skills within the travel industry, requiring certain knowledge, skills, and personality traits to ensure success. This text, intended as a guide for both the beginner and the veteran, covers every aspect of tour management from the planning stages to the post-tour activities.

This second edition of *Handbook of Professional Tour Management* has been completely rewritten, with statistical materials updated, all new examples provided, and four new chapters added. The format has also been improved to allow easy access to the material.

Each chapter begins with a list of terms found in that particular section, plus a synopsis of things to be learned in that lesson. At the end of each chapter, the material is highlighted, and at least two practical case problems for students are appended.

Throughout the book, there are ample illustrations to help students understand the variety of printed forms and other helpful materials that are available.

An anecdotal approach is followed in the copy, providing actual instances of tour management in action rather than citing theory. Students will learn that tour management is work, that it takes careful planning, and that it requires attention to detail. They will understand how such tours are costed, how promoted, and how conducted. A special chapter on unusual and emergency situations is intended as preparation for the unexpected. Not only are overseas tours discussed, but also domestic touring and the challenge of inbound tourism.

While this volume emphasizes "how to" methods, there are also many sections dealing with trends in the industry, data on travel patterns, and reference aids for further study.

EACH SITUATION DIFFERENT

Tour management takes on-the-scene experience to be truly effective. Many of the lessons do not hit home until someone has weathered the problems and challenges inherent in conducting others through a domestic or foreign tour. That is why this text should be viewed as a launching pad and not a set of stone tablets.

Each new assembly of tour members, each new destination, each variant set of circumstances—these alter the planning and program, and the good tour conductor adjusts to the situation. People and environment affect the chemistry of any tour and the escort never knows everything that will be required until the trip begins. Sometimes you can go by the book; sometimes you must improvise.

Experienced tour managers develop their own methods of employing group psychology and their own solutions to emergencies. Consequently, there are differences of opinion on procedures, and multiple solutions to any set of challenges. The bottom line must always be: Does this action work, both for the present emergency and for the future of this and other tours?

This "handbook" borrows from personal experience, from the reported experience of others, from the results of surveys, and from information gleaned from a variety of publications. To this must be added the perceptions of the instructor and the discoveries of the student.

ACKNOWLEDGMENTS

The author is grateful to those who took time to respond to survey questions; to a pair of graduate assistants, Janey Ashley and John Fogarty, who assisted with research for the first edition; and to the educators who reviewed the book in manuscript form and made helpful suggestions. In the latter group, special mention should be made of Kate Engle, Travel Trade School, Littleton, CO; Barbara McKenna, Columbia College, Columbia, MD; Ron Bernthal, Sullivan County Community College, Loch Sheldrake, NY; Dr. Katharine S. Heiligmann, Salem State College, Salem, MA; Sherry Getz, Lancaster, PA; Daren Bloomquist, El Paso Community College, El Paso, TX; and Robert Black, National College, Albuquerque, NM. A word of gratitude is also due to two professionals: Laurence Stevens, author and free-lance tour escort, who contributed heavily to Chapter Eleven; and to Rebekah Vohaska, director of tourism for the Raleigh, North Carolina Convention and Visitors Bureau, who performed a similar function for Chapter Twelve. Finally, thanks to all those firms and individuals who granted permission for the use of visual materials; and to Lisa Reale, Delmar editor, who took over the production of this book when the original editor, Cynthia Haller, assumed another post.

ABOUT THE AUTHOR

One of three books Bob Reilly has written for Delmar, this new edition of *Handbook of Professional Tour Management* joins *Travel and Tourism Marketing Techniques* (also in its second edition) and a new volume, *Effective Communication in the Travel Industry.* These books are widely used in colleges, universities and travel schools.

Reilly's other ten books, fiction and non-fiction, cover a wide range of topics, from the Indian wars to a textbook in public relations. Many of his works have Irish themes, including *Come Along to Ireland,* which combines a tour through Ireland with glimpses of the country's history and culture; *Irish Saints;* and *Red Hugh, Prince of Donegal,* which was made into a Walt Disney film in 1966. Reilly's books have been translated into seven foreign languages. He has also published over seven hundred articles in a variety of national magazines (including *Travel Weekly, Travel Agent* and newspaper travel sections); writes poetry, scripts for films and TV shows; and has produced material for Fred Waring, Mike Douglas, Capitol Records, and others.

A native of Lowell, Massachusetts, the author now lives in Omaha, Nebraska, where, until recently, he taught courses in writing, advertising, public relations, and Irish Literature at the University of Nebraska at Omaha.

Reilly spent over thirty years in the advertising/public relations field prior to his fifteen years of university teaching. During these years he worked on travel accounts in Boston and Omaha, served as public relations director for Creighton University, and was a partner in a major advertising/public relations firm.

Bob and his wife, Jean (who recently retired as a national sales executive with Travel & Transport, one of the country's largest independent travel agencies), have led numerous tours, with Ireland and the British Isles ranking as their favorite territories. Reilly has also traveled widely in Europe, the South Pacific, and the United States—first as an infantryman in World War II, and later on film and speaking assignments.

Reilly, who holds degrees in English from Suffolk University and Boston University, is also accredited in public relations. He has been a consultant to the Ford Foundation and once lost a close race for Congress.

His honors include a number of foundation grants, plus: the Fonda-McGuire Best Actor Award at the Omaha Playhouse, Hall of Fame Award from the American College Public Relations Association, Professional of the Year Award by the Nebraska Chapter of the Public Relations Society of America, Midlands Journalist of the Year, Boss of the Year, the Jameson Hibernian Award, the Henderson Medal, and the Kayser Chair at the University of Nebraska at Omaha.

Reilly, now a professor emeritus from UNO, is listed in: *Who's Who in Advertising; Who's Who in Public Relations; Who's Who in the Midwest; Contemporary Authors; The Dictionary of British and American Writers; Dictionary of International Biograpy; The International Writers and Authors Who's Who,* and *Writers and Photographers Guide.*

Even with work in travel, teaching, writing, and public relations, the busy Reillys managed to raise ten children—all of whom also like to travel.

Origins and Outlook

LEARNING OBJECTIVES

After reading this chapter you will:

- ❏ Have a general idea about how group tours developed through the years
- ❏ Possess some statistics on travel habits today
- ❏ Understand many of the reasons people take tours
- ❏ Be able to distinguish among various types of tours
- ❏ Have information on methods of travel chosen by tour members
- ❏ Understand some of the **trends** that affect travel

KEY CONCEPTS

Affinity tour	Cruise ships	Motorcoach travel
Airline Deregulation Act of 1978	Destinations	Package tour
	Foreign Independent Travel (FIT)	Pilgrimages
Airlines		Tour operators
All-inclusive tour	Group travel	Travel agent
Ask Mr. Foster	Guidebooks	Trends
Charter tours	Incentive tour	Wholesaler
Thomas Cook	Leisure travel	

Although we credit **Thomas Cook** as the father of the modern tour, his 1841 train excursion within Britain was hardly the first time a group of travelers set off together to have fun.

The origin of the tour is impossible to pinpoint. It is conceivable that prehistoric people banded together for protection or companionship and journeyed to some nearby site that promised hunting or recreational opportunities. We know there were roads built in China a thousand years before the birth of Christ, and that the Phoenicians and the Greeks used their ships not only for trade and warfare but also for occasional pleasure cruises.

During the relatively serene times of the *Pax Romana,* citizens of ancient Rome who could afford vacations, might trek to distant towns or resort areas, sometimes hiring carriages or renting hillside villas. On some trips, local guides were supplied to point out the scenic and historic sights.

While military and commercial demands probably sparked much of the initial interest in travel, other motivations eventually took over. With the spread of Christianity, **pilgrimages** to European shrines or to Jerusalem came into vogue, as people traveled for penance or in quest of healing. Not everyone, of course, was seeking a religious experience. Some travelers enjoyed the opportunity for companionship, sightseeing, and even the musical interludes that were part of some journeys. There were even **package tours** to the Holy Land from Venice, on large galleys scheduled for departure every few months.

Each advance in travel created changes in other phases of the industry. Roads allowed for carriages, and carriages promoted the development of inns and hostels. In England, for example, you can chart many old inn locations according to distances travelers could make in a single day while on pilgrimage. With the increase in travel, more attention was paid to road beds, with the Scotsman, McAdam, developing his unique tar and pebble surface in the 19th century. Sailing ships, river steamers, and canal boats gave way to railroads, automobiles, and airplanes.

During the Elizabethan Era, the exploits of adventurers and navigators thrilled the common citizen and provoked a desire to travel. Tourist attractions, like the Louvre in Paris, were publicized. Students became a target market for trips as an adjunct to education, and small group excursions sprung from the economic necessity of sharing expensive coaches. Some forms of travel licenses made their appearance as forerunners of the passport and visa.

By the 18th century, pioneering forms of guidebooks were fairly common. So was The Grand Tour—for those who could afford it. As many as forty thousand Englishmen might journey to the Continent, reportedly to enhance their knowledge of the world. For many of them, this was also a chance to escape the strictures of their local environment, and they made the most of it. Men and women, from vagabond gentry to journal-carrying young ladies, took months, even years, to cover the itinerary of today's three-week excursion: France, Germany, Switzerland, Spain, Italy, Greece, the Low Countries. Oliver Goldsmith and Lord Byron and Maria Edgeworth and Lord Chesterfield and James Boswell each made the trip. Their resultant letters, diaries, and memoirs commented on the various locales, even panning some amenities and praising others.

THOMAS COOK AND THE ADVENT OF MODERN TOURS

Tourism grew significantly in the last century. Both the Romantic and the Victorian periods had an impact on interests and on destinations. When

Thomas Cook arrived on the scene, the stage was already set for the expansion of the industry.

Cook, secretary of the Leicester Temperance Society in England, began chartering trains to take himself and his colleagues to distant temperance meetings. He had to sell the railroads on reserving seat space, which, in those days, was also related to the booking of hotel rooms the railroads owned. Cook personally escorted these groups, also providing printed itineraries, passenger lists, travel brochures, and vouchers to expedite payment to suppliers. As the idea caught on, Cook expanded his horizons, adding tours through Europe, a cruise on the Nile, and luxury rail journeys into exotic India. His son, John, organized tours through newly-opened Yellowstone Park and Civil War battlefields. In 1872, the senior Cook scored another first by personally circling the globe. It took him 222 days.

Others followed Cook's lead. Thomas Bennett, a former British consul, entered the travel agency business in 1850, and became a forerunner of Eugene Fodor and Temple Fielding by publishing standard **guidebooks.** On this side of the ocean, in 1888, Ward G. Foster inaugurated a chain of travel agencies, starting in St. Augustine, Florida. His **"Ask Mr. Foster"** slogan and name sprang from the habit of nearby hoteliers sending inquisitive visitors to Foster's gift and book shop when they had questions about train and cruise ship schedules. "Ask Mr. Foster," they advised, since Foster made a hobby of knowing this information. The book business gradually became a very successful travel business, and Foster concluded that women made better travel agents than did men. Today, in the six hundred Ask Mr. Foster Travel offices, with annual billings of $2.2 billion, some 90% of the employees are women.

Fig. 1-1. Train travel, once a major tour option, has been replaced as the leader by air travel.

TOURISM IN AMERICA

One might follow the progress of tourism in the United States by tracing routes and carriers. At first the waterways, like the Mississippi and the Missouri, were the passageways for travelers, starting as far back as the turn of the 19th century, when flat boats and keel boats transported explorers, soldiers, adventurers, and settlers. Steam navigation began in the second decade of the last century, with some of the river boats featuring grand salons and dining to rival the best inns. Hidden snags and sandbars, boiler explosions and occasional collisions added a bit of danger to what was otherwise a slow but pleasant journey.

Eventually, steamships made the Atlantic crossing, beating the time of earlier sailing craft but still taking the better part of a month. In 1838, Cunard Lines set about reducing that trip to little more than two weeks.

On land, the wagon trains familiar to western devotees were common in the 1840's and 1850's, spurred by the promise of free land or the gold of California. Stagecoaches provided an alternate means of cross-country travel before giving way to railroads. In the early years of rail travel, cities east of the Mississippi were linked, but by 1869, the system spanned the nation. Five years earlier, George Pullman had made the journey more comfortable with the introduction of the sleeping car.

Train excursions, the forerunner of more sophisticated group tours, were common even as the automobile came into vogue during this century. With the increase in the range of the motor car, roads were improved, inns became hotels, and hotels sired the notion of motels.

After the First World War, the building of airports moved rapidly, and, in the 1920's, **airlines** like United, Western, and Pan Am had their origins. As with other forms of travel, air passage was for the wealthy alone in the beginning. Eventually, it came within reach of the middle class. By the advent of the Second World War, there were thirty-four domestic airlines in service. However, transatlantic treks remained the province of the liners until the late 1950's when jet travel supplanted the seagoing ships. Cruising became more localized, surrendering the European touring market to the airlines.

Although tourism may have its roots in the past, it could be argued that modern tourism is a product of the past thirty years. In some countries, tourism became a significant contributor to the economy. Even within the United States, a variety of destinations were built up, ranging from the development of the National Park system to the creation of such man-made wonders as Disneyland and Disney World. The role of the **travel agent** became broader after World War II when they were able to book airline traffic and develop or tie into tours here and overseas.

NAMES AND SOURCES

There are many familiar names in the travel industry. One is Arthur Tauck who began his travel tour career over thirty years ago and is still highly visible as an active participant. Tauck specializes in adventure travel, and two of his sons and one daughter help manage Tauck Tours.

People like Cook, Bennett, and Tauck all share some similar characteristics. They are attuned to the interests of the public; they are innovative; they work hard; and they pay attention to details. These traits are worth emulation by anyone in the tour business.

Today there are more than twenty thousand travel agencies in the United States, and their total sales volume exceeds $20 billion. Virtually all of them are in the tour business, directly or indirectly, although some embrace rather narrow specialties. Even where business travel or independent travel constitutes the major share of an agency's income, tours remain the symbol of the industry. Tours incorporate color and romance, economy and companionship, profits and problems.

One recent phenomenon is the publishing of new editions of out-of-print travel books, volumes that gathered dust on bookshelves until this second shot at stardom. Isabella Bird's *A Lady's Life in the Rocky Mountains* has been around in paperback for several years, but Mungo Park's *Travels into the Interior of Africa,* an 18th century journal, was reborn in 1988; and *Travels in Asia and Africa* by Ibn Battúta, written in the 14th century, was also republished this decade.

U.S. News & World Report (April 4, 1988) attributes this trend to "a travel boom that has tourists seeking historical and practical insights, part nostalgic longing for the days of mystery and excitement that the jumbo jet has displaced."

More recent books that provide details of a previous era include: *Tourism in History* by Maxine Feifer (Stein and Day, 1985); *Tourists, Travelers and Pilgrims* by Geoffrey Hindley (Hutchinson, 1983); *Travelers,* by Horace Sutton (William Morrow, 1980); *A Book of Travellers' Tales,* assembled by Eric Newby (Penguin, 1985); *Take a Spare Truss (Tips for Nineteenth Century Travellers)* compiled by Simon Brett (Elm Tree Books, 1983); *Cook's Tours* by Edmund Swinglehurst (Blandford Press, 1982); *Writers and Pilgrims* by Donald Howard (University of California Press, 1980); *The Grand Days of Travel* by Charles Owen (Webb & Bower, 1979); *Beyond the Grand Tour* by Hugh Tregaskis (Ascent Books, 1979); and *A Book of Sea Journeys,* compiled by Ludovic Kennedy (Collins, 1981).

Also worth reading are *Medieval Travelers* by Margaret Wade Labarge (Norton, 1982); *Lord Curzon: Travels with a Superior Person,* by Peter King

(Sedgwick & Jackson, 1985); *Masters of Early Travel Photography* by Ranier Fabian and Hans-Christian Adam (Vendome, 1981); and *History of Travel* by Winfried Loschburg (Hippocrene Books, 1979).

Reading these volumes tells us how much has changed and how little has changed.

WHY DO PEOPLE TAKE TOURS— OR AGENCIES HANDLE THEM?

Despite the current emphasis on individuality, on doing one's own thing, and despite the media's frenetic image of escorted tours, package tours remain a staple of the travel business.

People travel for a variety of reasons. Business dictates much of American travel. According to the U.S. Travel Data Center in Washington, D.C., the number of business trips totaling more than two hundred miles increased more

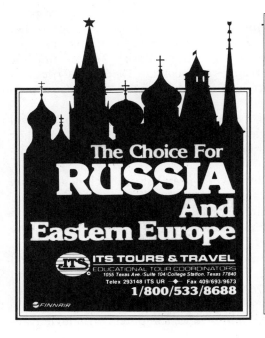

Fig. 1-2. Advertising appeals may be broad, embracing an entire country; or narrow, focusing on one special interest. (Courtesy of ITS Tours and Travel and Classic Tours International)

than a third in the 1980's, despite an economic slump and lean and mean budgeting. Some executives and salespersons become addicted to travel, boarding planes at every opportunity, driven by ambition, curiosity, even the pleasures of independence.

Other urgent matters may prompt travelers—illness of relatives, for example, or weddings of friends, or additional journeys where fun may be only a by-product.

Vacation travel is characterized by people whose aim is adventure, a climate shift, education, shopping, an antidote to boredom, a chance to meet people of the opposite sex, and even the experience of exotic foods. This form of recreation is popular. When asked what they would do if they received a $10,000 windfall, a majority of people surveyed by a travel trade association said they would spend it on a vacation. Next in line was a down payment on a home.

But why do certain individuals opt for tours?

Some people couldn't make it any other way. They can't cope on their own with the demands of an alternate culture, either because of physical problems or their own innate fears. Others, while perfectly competent to travel on their own, want to be free of hassles, want to have others attend to the details. Some are after companionship, the comfort of sharing experiences with others.

Tours provide a considerable amount of relief and safety, especially in countries where language and customs are unfamilar, or the political situation volatile. Members feel more secure with an experienced tour manager or leader. Other motives for **group travel** are economy of time and money, the assurance of decent accommodations, freedom from the responsibilities of driving, the educational aspects of intelligent commentary, and the availability of some destinations only through the tour route.

For travel agencies, tours, while not without headaches and financial risk offer an opportunity for wider profit margins. Agencies can build in profit in addition to commissions. Tours also enhance the image of an agency and give them something exciting to advertise. They lend a universal appeal. Tours also offer agencies a chance to develop leadership experience. Larger agencies will organize several annual tours of their own, along with the attractions available from **tour operators,** while smaller agencies may have to be content with a diet of pre-packed trips.

CLASSIFYING TOURS

Like tourists, tours also come in various shapes and sizes, with a choice of titles and themes. One constant, as far as the prospective tourist is concerned, is that you generally pay for what you get. Those making comparisons among tours should always study relative components, like the class of hotel, number and type of meals, fees paid, attractions included, and other details.

Some of the **generic categories** of tours are these:

❏ A **package tour** is one that combines at least two tour elements—like transportation and accommodations—but which normally offers at least hotels, land transportation, some meals, and some entertainment features. An **all-inclusive tour** connotes the coverage of all costs in the unit price, except for personal items.
❏ Not as prevalent today as in the past, an **affinity tour** describes a group with a common identity—like membership in a club or organization.
❏ To achieve lower fares, a **charter group** is sometimes assembled, and equipment is chartered from a **wholesaler,** carrier or tour operator.
❏ A **group tour** refers to any assemblage of travelers, whether using **chartered** or scheduled carrier, who are organized for the purpose of touring.

There are also consolidated tours, where individuals team up with already-established tours; **incentive tours,** where the trip is a reward for some achievement, like corporate sales; **FIT (Foreign Independent Travel),** which may embrace an individual traveling alone on a specific prepared itinerary or a group operating out of a single travel agency or an itinerary developed in conjunction with a wholesaler, and other variations, from convention extensions to business/pleasure excursions.

CLASSIFYING TOURS BY PURPOSE AND DESTINATION

Tours may also be classified according to purpose or destination. Some of these classifications are educational, ethnic, scenic, photographic, religious, historical, agricultural, scientific, health-related, recreational, romantic, or cultural. Their themes are limited only by the organizer's imagination and by the existence of a target audience.

Some tour destinations are traditional—places like the Caribbean, Hawaii, and Las Vegas, for example. While their advertising campaign themes may differ from year to year, their overall messages remain the same. They're selling a climate, an exotic setting, or the glitter of bright lights.

Other tour packages are more unique. The Chocolate Lover's Tour of Switzerland, for example; or a haunted journey through Transylvania; a deluxe visit to French wineries; a trip built around the Olympics; a chance to trace ancestors; an opportunity to gamble; theatre tours of London or New York; a week in Paris for the introduction of the new fashions; golf and tennis vacations; seasonal treks to cherry-blossom Washington, powder-packed Aspen, or tradition-oriented Dublin. The list is extensive.

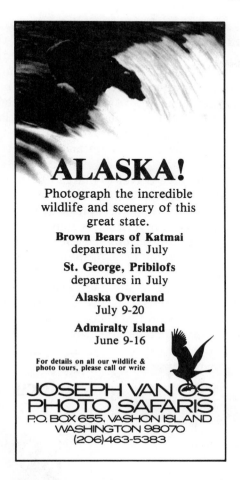

Fig. 1-3. Hobbies are used as a travel incentive. (Courtesy of Joseph Van Os Photo Safaris)

Some Current Tour Ideas:

❑ Battlefield Tours, Inc. specializes in returning veterans to the sites of their earlier service years. A typical two week trip might involve visits to combat areas, museums, and other familiar landmarks, for example: "A sensational DUGOUT EVENING," one brochure advertises. "We'll recreate the entertainment, nostalgia, song and comradeship of World War II." There could be receptions in the towns fought for or liberated by the veterans, plus sightseeing tours that include regular tourist attractions.

❏ Honeymoon packages are always popular. While nearly every hotel, resort and cruise line offers these vacations, not all of them make them part of a tour. Statistics show that nearly 98% of newlyweds plan a honeymoon, book early, and don't cancel. Over $2 billion a year is spent on honeymoons, with half of the married couples traveling within the continental United States. Better than two-thirds of the honeymooners book through a travel agent. Although places like Disneyland, Hawaii, Los Angeles, and New York continue to be popular with newlyweds, there are new sites appearing each year, embracing everything from river cruises to adventure treks.

❏ Photographic safaris involve travel to places like India, Death Valley, Iceland, Navajo Land, Fiji, Alaska, Honduras, and the Cayman Islands. There are visits to Canada to photograph polar bears and trips to Rwanda and Zaire to focus on gorillas. A tour to Quebec allows you to shoot the annual caribou migration, and some riverboat excursions have a western history theme. Some photographic tours include workshops and private instruction.

❏ The "adventure" traveler has many more choices today. From 5–10 percent of the nation's travel market is adventure travel, amounting to over $13 billion annually. Between two thousand and three thousand recognized tour operators specialize in adventure, and these are often escorted

Fig. 1-4. Adventure remains a prime attraction for tourists. (Courtesy of Questers Worldwide Nature Tours and SafariWorld)

by or accompanied by scientists, museum directors, or other experts. Climbing Mount Kilimanjaro is one option. So are cruises in Alaska's inland waters, aboard smaller, shallower craft that can reach destinations out of reach of the larger ships. There are llama trips, bicycle journeys, hunting expeditions. Observers consider this one of the growth areas in travel.

❏ Some adventure tours, like those of Rainbow Adventures, cater to women. Since many women already take vacations without their husbands, these trips tap into a market where the average age is fifty and the appeal is to avoid the couples-oriented standard tour. Destinations like New Zealand, the Galapagos Islands, Nepal, Kashmir, and Africa are featured, along with mountain and wilderness trips in the United States. Women, who account for one third of the skier population, are also the focus of special appeals, with ski seminars taught by women and length of stay options geared to the working women.

❏ Walking tours vary from leisurely-paced city tours to more difficult treks along mountain trails. Resorts are now promoting tennis under the lights. The Smithsonian lists over fifty travel options, from walks through England's Cotswolds or Lake District, to Danube cruises, "Scotland by Train," voyages through Hudson Bay, a horseback ride along the Lewis and Clark Trail, research expeditions in London and Washington, D.C., plus raft trips, sailing on a tall ship, and even a weekend in Brooklyn.

❏ In recent years, much has been made of the senior citizen market for travel. Discounts for air and hotels are common and more attention is being paid to special needs of older travelers, like appropriate lighting and tour guides who speak up. Within this vast market—people whose income is above average and whose time-away-from-home is twice that of those under fifty—there are sub-categories based on health, interests, and other factors. Christmas is a strong season for mature travelers and the sunnier areas are predictably popular.

❏ Tour operators are excited about the potential of the 19-million-member Hispanic market, with $130 billion to spend. In the decade of the 80's, the hispanic population grew about 35 percent. Many of them retained their Spanish language, making advertising copy writers more sensitive and bilingual. Almost every ethnic group has some specific tour directed to them. Carlson Companies Inc. (which owns Radisson Hotels and Ask Mr. Foster) makes a specialty of travel to Scandinavia. Several east coast cities tout packages to Ireland for St. Patrick's Day.

❏ A Florida travel agency does 85 percent of its business with labor union members. Casino Caravans caters to the "low roller" gambling market. There's an International Gay Travel Association and at least a dozen operators who serve this clientele.

❏   With affluence came an increase in the amount of luxury travel. No longer the province of the very rich, luxury travel may be within the means of those earning $40,000-$60,000 a year. Destinations go beyond the spas of Europe or the French Riviera. There are deluxe hotels in many places in the world. Some places, once unavailable to tourists, are now open. Of course, there are some tours which remain the province of the rich and famous. Travel pros calculate that luxury travel starts at $400-$500 a day—but it can be far more than that. One three-week Grand Tour of Europe, featuring the ultimate in accommodations, cost $750,000 per person!

Destinations

Besides viewing travel in terms of purpose and audience, one can also look at **destinations.** Places like Australia sometimes achieve sudden popularity, thanks to films, television, and other inducements. A tight economy or fear of terrorists can cause Americans to examine their own country, while the short-lived gasoline shortage encouraged other tourists to try Europe. While a number of resorts gear themselves for family stays, others counter with "adults only" campaigns. Despite unrest, Israel continues as a part of Christmas in Jerusalem tours. Deep sea fishing and scuba diving off the Great Barrier Reef has become a winter getaway spot. Calgary plugs its colorful "Stampede." One art museum builds its trip on collections in the Low Countries. See "Outback China" advises one brochure. Another reminds travelers that *glasnost* makes Russia and Eastern Europe more attractive than ever. Manor House tours to Great Britain are growing. Country homes in New Zealand have similar potential for tourists. Experts are advising travelers that now is the best time to see Africa, thanks to cost and an enhanced consciousness of tourist needs.

A recent poll in *Tour & Travel News* (August, 1988) listed top destinations for American travelers in this order: Canada, Mexico, Great Britain, the Bahamas, France, Puerto Rico, Italy, Virgin Islands, West Germany, Spain, Switzerland, Hong Kong, Jamaica, Netherland Antilles, Dominican Republic, Bermuda, Netherlands, Ireland, Israel, and Australia. Eastern Europe may now become an emerging destination. Within this country, Los Angeles leads as a tourist favorite, with nearly fifty million visitors annually, followed by Anaheim, San Diego, Atlantic City, Washington, New York, and Las Vegas. Myrtle Beach, Cape Cod, and Orlando precede Boston, the Poconos, New Orleans, Philadelphia, Nashville, Reno, Miami, and Hawaii. Lake Tahoe, Clearwater, Fort Lauderdale, Williamsburg, San Francisco, Tampa, Virginia Beach, the Ozarks, and the Catskills complete the list.

Special Tours

Some companies specialize in tours for the handicapped, carefully selecting hotels designed for easy access, or offering escorts who speak sign language. There are other firms whose specialty is the city tour, centering on convention-eers or the casual traveler, plus incentive marketers whose business is built on pleasing corporate high achievers.

All of these packages have their own organizational and promotional tech-niques, their own vocabulary, and their own problems. The job of the tour manager varies with each set of circumstances, and few men or women would be adept at handling every specialty.

MODES OF TRAVEL

Air

Travel by air is the predominant method of tourist travel, both in terms of passenger miles logged and money spent. Even though there has been a re-newed emphasis on **leisurely travel,** most tourists prefer to spend the time at their destination, rather than in getting there.

This is a volatile industry. In recent years, the **Airline Deregulation Act of 1978** created a spate of fare wars, pleasing many passengers but causing problems for travel agents. Hundreds of different fares for a single destination made bookings a nightmare, even with the invaluable aid of the computer. Flight delays continued to surface, with some major airlines showing a third of their flights late at least fifteen minutes. Travelers were also upset about lost luggage and about overbooking. Safety then became a prime concern, prompted by acts of terrorism and by the structural failure of certain types of aircraft. From the domestic airline viewpoint, the increased costs of operation, plus the effect of competition, has made it more difficult to show a profit. A number of airlines have gone out of business; others have merged or succumbed to a buyout.

Still, millions of American tourists start their journeys by air. Charters, especially to standard resort areas, remain a factor, but regularly scheduled air is more common, more reliable, and much more flexible. For larger groups, airlines may offer dollar incentives, and will provide other assistance, from block seating to personal attention at gateway cities.

Some airlines also promote their own tour packages, a fact that may annoy some tour operators. A few airlines even have their own in-house tour divi-sions, but most use tour operators to market either part or all of he tours that bear their names.

Airlines may also be part of a combination of arrangements, from "Fly-Drive" packages, to links with cruise lines, to offerings pairing an airline with a hotel chain owned by the parent company. Many tour operator brochures cite land costs only, leaving the air arrangements to the individuals, while others list a price combining air and land.

Current airline leaders in this country, in terms of scheduled passengers, are American, Delta, and United. Among foreign airlines serving American passengers, British Airways leads, followed by Japan Air Lines, Lufthansa, Alitalia, and Air France.

Motorcoach, Cruise Lines and Trains

Motorcoach travel is another major source of tourist transportation. In the United States there are ski trips, fall foliage tours, cross-country runs and other vacations that rely solely on the bus. Many are built around themes, like Old West Trail trips and Civil War Battlefields. Abroad, the air passenger is likely to be met at the airport by a bus which will become the sightseeing outlet. Europabus, the motorcoach system of European railways, has shown a dramatic increase in American passengers over the last few years. Most of these trips are seven days or shorter and visit as many as sixteen different countries. Some tour operators own their own fleet of coaches while others rent them as needed, relying on allied firms to service them. Among the many bus companies vying for the tourist dollar there are government-backed giants and small independents. The coaches may range from compact units seating less than twenty to much larger coaches equipped with toilet facilities and a built-in bar.

Fig. 1-5. Cruises have increased in popularity. (Courtesy of Questers Worldwide Nature Tours)

Cruise ships have been riding high in the waves for more than a decade. They promote a more relaxing way to travel, plus excellent cuisine, ample recreation, and a hint of romance. Their destinations may be insular, such as the Greek Islands or the inland passage to Alaska, or they may be extended round-the-world cruises with numerous ports of call. The average age of cruise passengers is getting younger, with women outnumbering men. Yet, despite the quadrupling of the number of cruise patrons in the last twenty years, more than 90 percent of Americans have never taken a cruise. So the market potential remains vast. If this 90 percent did opt for a cruise, the Caribbean would be their first choice, followed by the Mexican Riviera and Acapulco. While there are over eighty cruise lines worldwide, Americans are likely to use about one-fourth of that number, with a choice of over seventy ships. Besides the more familiar ocean destinations, there are also river cruises, from paddleboats on the Mississippi to steamers plying tropical rivers. As with airlines, there are also bargains on cruise tours, with special fares available to seniors, to those traveling off season, and to those willing to settle for the less desirable accommodations.

Trains were once *the* carrier. In Europe they remain a strong contender for vacationers, but their role has diminished in the United States. There are some attractive train packages using items like the Eurailpass or, for foreign visitors to our shores, the Discover America pass. Trains also have their own form of romance, particularly lines like the Orient Express, the Flying Scotsman, Trans-Siberian Railway or the rapid Osaka-Tokyo run. It used to be like that in the United States. Amtrack continues to offer some exciting rides, although the scheduling is much more restricted. For train enthusiasts, there are tours on several continents. The Orient Express continues to operate, or you can see Great Britain from inside those coaches made famous by British films. In the last several years, train travel through the Scottish Highlands has been promoted. Steam, diesel, and electric trains are featured in Trains Unlimited Tours through five Latin American countries. Some of the equipment used is over a century old and still functioning. Short trips on vintage rail coaches are spotted throughout the United States, often through scenic areas, or tied to meals and excursions. A new trip arranged by Sentimental Rail Journeys combines air and train on round trips from Los Angeles to New Orleans. Rides on a stern-wheeler and trolley are part of this nostalgia tour.

Other forms of transportation include everything from private touring cars and limousines to tramp steamers and hydrofoils. Some tours offer self-drive options, rented bicycles, camera caravans, rickshaws, and rafts. It all depends on the territory, the time, and the amount of adventure one wants and can afford.

TRENDS IN TOURING

For reasons cited earlier, tours will always be a popular option. Other methods of travel have their own advantages, but those who want a more worry-free trip at a fair price will always gravitate toward the tour. Still, tour conditions vary and new destinations, new combinations of attractions enter the scene.

A University of Massachusetts professor, speaking to that state's conference on tourism in 1988, declared that tourism would be the biggest business in the world by the turn of the century. He predicted an increase in foreign visitors to the United States, a decrease in leisure time of Americans, an increase in the number of shorter vacations, a decrease in touring-type trips versus primary destination stays, more careful planning, and continued demand for "back-to-nature and personally enriching" vacations.

Surveys also show that Americans remain a comparatively fertile market for overseas tours—if they can be motivated to try them. From 1985-1988, only one out of every five Americans traveled outside the U.S. mainland. Of this number, only a small fraction went to Europe or Asia, with the others landing in Hawaii, Canada, Mexico, Alaska, or the Caribbean. Even so, in terms of Europe, the overall figures are up nearly 20 percent every year in the 80's—except for 1986 when fears of terrorism sabotaged European travel. When one compared money spent by Americans abroad with money spent here by foreign visitors, the United States showed an $8.5 billion deficit. This trend, however, is showing signs of reversal.

Although business travel has accelerated, vacation travel still accounts for the majority of visitors overseas and to Mexico, and tourists from the east and west coast are the most frequent travelers. Even though hectic tour schedules are satirized in the media, more than half of American travelers focus on a single destination. Mexico has been experiencing a travel boom in recent years, thanks to the mixed blessing of the plunging value of the peso. Over two billion tourist dollars have been poured into the Mexican economy, mainly by Americans.

It is well to remember, however, that, as a percentage of all bookings by travel agents, domestic travel has increased sharply while international travel has declined steadily. More people are traveling, but more of these tourists favor seeing America first.

Other Trends:

❏   Big increase in the family tour market, especially in ski and cruise areas.

❏ July is the most popular vacation month for Americans, but the destination would also have an effect on what time of year the traveler chose.

❏ New York tops the list of states in budgeted funds for travel promotion, followed by Illinois, Hawaii, Pennsylvania, and Texas. New York's expenditures in 1988 topped $20 million.

❏ More government interest in tourism as an economic factor and as a means of promoting peace is seen in attempts to establish a panel or commission at the federal level.

❏ Frequent flyer programs, now mirrored in various hotel chain plans, will find echoes in other tourist areas.

❏ A population decline in the United States affects the travel industry directly, both in terms of employee availability and the market for tourism. Much of this market will be older, making service even more important.

❏ If the American economy slows down, as some predict, the impact will be felt immediately on both business and leisure travel.

❏ Backed by an increasing number of complaints from travel agencies and tour operators, some congressmen are investigating the taxing of non-profit groups who sponsor their own tours, sometimes undercutting the established tour firms.

❏ Airline computer reservations systems are much more global than in the past and will eventually be interconnected with airlines on other continents. Other innovations include access to video scenes of various destinations, plus video maps of any area.

❏ Corporate travel managers are increasing as business travel becomes more complicated, and their presence will also affect some phases of tour marketing.

❏ More attention is being paid to alternative tourist markets, those specialized groups who are attracted by health-related trips (hiking, adventure, cycling, spas), camping, education (e.g., the study of other cultures and political systems), off-season trips for retired persons and many other travel segments within the overall market.

❏ Some observers note an increase in travel fraud, from falsely advertised tours and inflated prices, to outright theft by phony operations.

❏ The relative strength of the dollar is considered to be the major factor affecting travel to Europe. More favorable exchange rates may boost travel to Eastern Europe. This same decline in the dollar vis-a-vis other currencies means an increase in foreign visitors to the United States.

There are many more people who swear by tours than swear at them. So the destinations may vary, the length of stay will differ, the prices may fluctuate, but the advantages of group touring will always find acceptance.

❏ *CHAPTER HIGHLIGHTS*

❏   Traveling as a group can be traced back to ancient times, but Thomas Cook is considered the father of the modern tour.

❏   The sales volume of the twenty thousand travel agencies in the United States exceeds $20 billion.

❏   People travel for adventure, climate, education, shopping, companionship, dining, and a host of other reasons.

❏   People take tours to avoid hassles, to share the experience, or because they prefer not to travel alone. Cost may also be a factor.

❏   Generic types of tours include: package tours, all-inclusive tours, affinity tours, charter tours, and incentive tours.

❏   Tour packages are built around destinations, themes, events, exercise, adventure, even nostalgia.

❏   Travel by air predominates in terms of carriers, with motorcoaches, cruise ships, even trains, getting a share of the tourist market.

❏   Tourism will continue to be big business, but various trends will influence frequency, destinations, types, length, and other elements.

❏ *CASE PROBLEMS*

1. A friend of yours is planning to spend two weeks in France and Germany. This friend is forty-five years old, has never been to these countries before, and speaks no foreign languages. He plans to travel independently, convinced this will be more enjoyable, and that he will have no problems finding people who speak English. While you do not disagree with this assessment, you would like to get him to at least consider a tour. What arguments would you use? Be specific.

2. Take each tour type listed in this chapter and, using the travel publications and travel sections available in your libraries, find an example of each type. Identify the ways that each is similar or dissimilar.

PLANNING THE TOUR

LEARNING OBJECTIVES

After reading this chapter you will be able to:

- ❏ Identify different appeals offered by different types of tours
- ❏ Sensibly establish dates for a tour, weighing a variety of factors which influence the decision
- ❏ Understand how an **itinerary** is organized and what goes into it
- ❏ Compare the relative merits of using a tour operator versus building your own tour
- ❏ Understand the elements necessary to secure information to help with the itinerary
- ❏ Identify the actions necessary to register the tour

KEY CONCEPTS

Balance in itinerary	Hotel availability and location	Rest and luncheon stops
Budget		Scheduling
Client preferences	Hotel ratings	Shopping
Dates of tour	IT number	Special events
Dollar devaluation	Itinerary	Tour operator
Emotional appeal	Optional entertainment	Tour package
Free time	Pacing	Weather
Geography	Profit	Wholesaler

A lot of work goes into planning a tour. Even when the proposed route is familiar and even when the entire package is a repeat of previous years, there are still many details to review. Besides that, tour operators like to keep their offerings fresh, so they may add new destinations or new wrinkles to old destinations.

19

Political unrest and terrorism inhibit travel to some previously popular areas. Even a reputation for being too crowded or too expensive restricts leisure travel.

Certain locales appear in brochures and on travel agency racks year after year. Scan the offerings of the major tour companies and you'll note little change annually. European countries are toured individually or in combination. There are Rhine and Nile cruises. African safaris still find an audience. But there are also changes. After Hurricane Hugo in 1989, the Caribbean braced for some drop in tourism, while Australia emerged as a favored new destination.

VARIETY SELLS

Though standard tours may continue to thrive, today's traveler may be looking for something extra, something different, something to experience and later talk about. When Bhutan opened its borders to tourism a decade ago, a number of travel agencies discovered a ready list of clients eager to be first. When tours to China became a reality, one agent booked his quota in twenty-four hours—with one piece of direct mail, a few phone calls, and word of mouth. With the dramatic changes in the political status of Eastern Europe, a whole new set of tours can be anticipated.

A Chicago **tour operator** pioneered out-of-the-way spots by introducing air-conditioned vehicles to East Africa and by augmenting the few hotels on Easter Island with facilities in private homes. The same operator takes visitors to Patagonia, pre-Incan villages in northern Argentina, New Guinea, Marrakech, and Tierra del Fuego. In recent years, thanks to a reported spiritual apparition, a tiny Yugoslavian village plays host to thousands of vistors annually, even though bereft of hotel facilities.

Obviously, not everyone is a candidate for every tour, but the variety of available itineraries reminds us that there are many places to see and things to do that lie outside of the typical **tour package.** Observe how some tours are promoted today. Sex and romance are promised to a generation accustomed to a freer lifestyle. Tours may cater openly to these **emotions,** featuring everything from heart-shaped, mirrored tubs in the Poconos, to bikini beaches in the Caribbean. This, too, will pass, and we're already seeing an emphasis on attracting more mature travelers, even to exotic locations.

Some tours concentrate on unusual facets: a hydrofoil cruise, a treehouse sojourn beside a jungle oasis, or a three-day trail ride into the Superstition Mountains, with perhaps a glimpse of the Lost Dutchman's Mine. People-to-people itineraries reflect the interest in closer ties with other nations. Folk music and art have replaced the heavier cultural attractions. Many tours are built around sports and hobbies, capitalizing on the pursuits spawned by dozens of special circulation magazines.

What the careful planner must do is try to anticipate future demands of a fickle public: roots, mythology, a new love boat? There are unlimited possibilities. Some are risky; some are dynamite. But caution is the key. Just because a tour of the villages of Britain and Ireland seems charming to the experienced tour operator doesn't mean a price-conscious, first-time tourist will want to forego the glamor of London, Dublin, or Edinburgh. Consider the drawbacks before announcing a tour. Hindsight is accurate—but expensive.

Planning varies with the company and with the nature of the tour. Large tour operators have many of their itineraries set from year to year. Their planning may revolve more around the **availability of hotels,** certain events, and their own escorts. They may also focus on promotion and on a new tour or two. Smaller tour operators also repeat their winners. Travel agencies get involved in planning only when they produce their own tour or some variation of an established trip.

But, even with the traditionally popular tours, someone had to establish the initial program, and someone has to keep the diversion fresh and exciting. For purposes of this chapter, let's assume we are starting from the beginning and have to pull together the diverse elements that go into any tour.

PLANNING AS A SCIENCE

Planning for any activity normally includes four steps: a searching look backwards, a wide look around, a deep look inside, and a thoughtful look ahead.

The planner should know what success this firm has had with similar tours in the past, and should be familiar with any problems that occurred. Considerations like the difficulty of promotion, or the potential for **profit** must be analyzed, based on previous experience. In-house files and reports are a primary source, but conversations with experienced colleagues must be added. The planner learns from what has been attempted.

Next, tour planners broaden their scope, tuning into the experience of other tour managers or operators, gleaning what they can from extant publications or trade journals, soliciting help from tourist bureaus or government sources, and reading thoroughly the numerous sources recommended throughout this text. Just about everything has been tried elsewhere, and only the fool ignores the lessons available from travel counterparts.

Once past and similar experiences have been tapped, the planner must dig deeper within the proposed program. Live the tour day by day, looking objectively at scheduling, events, and other variables. Where are the potential problems? Where are the opportunities?

After these three steps have been accomplished, it's time to take a long look ahead. How will this tour impact on the goals of the agency or operator? How will it affect other plans and other people? Is there potential for long range negative results?

Throughout these planning phases, the tour manager takes advantage of any research materials that will assist intelligent deliberation, and will probably consult with others to secure their input. Ultimately, a consensus emerges, a decision is reached, and the program is launched. However, wise planners monitor every step along the way, remaining alert for any difficulties and adjusting immediately to handle them. If the total plan seems unworkable after the scrutiny suggested above, the tour planner returns to step one, initiates a fresh plan, and again sifts through the four phases.

Among the specific considerations are those listed on the following pages.

Setting the Dates

Intelligent **scheduling** is a combination of factors, some of them uncertain. You're looking for the right place, at the right time, for the right people, and at the right price. To come up with this combination, several items require consideration. Setting the **best dates** depends on these.

Client Preferences

Depending upon your assessment of the potential clients, you'll want to ascertain good and bad times for these groups. Teachers are best bets for summer or Christmas forays; parents with small children will opt for vacation months; CPAs find it hard to get away during tax time; farmers are stronger targets in winter than in spring or fall; office staffers still lean more heavily toward traditional vacation times; students are limited by class schedules; most people want to be home for important holidays, like Christmas and Yom Kippur. The trick is to pinpoint your audience and then consider all aspects of their lifestyle and occupational routines, trying to capitalize on the most propitious seasons.

Weather

Weather becomes a factor in two ways. Travelers often flee their most unpleasant seasons for better weather, trading winter for summer, summer for spring. In addition, planners have to consider weather at the destinations. South Seas resorts have their dry and rainy seasons; England has its raw and mild months. Then, too, some people are chasing snow while others are eluding it. Guidebooks provide some general help in ascertaining likely weather conditions, but the charts of average temperatures give only broad parameters.

Since most of these statistics are provided by tourist-conscious staffs, they tend to accentuate the positive. The best course is to discuss your routing with a reliable **wholesaler** or with someone who knows the country in question. They'll tell you if the temperature registers fifty but feels like thirty, and if the annual average rainfall is concentrated in one month. No one can guarantee good weather, but, unless you're bent on skiing or attending a string of plays, you shouldn't deliberately head into a foul climate.

Special Events

Occasionally the tourist may want to avoid **special events.** Such events mean crowds and higher prices, causing delays and cramped facilities. If tour planners have customers who want the spirit of Mardi Gras, then they work toward it; if not, they should book earlier or later.

Most of the time, however, you want to build in some activities that add lustre and entertainment to the tour: Oktoberfest; the Galway Bay Oyster Festival; the opera season in Milan; the Kentucky Derby; Oberammergau's Passion Play, which occurs every 10 years. Most nations supply brochures listing principal events of the year and chambers of commerce or tourist bureaus dispatch similar materials for cities. Wholesalers are also a source of such information.

These events must be balanced against considerations such as time, cost, crowds, and the appropriateness for certain target audiences. An elderly group won't be partial to a rock concert at London's Palladium, nor will avid shoppers vote for two days at the London Horse Show. For a two week tour, a few major attractions, a few minor ones, and a handful of options should more than suffice.

Planners should also consider adding events of their own, ones that may have even more appeal than the routine tourist attractions. A local professor might lecture to the group, or a local musical group stage a concert, or an amateur theater troupe present a play. The planner should be familiar with this talent and may arrange to pay them on some equitable basis.

Cost

Although price is usually factored in after the variables are known, overall consideration of cost may disclose some initial handicaps. Some tours, though attractive, come with such high price tags that they don't prove feasible for the clientele of certain agencies. In any tour, planners must begin by assuming there must be profit in the venture. This is true of prepackaged trips as well as specially designed ones. If profit seems doubtful, a more marketable tour might be selected.

Weather

Gilbraltar: Temperate, with winter rains. Average temperature range from 45–60 degrees in February, to 68–84 degrees in August.

Afganistan: Temperatures in the capital of Kabul range from 18–36 degrees in January to 60–90 degrees in July.

Poland: Continental climate, with an average high temperature of 32 degrees in January, and an average high temperature of 75 degrees in July.

CITY	TEMPERATURES (F) (NOV)		Precip (Inches)	Precip (Days)
	Min	Max		
Beijing	50	30	.4	1
London	49	40	2.5	6
Moscow	36	27	1.7	15
Paris	50	41	2.0	15
Rome	61	48	4.4	11
Tokyo	60	42	3.8	7

*   *   *   *   *

Average Temperatures (in degrees Fahrenheit) *in Ireland*

	Jan Feb	March April	May June	July Aug	Sept Oct	Nov Dec
Day	47	51	61	66	59	49
Night	35	36	45	51	44	37

Fig. 2-1. Climatic conditions are reported in a variety of publications, ranging from daily lists to weather maps.

Costing a tour is covered in the next chapter, but it's well to realize here that, besides considering the price of the trip, the tour planner should also look at what the tour member will get for the American dollar at a foreign destination. In 1988, the dollar dropped approximately 20 percent against major foreign currencies, and this may deter travelers for whom **shopping** is a prime incentive.

There are ways travelers may cut down on their personal expenses while on tour, and the tour manager may make them aware of these savings hints. Changing their dollars at a bank rather than in hotels, travel bureaus, or stores is good advice; and so is the suggestion to shop shrewdly, tip according to local custom (noting whether the service charge is already included in their meal costs), and to carefully choose the restaurants and entertainment sources they select to fill their **free time.**

European countries, conscious of the reaction against the **dollar's decline,** have also promoted a variety of bargains for the cautious traveler. A week in Rome, for example, might be as low as $250; and a London operator tosses in an evening at the theater and a Thames cruise.

Space

Travel agents know—or should know—when certain areas are crowded and likely to be overbooked. Expect rooms to be tight during the Cannes Film Festival, the New Orleans Mardi Gras, a bowl game, or a coronation. If planning time is short, it's foolish to embark on tours into these areas, particularly if tourists are expecting Class A accommodations. Better to shift the scene or wait until next year.

The wise agency also keeps its regular clientele in mind and won't risk losing them because of marginal housing. Recently, when a football team was chosen to represent its state in one of the minor bowl games, many of that state's travel agencies backed off on selling tours because they felt the host city's accommodations were inadequate. Rather than field a ton of complaints, they preferred not to market the tours.

Leader's Availability

If the tour leader is a part-time or occasional leader—a minister, teacher, TV personality—he or she may not be available except at certain periods. Tours have to be built around their leader's schedules. Even with the professional tour leader, other commitments have to be considered.

The Agency's Own Operation

Travel agencies rarely have time on their hands; they are busy shops. As a result, any new enterprise has to be weighed against the agency's ability to deliver. You can't tie up a small staff on a single tour; neither can you add so many tours that you don't properly promote any of them. Moderation is the watchword. Handle whatever can be efficiently, profitably managed, and give only cursory attention to the others.

Even where the bulk of the promotion and selling, and all of the details, are being handled by a national or international tour operator, the small agency still has to ask itself just how much time and money it can spend on behalf of that tour, or how cluttered it wishes to make the office sales program.

ORGANIZING THE ITINERARY

In terms of volume, most tours are prepackaged. They have lavish folders and drop-in ad copy. Their itineraries and tour personnel are set. All the travel agency has to do is review the literature and, perhaps, request some alterations. Then come promotion and selling. Agencies which put together their own tours have many more problems.

Distance and Geography

Americans have never been too proficient in destination **geography.** Even travel agents, who should be global experts, frequently fall short in this category. In making itineraries, however, there is little margin for error. This means you must calculate distances with accuracy, considering all facets of the journey and terrain, and not merely counting inches in an atlas. If you schedule a six-hour bus trip between Point A and Point B, arriving in time for a meal and a play, are you certain you can make it? Are you able to work in all the scheduled stops en route? Are you putting too much of a burden on passengers by asking them to travel long distances in a single day?

Wholesalers may be helpful here, reminding you when you have overextended yourself, but they are not infallible either. Many of them stick to

May 28, 1991	Leave New York for Scotland
May 29	Arrive Prestwick, clear Customs, take coach to Edinburgh for beginning of 3 night stay at the Mount Royal Hotel on Princess Street with a great view of Edinburgh Castle. Day and evening on own.
May 30	Morning tour of historic Edinburgh (Castle, Holyrood Palace, Royal Mile, St. Giles Cathedral etc.). Afternoon free. Banquet at Dalhousie Castle.
May 31	Day tour of the Trossachs, Loch Katrine, Rob Roy and Lady of the Lake Country, Stirling Castle, battlefield of Bannockburn, along the shores of Loch Lomond. Scottish meal this evening, featuring the haggis!
June 1	North to lovely Inverness, with stops at a whisky distillery, the Pitlochry Dam, Highland Museum at Kingussie, sports center at Aviemore, and the battlefield of Culloden, where the last battle fought on British soil was waged. Overnight at the Caledonian Hotel . Evening bagpipe concert.
June 2	Early departure for tour of Loch Ness, Fort Augustus, the

Fig. 2-2. The initial itinerary sent to prospects may be condensed, and it's this form that usually finds its way into the brochure. On departure, however, or at the initial destination, the tour member may be supplied with a more detailed itinerary.

traditional routes, and deviations from this pattern may be both unfamiliar and unwelcome to them. You should know yourself just what can be comfortably covered within the time frame you've set. Travel agents may also be expected to know geographically-related information, like whether the water in a particular spot is warm enough for swimming, or which locale on tour might be the best departure point for a traveller who wants to spend a day checking on relatives.

On a bus tour crossing the Great Plains you may cover five hundred miles or more in a day (although you have to stay within driving limits imposed by touring companies or the Interstate Commerce Commission), but this is no guideline for Europe, Africa, Asia, or Latin America. Sightseeing opportunities and road conditions enter in. Two hundred and fifty miles can be a very long day, especially if rest and lunch stops are factored in.

Keep in mind, too, the limitations of passenger endurance. You have to **"pace" a tour** so that travelers are not continually pushed, tired, and irritable. They'll fall asleep during an evening play, and they'll get sick more easily. The tour should be reasonable, with longer and shorter touring days, plus some two- or three-night stopovers. New York City runs an ad campaign encouraging American tourists to spend an extra night or two in the city when heading to or returning from Europe. People destined for the Far East may opt for an extra day in California. When visiting a foreign country, it's refreshing to have the occasional longer hotel stay, allowing time to catch up on rest or laundry. Fight for what you want with wholesalers, but don't be stubborn about it. If they say you can't drive to Perth in four hours, they're probably right.

Special Events versus Free Time

Tourists generally expect some activities to be provided for them. They don't want to spend three successive nights in an outlying village with nothing to do but count the limited traffic.

On the other hand, you can overdo the entertainment bit. Some tours have people going all the time. Everybody out for shuffleboard! Tonight, *The Merchant of Venice.* Is everyone set for the moonlight picnic? Sitting at home, drafting the itinerary, it looks great to have all those salable attractions but, on the scene, you can watch travelers wilt. They'd appreciate a quiet night in their hotels or a chance to see and do something on their own.

Balance, that's the program. Combine a few group sessions with some free time options: perhaps a play, a pub crawl, a tour of a winery, a ballet, a lake cruise, native dancing, all tempered with suggestions for **individual entertainment.**

Some people love night life, others loathe it. Some want to experience exotic cuisine while their companions are more timorous. Giving them **personal choices** takes away the feeling of being constantly herded, and it also frees up the tour manager for record keeping, making contacts, or catching up on rest. Experience dictates some procedures. The average age of the group may be a consideration. Although there are exceptions, a younger crowd is more likely to want to party later than an older group. Regardless of age, every tour member wants some restful or optional evenings. Experience also tells you to blend entertainment features that are popular with those that may be a bit highbrow. Ballet is for some folks; folk dancing is for others; still others want to attend a contemporary disco.

Shopping

Even though sightseeing will be nominated as the chief pleasure in traveling, only the foolish planner will neglect to schedule ample shopping time in the right places. This means organizing arrivals and departures properly, avoiding holidays and half-holidays, and building in sufficient free time so that bargain hunters don't feel hurried.

Certain cities are a must for shopping, but even on tours to destinations where there are no world-famous marts, tour members still want an opportunity to find something special for themselves, or collect souvenirs, or purchase gifts for family and friends. On a two-week tour, travelers will expect a couple of good shopping days along with periodic short stops.

There are even "Born-to-Shop Tours" for the serious shopper. Many are short and combine a little sightseeing with the shopping sprees. Icelandair gives those looking for woolen sweaters, coats, and blankets a package that includes RT air, first class hotels, and some meals, all in Reykjavik. Abercrombie and Kent takes travelers on a luxury shopping tour of Bangkok and Hong Kong. Ireland offers a weekend shopping excursion. Even New York, Los Angeles, and Honolulu are in on the act. Prices for these trips may range anywhere from a few hundred dollars for the domestic splurges to over $2500 for the more expensive foreign trips. *Born to Shop* guides help you find these programs.

Location of Accommodations

Tour planners can't always secure the kind of accommodations they seek in exactly the right places. The earlier you book, the better selection you have. You end up with Class A hotels instead of places with limited private baths, diminutive towels, a handful of coat hangers, poor lighting, and no in-house restaurant. When you have to change locales in order to get satisfactory facilities, this may mean that some entertainment will have to be shifted or eliminated, and that some tours may require alteration.

The hotels should be spaced so there is some equity in the miles traveled daily, but also with an eye toward the attractions available in that area. Staying outside a big city may be more economical and restful, but it also

Fig. 2-3. Scheduling air and booking hotels must be done very early in the planning stages.

curtails the opportunities for shopping, browsing, sampling restaurants on one's own, and other pleasures.

There are a variety of **rating services** for hotels—some of them helpful, some of them not. The top-of-the-line hotels which are rated AA or given four stars may be reliable bets, but once you get into the "B" or two-star categories, there could be a wide range of facilities. Finding a guide you can trust is one method of selecting hotels. Relying on the advice of the tour operator or travel agent is another. You may wish to check with someone who has stayed at the facility. Best of all, of course, would be a visit to the accommodation yourself. Travel agent familiarization trips attempt to accomplish this. These "FAM" trips usually allow agents to visit several hotels a day. Naturally, the hotel manager will try to have the place in A-one condition, but the experienced agent can still spot flaws or problems.

Do the doors have dead-bolts on them for privacy and safety? What does the furniture look like? Is there a shower or tub or both? Television set? How efficiently does the desk operate? How are the food and service in the restaurant?

Managing a tour is enough work without adding the problem of dealing with dissatisfied tourists in a sub-par hotel. Be sure you know what you are getting and be sure the location is apt. Above all, keep your information current. A change in management, purpose, or economic status can make a major difference in improvement or deterioration.

Tour members—especially first-time travelers—should be made aware of the different hotel standards in different foreign countries.

Rest and Luncheon Stops

These may not appear on the itinerary or in the brochures, but tour managers have to think about them. Even in the more economically developed and highly-populated countries, adequate rest stops and lunch stops are not automatic. Some forethought is required. Obviously, certain tours and regions demand more caution than others but, in plotting the itinerary, it is always wise to have some notion of the most likely locales for breaks. Experienced drivers and couriers are helpful in making these decisions; and there are domestic guidebooks which catalogue restaurants, including some fast food chains available at interstate exits.

The size of the tour group has some impact on this decision, and as does the nature of the stops. In larger places, for example, where there are many dining choices, the tour manager may mention some options, give the passengers a couple of hours, and remind them where to meet the coach when finished eating. In locales with fewer options, reservations may have to be made.

Keep in mind that the luncheon stop can also be a pleasant experience, something the tour members will view as a bonus, rather than a necessary and uninspiring meal.

While American cross-country buses are normally equipped with rest rooms, foreign touring coaches may not be. You can't remain on the road too long without providing an opportunity for a rest stop—generally every two hours. Even when the vehicle has a built-in toilet, rest stops should be encouraged.

Tour Members

Solid itineraries also reflect the makeup of the tour members. Youth hostels or their equivalent are no lodgings for older citizens. Camera bugs will demand more frequent stops; a wine tasting tour can't be rushed; a farm tour must be loosely programmed.

Handicapped persons may have to forego some of the more rigorous excursions, although one travel agent recalls a man in a wheelchair who inched himself up the myriad steps of Blarney Castle, sans chair. The more elderly are susceptible to fatigue and shouldn't be expected to tolerate a succession of long

DATE	*PLACE*	*ITINERARY* *Page 3*
June 2	Ballachulish Call ahead to Windermere Check on Burns reading	Breakfast at the Caledonian Hotel. Depart at 9:00 a.m. for a tour of the west shore of Loch Ness, a stop in Fort Augustus, and then on to the spectacular Eilean Donan Castle, before heading "over the sea to Skye" via ferry. After a short tour of this island, off again by ferry to Mallaig, followed by a visit to Glenfinnan where Bonnie Prince Charlie gathered the clans. Through Fort William and along Loch Linnhe to Ballachulish. Check into the beautifully-sited *Ballachulish Hotel* (one of the oldest inns in Britain), with striking views of the loch, and of Ben Nevis, the highest mountain in the British Isles. Dinner at the hotel, followed by an evening with a Scottish folk singer in the lounge.
June 3	Ayr Call Jan MacDougall in Glasgow 45792	Breakfast at Ballachulish Hotel. Leave at 9:30 a.m. for morning stop at the massacre site in eerie Glencoe, then south via the Bridge of Orchy, along the west shore of Loch Lomond, lunch in Glasgow, then on to Bobbie Burns country. Visit Burns' home and tour other sites made famous by the poet. Check in at *Ayr Caledonian Hotel.* Dinner at the hotel, followed by readings from the work of Robert Burns by a local actor.
June 4	Windermere	Breakfast at the Caledonian Hotel. Through Dumfries to Gretna Green for a look at marriage "over the anvil," and then on to Carlisle,

Fig. 2-4. Tour members are supplied with a detailed itinerary, and the tour manager may use this to make notes on things to be done at each stop.

driving days. Minor illnesses are more common in this age group and things like meals are more important to senior citizens—particularly the experience of sharing a meal together. On the other hand, many tour leaders swear that the older person is the best traveler.

As much as possible, try to match the tour to the target audience, or you make certain those who plan to travel with you are aware of the conditions, and of responsibilities toward fellow passengers. Prospects may inquire, "Is there going to be a lot of walking?" or "Do you allow smoking on the bus?" or "Will I be the only single person going on the trip?" You must answer these questions honestly.

Other Sources of Itinerary Information

Reading old itineraries, or wholesaler itineraries, or package itineraries, or competitive itineraries provides clues to forming an independent travel schedule. Materials may be garnered from tourist boards, carriers, hotels, embassies, libraries, guidebooks, international travel groups, and the comments of agency personnel and veteran travelers. Familiarization tours are supposed to be used for this purpose, to gather details on destinations. Conscientious agents file reports when they return, establishing a catalogue of materials for their colleagues to draw from.

The most dangerous thing to do is guess about any aspect of the itinerary, or to act on sketchy information. Before anything is offered to the public, the tour planners should satisfy themselves that the item is as represented and that it meets all the tour standards.

Budget

Some economies may be practiced in routing, accommodations, and activities without cheapening the overall tour. A play by an amateur group in an intimate setting may be more fun than occupying poor seats at an indifferent performance in a crowded metropolis. Some perfectly good hotels may offer reduced rates while building their reputations. And everyone knows that the highest prices don't always indicate the best restaurants.

From the agency's and the leader's viewpoint, however, it would be a mistake to try to go second class. Stateside tourists think this sounds exciting and democratic but, when exposed to such conditions after a long day of touring, the passengers—except, perhaps, for students—get surly. Life becomes much easier for those in charge when complaints are minimal.

Every item you add to the itinerary affects the **budget:** A medieval banquet—add $30 per person; tickets to a London play—add at least another $30.

Then there are yacht cruises, private limousine tours, pub crawls, elegant oriental cuisine. All of these items increase the tour price. Some are necessary; others may not be. The successful planner balances appeal against the effect on the total cost of the package. If the group tour is an incentive package for some institution or industry, the budget may have to include a number of things outside the normal tour expenses. Special parties or meetings may be called for, plus speakers, equipment, gifts and other items. These costs, too, should be added to the budget.

COSTING THE TOUR

The following chapter covers the subject of "costing" a tour. Touring, while recreation for the traveler, is obviously a business for the tour operator or agency. So planners have to anticipate and program for profit. This includes an item-by-item pricing, but it also involves knowing how many tour members it will take to make a trip feasible, knowing the deadlines for payment to hotels and airlines, and keeping in mind both inflation and the condition of the dollar.

Determining the most convenient and cost-efficient air fares is a science of its own. There are hundreds of ways to figure air fares to Europe, and these fluctuate from time to time, driven by competition and by an airline's own economic situation. The client must be considered first, before any special travel agency or tour operator relationships with specific airlines. The air package must be both sensible as a schedule and reasonable as an expense item.

To help with the profit line, many agencies have added articles that can be marketed along with the trip. Insurance is a major one, including health and accident policies, luggage protection, and a guarantee against cancellation of the tour. Maps and guidebooks, foreign currency packets, luggage, adapter plugs and converters, and even emergency services are potential sales items. Many travel agencies own Minportrait cameras from Polaroid and use these to supply color passport photos. Of course, the travel agency will also book cars and hotels for tour members who want to extend the trip on their own.

Chapter 3 goes into the subject in more detail.

Using a Wholesaler

It is possible, of course, to deal directly with carriers, hotels, restaurants, and entertainment centers, if you are a travel agency—but this is a lot of work and

IRONIC THAT A COUNTRY SO RICH IN HISTORY AND CULTURE WOULD COST SO LITTLE TO VISIT.

low price. The Highland Games of Scotland and the Morris Dancing of England also go for a song.

Conveniently, the most refreshing way to break up a day of sightseeing in Britain is in an authentic British pub.

There you'll find the same refreshment, renewal, and inspiration (not to mention bitter, lager, and stout) that the British have been enjoying for a thousand years.

While you're at it, get a "Ploughman's lunch" for less than five dollars.

In Britain, you can truly become part of the fabric of another culture, without paying a King's ransom. All you need is a hearty appetite for the sights Britain has to offer.

And a slight thirst may be helpful as well.

For more information, just contact Dept. TW at one of the British Tourist Authority offices listed below.

Britain
BRITISH TOURIST AUTHORITY

It's been said that a vacation in Britain is priceless. This is true in many respects.

For example a visit to the Houses of Parliament, St. Paul's Cathedral or the British Museum costs absolutely nothing.

Nor does a village cricket match, the Changing of the Guard at Buckingham Palace, a walk around the medieval walls of York or any one of hundreds of museums, galleries, and exhibits that are completely free.

However, it should be pointed out that many of Britain's most popular attractions are — if not completely priceless — quite reasonable.

A Great British Heritage Pass opens the gates to over 600 castles, stately homes and gardens for one

625 N. Michigan Avenue, Chicago, IL 60611
Tel: (312) 787-0490

Cedar Maple Plaza, Suite 210,
2305 Cedar Springs Road, Dallas, TX 75201
Tel: (214) 720-4040

Room 450, 350 South Figueroa Street,
Los Angeles, CA 90071
Tel: (213) 628-3525

40 West 57th Street, NY, NY 10019-4001
Tel: (212) 581-4700

Fig. 2-5. Tourism bureaus provide overall appeals which may then be supported by specific tour operators for specific tours. (Courtesy of British Tourist Authority)

rarely worth the effort. It's like baking from scratch compared with using some available packaged goods. Often the packaged tour, booked through a wholesaler, means less effort, more profit, and a lower cost to the traveler.

As a matter of fact, almost every tour relies on wholesaler input, expertise, and labor. When the travel agency manager wants to put a tour together, he or she submits a rough itinerary to several wholesalers for their bids. As in any business, getting several bids is sound policy and enables you to make a selection based on cost, services, and company reputation.

Certain wholesalers have near-impeccable reputations and the agency is pretty safe in dealing with them. Periodically, *Travel/Holiday* magazine polls its readers regarding their choices of carriers, hotels, tour companies, and other travel suppliers. *International Travel News* also supplies hints. Names like Maupintour, Cartan, American Express, Olson, and Thomas Cook, appear with regularity among the firms specializing in package tours. But there are also hundreds of smaller tour companies vying for the tourist dollar.

It makes sense to examine some of the smaller wholesalers about whom good reports circulate. Anxious for new business, they may extend themselves even more than the giants. Larger wholesalers do have more clout, at least in most situations, and they may have stronger claims on specific hotels or chains. But they can also get careless and sloppy and lose the personal touch they once possessed. They may also be more intractable than the smaller company. One considers these things when reviewing bids, augmenting that information with personal calls or letters, plus a check of clients or references.

Reading the travel trade journals helps the planner stay current, especially about changes in things like air service, hotels, and the rise and fall of the dollar. For situations which are more volatile, the tour manager should stay abreast of the news, especially those sources that report in depth, and , as a final check, may wish to contact the appropriate government agencies in Washington to secure an update. There are also special travel services, like the Fuller-Weissmann Report (810 St. William Ave., Round Rock, TX 78681) which focuses on a different country each issue. The diverse information includes tips on when to go, what to do and see, how to get there, where to stay, what to eat, cultural do's and don'ts, shopping, health advisories, and even a sample itinerary. If there is political unrest, as we witnessed in the Philippines in late 1989, this report provides facts along with hotline numbers to check for updates. A list of holidays may be added, plus details on credit card acceptance, and even some basic phonetic conversation helps. Some of this information may be stored in computer reservation systems.

Planning a tour shouldn't involve guesswork; it should concern itself with gathering all available information, including personal visits, and then sensibly scheduling the proposed trip.

NEW

West Country Explorer

Sample Somerset, Devon, Cornwall, the Isle of Wight and more.
4 days from $298, or 8 days from $549, plus air fare.

● OVERNIGHT STAY
✈ EN ROUTE
— MOTORCOACH

ENGLISH CHANNEL

This new Top Value tour wraps up the city sophistication of London with the traditional towns of Western England in a single eight-day vacation. If you have already seen Stratford and Windsor, it is the perfect next step, acquainting you with a region of England full of legends and tales. And if you're already familiar with the capital and wish to join only the four-day countryside portion of this itinerary, you're welcome to do so.

As the private motorcoach travels westward, you'll discover sparkling waters around the Isle of Wight and the delectable sparkle of Devonshire cider – dangerously strong and delicious! Visit Glastonbury Abbey and see the grassy grave of King Arthur, visit the Roman spa of Bath and see the steaming hot springs of the god Sul. You'll take a guided tour of the Fleet Air Arm Museum in Somerset and explore Queen Victoria's summer home, Osborne House. See the rocky tors of Dartmoor and the giant stones of Avebury and Stonehenge. It's a magical British vacation, available at a very down-to-earth price.

TWA FEATURES

ACCOMMODATION First Class and Superior Tourist Class hotels throughout. All rooms have private bath or shower. Service charges, tips and taxes are included.

MEALS Continental breakfast with juice daily in London; full breakfast elsewhere. Dinners in Lynton, Exeter and Winchester.

SIGHTSEEING In all major cities, including admission and guide fees.

ON TOUR Land transportation by luxury, private motorcoach and ferries. Round-trip transfers between airport, quays and hotels, including baggage handling. Hostess service in London; experienced Tour Director on tour.

BEFORE DEPARTURE TWA Getaway flight bag, tour documents and boarding passes, plus TWA's exclusive Getaway Tour Warranty.

BONUS HIGHLIGHTS

LONDON ★ Tour of Westminster Abbey.

AVEBURY ★ Walk amidst the ancient stones.

BATH ★ Guided tour of the Roman baths beneath the Georgian Pump Room.

GLASTONBURY ★ Visit to the ruined abbey containing King Arthur's grave.

DARTMOOR ★ Scenic drive across the windswept heathlands.

PLYMOUTH ★ See famous Plymouth Hoe and the Mayflower Steps.

YEOVILTON ★ See antique airplanes in the Fleet Air Arm Museum.

STONEHENGE ★ Visit the circle of stones.

WINCHESTER ★ Visit to the massive Norman cathedral.

ISLE OF WIGHT ★ Guided tour of Queen Victoria's Osborne House.

Please note: accommodation, features and highlights in London are only included on the 8-day tour (no. ITOTW17870).

YOUR 8-DAY TOUR BEGINS HERE

Day 1 **USA – En Route** Enjoy cordial TWA service on the way to Great Britain.

Day 2 **London, England** Your Travellers Hostess meets you at London's airport and eases the transfer to the hotel in town. Balance of the day free; perhaps listen to the Evensong service at St. Martin-in-the-Fields church, right on Trafalgar Square.

Day 3 **London** See the sights this morning, rolling down the Mall to Buckingham Palace then around Parliament Square to see Big Ben and visit Westminster Abbey. You could devote free time to studying the monarchy in the Tower of London and Kensington Palace, or gaze at royal portraits in the impressive National Gallery. This evening, treat yourself to a West End musical or a showboat dinner on the Thames.

YOUR 4-DAY TOUR BEGINS HERE

Day 4 **London – Bath – Glastonbury – Lynton** Let the bustle of London retreat as we set off by luxury motorcoach for the countryside. Our first stop is the stone circle of Avebury, pre-dating even Stonehenge, and its mysterious man-made neighbor, Silbury Hill. Next, to Bath, where you can lunch after a guided tour of the spa complex. In the afternoon, we visit Glastonbury to see the ruined abbey and the thorn-tree legend says was planted by Joseph of Arimathea. Now we turn to the coast, passing Dunster Castle on the way to our hotel in Lynton, where dinner awaits.

Day 5 **Lynton – Looe – Plymouth – Exeter** We leave Exmoor today and enter the county of cream teas – Devon, with rich rolling farmland on all sides. On Dartmoor, the tors and heath are more forbidding! We break for lunch in Looe, one of the prettiest villages on the Cornish coast. Now to Plymouth. We'll see The Hoe, a broad grassy field, where Sir Francis Drake waited for the Armada to attack, and the Mayflower Steps, embarkation point of the Pilgrims, during a brief sightseeing tour. Again skirting Dartmoor, we come to Exeter and our hotel, where dinner is included tonight.

Day 6 **Exeter – Yeovilton – Stonehenge – Salisbury – Winchester** From the university center of Exeter, we go to Yeovilton for a visit to the Fleet Air Arm Museum, an interesting collection of antique airplanes. Then we visit Stonehenge before crossing Salisbury Plain to stop in Salisbury, where there's time to see the beautiful cathedral. Later, we'll visit the cathedral of Winchester, the severe Norman architecture contrasting with the green lawns and gardens all around, then dine at the hotel.

Day 7 **Winchester – New Forest – Isle of Wight – Portsmouth – London** We drive beneath the huge trees of the New Forest on our way to the ferry for the Isle of Wight, a chalky island separating the Solent from the English Channel. There, we'll visit the superbly preserved Osborne House, Queen Victoria's favorite summer home until 1901. Leaving the island at Fishbourne, we ferry to Portsmouth, home port of the Royal Navy. In late afternoon, we return to London.

Day 8 **London – USA** To the airport this morning for the TWA flight home, arriving later today.

Fig. 2-6. Printed itineraries may compose a single brochure or, as in this instance, may be part of a larger book of tours. (Courtesy of Transworld Airlines Inc.)

MOUNT ROYAL
TWA Tour Category: Top Value
Unbeatable location right on Princes Street, facing the Castle and in walking distance of the Royal Mile. Full meals are served in the restaurant, while snacks are available until late in the bar. The comfortably furnished rooms are centrally heated, all with TV.

POST HOUSE
TWA Tour Category: Budget
This attractive contemporary hotel is located just out of city center, next to the Zoo and gardens. Ravelston restaurant has panoramic views of the Pentland Hills, and there is an informal coffee shop and bar. Guest rooms are well-furnished, with color TV, in-house movies and tea/coffee-making tray.

EXETER
ROUGEMONT
TWA Tour Category: Top Value
A tastefully and traditionally styled Victorian hotel, situated close to the remains of Rougemont Castle, and within a short walk of the center of town. This superior tourist class hotel has its own restaurant and bars, even a ballroom. The guest rooms are well-modernized, with color TV.

GALWAY
ARDILAUN HOUSE
TWA Tour Category: First Class
Once a private home, this 1840's mansion is now a secluded first class hotel. It is set in extensive grounds on Taylor's Hill, about one mile from Galway town center. There are bright, spacious lounges, a bar and dining room. Guest rooms are unusually large, with central heating and TV in all.

GALWAY RYAN
TWA Tour Category: Top Value
A first class hotel situated about a mile from the heart of Galway. Hotel amenities include a lounge, bars and restaurant. Bedrooms are comfortably furnished, with direct-dial phone, color TV and central heating.

GLASGOW
HOSPITALITY INN
TWA Tour Category: First Class and Top Value
A comfortable, modern hotel rated "5 Crowns" by the Scottish Tourist Board, set in the heart of Glasgow. Hotel has a large restaurant and cocktail lounge plus a garden café. Spacious guest rooms are centrally heated and air-conditioned, featuring color TV with movies and tea/coffee-making facilities.

BEDROOM IN THE ALPHA ROYALE

MOAT HOUSE INTERNATIONAL, HARROGATE

HARROGATE
MOAT HOUSE INTERNATIONAL
TWA Tour Category: Top Value
Modern high-rise hotel within walking distance of the parks and pretty streets of the spa center of Harrogate. Spacious lounges, a bar and restaurant, all with friendly, efficient service. Pleasant guest rooms all have trouser press, hair dryer, tea/coffee-making facilities and color TV with in-house movies.

HULL
STAKIS PARAGON
TWA Tour Category: Budget
Contemporary hotel in the center of the Hull business and shopping area, a short walk from the historic docks. There is a large buffet restaurant with carvery service and a lounge bar. Bedrooms are compact but well-furnished, with hair dryer, hospitality tray, color TV and tea/coffee-making facilities.

KILLARNEY
KILLARNEY RYAN
TWA Tour Category: Top Value
The lakes and the village of Killarney are just a few minutes away from this first class hotel. It has a restaurant and lounge bar, plus two tennis courts. The comfortable rooms are all centrally heated.

LIMERICK
LIMERICK RYAN
TWA Tour Category: Top Value
A first class hotel combining an old manor house and modern premises in attractive surroundings, close to the River Shannon and less than a mile from the town center. Amenities include lounge, bar and restaurant. The centrally-heated bedrooms have direct-dial phone, hair dryer, trouser press and color TV.

LIVERPOOL
ATLANTIC TOWER
TWA Tour Category: Top Value
Large first class hotel, next to St. Nicholas Church and the Pierhead on the Mersey River. The building is completely air-conditioned, with two restaurants, lounge bars and a more intimate cocktail bar. All rooms and suites have direct-dial phone, color TV and in-house movies.

MOAT HOUSE
TWA Tour Category: Budget
With views across the Albert Dock and the River Mersey, this hotel is close to the city's shopping and commercial center. It features a restaurant, a bar and leisure center with indoor pool, whirlpool spa and gym. Bedrooms all have trouser press, color TV with in-house movies and tea/coffee-making facilities.

LONDON
ALPHA ROYALE
TWA Tour Category: Budget
A very attractively renovated hotel, now with a first class rating, in the residential area of Bayswater, near Hyde Park and the West End. Two restaurants, one specializing in Indian cuisine, bar and leisure complex, with a small pool and gym. All bedrooms have direct-dial phone, hair dryer, trouser press, color TV with movies and 24-hour room service.

BLOOMSBURY CREST
TWA Tour Category: Top Value
Conveniently located in Bloomsbury: close to the British Museum and a few minutes' walk from main shopping streets, theaters and Soho. Completely renovated in 1989, the hotel features a lobby and public rooms, including café bar, brasserie and restaurant. Bedrooms all have trouser press, color TV with movies and tea/coffee-making facilities.

IN LONDON
HAREWOOD
TWA Tour Category: Budget
Built in 1974, the Harewood is in Marylebone, close to Baker Street and Regent's Park. The Colonnade Restaurant offers a choice of menu, with popular Deckers wine bar serving snacks, wine and beer. Bedrooms have direct-dial phone, hair dryer, trouser press, color TV with in-house movies and tea/coffee-making facilities.

HILTON INTERNATIONAL KENSINGTON
TWA Tour Category: First Class
A modern hotel to the west of Marble Arch and Hyde Park, but with easy access by taxi, bus or subway to the West End. Usual high Hilton standards: facilities include Hiroko Japanese restaurant plus the Market Restaurant and wine bar. All air-conditioned guest rooms have mini-bar and color TV.

HILTON INTERNATIONAL KENSINGTON

Fig. 2-7. In the larger tour brochures, hotels become one of the features. (Courtesy of Transworld Airlines Inc.)

COORDINATING THE PACKAGE

When you go through a tour operator and merely advertise that tour for your clientele, the details are pretty well set. Your people enlist for what is offered.

If you go the route of organizing your own itinerary with the aid of a wholesaler, there's likely to be some give and take before the journey is finalized. Sightseeing, hotels, and entertainment must interlock. Regional geography and the pace of the tour must be reviewed. You have to make certain space is available and that the proper blend of elements is considered in order to make the trip efficient, pleasurable, economical, and salable.

When these variables are properly positioned, the itinerary may be committed to brochure form (see Chapter 4). The tour is then registered with the appropriate carrier and given an **IT (Independent Tour) number** which is used on all printed materials. This coded number is necessary if the tour company or travel agency wishes to receive its full 11 percent commission from the carrier. Additional forms may also be required by the airlines or by organizations like the International Air Transport Association (IATA) or the Passenger Network Services Corporation.

❏ *CHAPTER HIGHLIGHTS*

❏ Tours come in many varieties, because travelers' tastes are different and because external conditions also affect the popularity of specific destinations.

❏ In setting the dates for a tour, the tour manager (or travel agency or tour operator) considers the prospective client base, potential weather, availability of special events, cost, tour leader's availability, and the agency's convenience.

❏ In organizing the itinerary, distance and geography are factors, along with a balance of activities, hotels, shopping opportunities, rest stops and luncheon spots, the nature of the tour group, and the budget.

❏ Costing a tour is important, since the idea is to make money on the trip.

❏ Working with a tour operator or wholesaler is the usual route for planning group travel.

❏ Tour planners have to avail themselves of as much information as possible, including printed materials, testimony of those who have traveled the area, the advice of tour operators, and preferably, their own on-site inspection. Sometimes government agencies are used to provide updates.

❏ All tours must be registered in order to earn the sponsoring agency the highest commission.

❏ *CASE PROBLEMS*

1. Using the guidelines in this chapter, plus information available in guidebooks, prepare a recommendation for your travel agency boss regarding the best potential dates for an educational tour of Italy for a group of high school history teachers. Justify your selection.

2. Just before Thanksgiving, a corporate client contacts you as his travel agency manager, and asks you to pull together an incentive package for his sales force. The twenty top salespersons (and their spouses) will get to spend New Year's Day at the Fiesta Bowl in Phoenix, Arizona as part of a week long vacation trip. The sales contest covers the first three weeks of December. The client apologizes for this late request but says sales are down and he is looking for some way to boost them before year's end. You say you'll do your best. What are some of the problems you might expect to encounter?

COSTING THE TOUR

LEARNING OBJECTIVES

After reading this chapter you will be able to:

❏ Distinguish the ways various elements of the travel industry price their tours
❏ Understand how tour operators and travel agencies build in profit
❏ Categorize the various costs that go into a tour
❏ Actually build a tour cost sheet, using materials provided in this chapter, plus individualized information you secure on your own

KEY CONCEPTS

All-expense tour	Incentive Travel	Porterage
Contingencies	Independent tour operator	Profit margin
Costing	Land cost	Room rate
Entertainment	Net price	Special events
Entry fees	Off-season	Tipping
Foreign Independent Travel	Override	

While **costing** a tour may sometimes become complicated, the principles are rather simple. You have to cover expenses, and you want to make a profit. It's the same as any service industry. You determine what it takes to provide the service and you build in both **contingencies** and your own potential **profit margin.** Obviously, the total must be competitive, or, if higher than other tours, must justify the increase.

Each segment of the travel and hospitality industry approaches the task of costing in a slightly different way, even though the principles remain the same. Before assigning a menu price to a specific meal, for example, the restauranteur considers a multitude of things, ranging from the cost of produce and utilities to the staff wages, space rental, tableware, advertising, and dozens of other items. Even the reputation of the establishment may figure in, along with the reality of competition. The restaurant also builds in its profit.

In costing tours, there are different levels. Large tour operators do things somewhat differently than smaller tour operators; travel agencies look at the situation in yet another way; and the independent tour manager (like the educator or minister) may figure costs in an entirely different manner.

DETAILS ARE THE KEY

The key to costing a tour is the same as the key to all sensible planning: *pay attention to details*. You don't want to forget some hard costs, you don't want to underestimate potential charges, and you want to be sure you're properly compensated for your own investment of time.

Basically, on tour, you are looking at these standard items:

- ❑ Cost of air, ground, or cruise transportation
- ❑ Cost of accommodations
- ❑ Cost of meals
- ❑ Cost of entertainment features
- ❑ Entry fees, local guides, porterage (the transfer of luggage by airport and hotel porters), airport taxes
- ❑ Expenses of the tour manager
- ❑ Miscellaneous costs, ranging from advertising and mailing costs to periodic treats for tour members
- ❑ An emergency fund
- ❑ Profit

Let's take a look at how an independent tour company, a travel agency, and an individual organizing a tour might determine their costs.

The **independent tour operator** planning a ten-day tour will want to arrange for nine nights lodging. Once the route has been determined, the operator contacts the available hotels in the designated areas to learn if they have sufficient rooms for the anticipated number of guests. Any one of the tour planners has to have some notion about the minimum number of tour members in order to sensibly gauge needs and prices. Let's assume this tour operator is working with a figure of twenty-five tour members needed to meet the desired profit margin.

The hotels will give the tour operator a **net price** for the rooms—let's say $40 per room, including breakfast. (The operator will, of course, be costing this in his/her native currency, then converting for the convenience of the traveler.) Even within this single area, there are numerous variations. The tour operator could be dealing with a chain and using only their hotels; or working with some hotels with which the operator has a special relationship; or arranging for space in accommodations with a wide range of prices. There are also **off-season** prices, weekend prices, group rates, and other variations. The tour operator tries to get the most competitive rates possible while considering the quality and location of the facilities as well as their appropriateness for the specific tour. To simplify things, we'll say the per night cost of the hotels averages $40. So, nine nights at $40 gives us the initial tour cost of $360.

If the hotel bases its net price on a room basis, rather than an individual basis, the cost per person may be arrived at by dividing the room cost by the number of occupants. If we use the above example, and the **room rate** is $40 per night, then the net cost for a couple sharing this room would be $20 per person. Triple occupancy would be figured in a similar vein.

It's common to base the rate on two persons sharing, meaning that an individual opting for a single room is assessed a "single room supplement." This is quoted in a lump sum for the entire tour and not on a per night basis. This sum is, basically, the difference between the tour package room rate for individuals sharing and the actual net cost per room.

MEALS AND OTHER LAND COSTS

Then the tour operator must decide which meals will be included. Lunch is often omitted, except where the location requires that it be included—as when you're in a place with only one restaurant large enough for your group, and that restaurant demands reservations. Even in this situation, you could have the tour members pay their own luncheon bills, but an assessment might be easier. Similarly, a luncheon cruise might require you to book in advance. Normally, though, lunch would not be part of the tour, except for the situations mentioned above, as well as the cruise tour and the somewhat rare **all-expense tour.** There is a good reason for skipping lunch. Many travelers prefer a light lunch and want to choose their own repast. If they are locked into three heavy meals a day, they may be dissatisfied—or ill.

Dinner is commonly part of the tour, although most tours allow at least one free night to sample restaurants on one's own in the larger cities—like London, Paris, or Melbourne. Frequently, the on-tour dinners are at the hotel where the group is staying. These might be included as part of the hotel's net cost to the tour operator, or they might be billed separately. Sometimes too, the tour arranges for evening meals at a series of popular restaurants. For purposes of this exercise, let's assume breakfast is included as part of the hotel charge, that we are going to include one lunch, and that six dinners will be part of the tour package. Again, the tour operator gets a net price for these meals—say, $70. Our total, per person, for rooms and meals is now $430.

No, that price doesn't mean your clients will stay in a tent beside the Tiber River. It's just one more sensational off-season value from CHT. For $79, they'll get five nights, continental breakfast daily, free dinner, guided tour, transfers, and more. Call CHT today for your free supply of Italy/Fall-Winter brochures. *Per person, double occupancy.

CENTRAL HOLIDAY TOURS
206 Central Avenue, Jersey City, NJ 07307
800-526-6045

Fig. 3-1. The price offered to tourists comes only after considerable costing by the tour operator. (Courtesy of Central Holiday Tours)

Three **special evening events** are made of this tour—a play, a dinner/cabaret, and a concert. Net costs of these three attractions come to $80, making our running total $510.

Since charges differ from country to country, the cost of **porterage** (the transfer of bags in and out of the hotel) may vary. Let's average this out to $15 per person for the nine days. This would also include the airport transfers. New total: $525.

Tour operators would have a set figure for the cost of running a motorcoach for a day. Let's make that $250 per day. Since we have 25 passengers, that comes to $10 per day for each, or a total of $615 when averaged into the tour costs.

There may be other known costs—like taxes, **entry fees** to cathedrals or museums, other anticipated tipping (although much of this may be built into hotel or restaurant charges), payment to local guides in the larger cities, and similar expenses. Let's make this item $30 per person, bringing the total to $645.

These, then, become the **land costs.** If the tour operator is offering only the land package, this is the basic cost. Now the tour operator adds his profit margin to these net costs—perhaps 10–25 percent. The total land cost becomes $709.50 or more for the ten-day tour.

To this must be added the cost of transportation to the foreign destination, if applicable. If we are talking here solely of a bus trip within the United States, this charge may be minimal or non-existent. If the tour takes place overseas, the air costs may be substantial. Just for the purpose of this example, say the RT air from Chicago to London is $800. Adding this to the previous figure of $709.50 gives us a new total of $1509.50.

And we may not be through yet. The tour operator may decide to cover other costs, like advertising, or the profit percentage could be raised. A tour operator might, for example, get an exceptionally good price on hotels. Even when plussing this figure by 10 percent, the resultant cost to the tour member would still be far below the regular room rate. To balance this off, assuming the increase still leaves this tour operator competitive, the operator may take a larger markup.

Let's summarize this independent tour operator's cost sheet:

Hotels (these would be calculated individually)	$360.00 per person
Meals (6 dinners, 1 luncheon)	$ 70.00 per person
Entertainment (play, cabaret, concert)	$ 80.00 per person
Porterage	$ 15.00 per person
Coach costs (pro-rated)	$ 90.00 per person
Miscellaneous costs (fees, tipping, gifts)	$ 30.00 per person
Profit (10–25 percent of total)	$ 64.50 per person
TOTAL LAND COSTS PER PERSON	$709.50

VARIATIONS OF COSTING ELEMENTS

It is worth stressing that the costing process above is merely one example. There are myriad potential variations. Tour operators are often able to negotiate special deals with hotels, restaurants, and attractions managers, so their profit could be greater, or their trips cheaper. Some countries are far more expensive to visit, so the basic costs would be much higher. The time of year affects costing, and so do numbers of tour members. Some tour operators maintain their own fleet of coaches, while others rent theirs seasonally.

In addition, large tour companies have more clout and can negotiate better deals—in some instances. But they also expend more on promotion and perhaps on personnel. A smaller tour company may be employed by a larger travel firm that handles overseas bookings. In this instance, the travel agency deals with the umbrella booking firm and this company engages the on-site operator. Obviously, this adds to the cost, because more people are getting their percentage of the action.

Fig. 3-2. Tours to the same destination may be marketed differently, with the accent on scenery or on price.

Other Considerations

In costing a tour, planners normally work with **net** costs as we have done here, basing their markup on these costs rather than on gross prices for the various elements.

Planners also take cognizance of **fixed** versus **variable** costs. Fixed costs are those which do not vary depending on the size of the tour. You may negotiate things like hotel and meal rates, **entertainment** features, and other variables, but items like airfares, advertising, the tour manager's salary, and other charges may well remain the same whether twenty-five or fifty people opt for the excursion.

Taxes were mentioned earlier. These could be assessed by foreign or domestic governments on rooms, meals, entertainment, even on landings and departures from airports. These become part of the cost of the tour and have to be factored into the final price to tour members.

HOW THE TRAVEL AGENCY COSTS A TOUR

Let's turn to the travel agency's costing of a tour. Again, it makes a difference whether they are merely sending prospects to a large tour operator to become part of that company's tour membership, or whether they are negotiating with a smaller tour company to handle a group of their clients (like a football tour package, for example), or whether they are building up one of their own tours virtually from scratch.

When travel agencies refer clients to the larger tour companies—like Caravan or Maupintour—there is little real costing to be done. People are really traveling on an FIT (**Foreign Independent Travel**) basis, even though they eventually become part of a group. The agency may book the air and earn a commission on it (perhaps 11 percent) and will also earn a commission from the tour company for booking the client. These tour company commissions vary considerably, but range from 12–15 percent among the top scale tour company. One major tour operator, anxious to increase its business, currently pays 17.5 percent. The idea, of course, is to get the travel agent to recommend their trips in order to earn a higher commission.

When a travel agency works with an independent tour operator in putting together a tour for its own clients, it tries to get the best price possible for the land portion. This may require some negotiation, and the success of the travel agency in scaling down charges will depend on how low the costs are already and on how much the operator wants (or needs) the business.

Let's say the travel agency decides to tie into the tour package mentioned earlier—for $709.50. This is net to the travel agency, but, of course, it contains the tour operator's profit margin. The travel agency then adds a percentage markup to this figure to establish its profit.

How high a percentage?

This may vary wildly, from 5 percent to 100 percent. Part of this difference may be attributable to agency costs, but a lot is based upon how the final package looks to the consumer. If a high add-on figure can be used while keeping the cost to the client competitive, this may be done. Before this tactic is set down as pure greed, it should be stated that some travel agencies may add features, may be heavier into advertising, or may be trying to balance out some losing or marginal tours with this successful one. Another factor mentioned earlier may be at work here. Suppose the hotel package is exceptionally low, because of a seasonal lag or other reason. Maybe a room that normally rents for $140 could be netted to the tour operator or travel agency at $50. Should the operator or agency then take only a 10 percent markup, billing the room at $55, or is it entitled to a more realistic markup which would bring the room rate to a reasonable figure, though still a bargain?

Rarely is the airfare marked up. The land costs are the basis for the agency markup. Simply put, the agency is interested in—and entitled to—a reasonable profit. Every expenditure of time and money must be included in determining this figure, and so must any fees due other selling agents who may be providing clients or services to the tour.

For purposes of this illustration, we'll assume the travel agency adds 12 percent to the tour operator figure of $709.50, making this $794.64.

Then there is the air—if this tour involves air. While the standard commission to the travel agency for tour-related air might be 11 percent, there is sometimes room for negotiations in this area. **"Overrides"** or bonus commissions of 20 percent or higher may be worked out. This sort of deal is not cut, normally, because the particular travel agency is a good customer, but more because the airline needs or wants the business. There is sometimes a very liberal interpretation of the rules in this area. Travel agencies might classify their ticket purchases as overseas tour buys, even though they may actually fall in other categories such as independent or business travel. Even when airlines suspect this, they may turn the other way.

Again, sticking with the earlier example, we'll calculate the air at $800. This is the price to the client, with the travel agent earning commissions from the airlines. Commissions, it is worth remembering, are normally less significant as a profit factor, than the markup.

There may be other travel agency considerations. Will the agency supply a tour escort? If so, that person's expenses must be considered, adding perhaps another 10 percent to the cost. Will the agency want to build into the tour package any extra events, or the cost of promotion and advertising, or the charges associated with pre-and-post tour meetings? Will it supply things like carryon bags or map portfolios or other items? What about an expense account for the tour manager (or escort) for personal expenses, **tipping,** gifts, and emergencies? Will they pay the tour manager for his or her work? Are site inspections called for before the tour takes off, and are these costs covered?

The travel agency carefully analyzes all potential costs and bases its price on these costs (plus profit), keeping in mind that the result must be attractive to a prospective client. A *Group Tour Pricing Sheet* is shown in Figure 3-3. This assumes the travel agency may be building the tour from scratch, more or less, but the use of an overseas or domestic tour operator would be far more common. For one thing, travel agents may book hotels on their own, but they are more reluctant to get in the business of booking coaches and drivers. They'd rather use an established operator. Before we get into some variations on the agency scene, let's see how an agency costing might look, based on the tour operator's model.

Land costs (plus 12 percent agency markup)	$794.64
RT Air	$800.00
Escort Costs	$150.00
Expenses	$ 75.00
TOTAL TOUR COST TO CLIENT	$1,819.64

This might be rounded out to $1,820. How much will the travel agency make? That depends. What sort of a deal were they able to get on the air

GROUP TOUR PRICING

Group Name:_____

Destination: _____

Approximate Number of People: _____

Type of Program: _____ (Incentive, Awards, Social, Etc.)

$_____   Transportation :_____

_____

$_____   Lodging :_____

_____

$_____   Baggage: _____

$_____   Transfers: _____

$_____   Sightseeing: _____

_____

$_____   Meals/Cocktails: _____

_____

$_____   Special Tickets/Admissions: _____

$_____   Entertainment: _____

_____

$_____   Tips: _____

$_____   Escort: _____

_____

$_____   Advertising: _____

$_____   Promotions: (Telephone/Postage/Printing) _____

_____

$_____   Site Inspections: _____

_____

$_____   Miscellaneous: _____

_____

_____

$_____   Total Net
$_____   Mark-Up

$══════════   Selling Price   10-88-TG-kk

Fig. 3-3. This handy sheet enables planners to enter all known and anticipated expenses when costing the tour. (Courtesy of Pegasus Travel Center)

portion? If they priced the tour on the basis of 25 people, how many did they actually get? If fewer, they could even suffer a loss (unless the tour operator or hotels are willing to negotiate); if they attract more, that's a plus for the agency and means more money. Figuring a normal commission on air, and a normal markup on land, the agency would earn approximately $175 per person. If twenty-five tour members actually showed, the profit would be $4375—a modest profit for the work entailed. This could be augmented if the expense money were not used totally, and it could be diminished by advertising or other expenses, or by a failure of the twenty-five members to materialize. Normally, tour costs will be projected on the basis of some minimum enrollment.

As any travel agency manager will tell you, this arithmetic oversimplifies the costing operation. So many other factors may be involved. An agent may call a cruise line, for example, and ask what time of year that line might give them the best deal for sixty people. Armed with that information, the travel agency could then sell the cruise for that time slot, and at a reduced rate. Similarly, a travel agency that regards its profit margin as too thin and risky, may call the airline or tour operator to see if a better arrangement can be made. At least one major American airline trains its people at all levels to negotiate with travel agents. Most airlines force you to talk with one of the higher-ups.

There are also occasions when the travel agency may operate a particular tour at a loss, simply because it doesn't want the bad publicity of a failed tour. Hopefully, they will recoup on another trip.

As far as tour operators and travel agencies are concerned, the whole exercise described in the preceding pages comes under the heading of *costing*. This is distinct from *pricing,* which is the dollar cost of the tour when offered to prospects. Pricing is affected, not only by fixed and variable costs and by markup, but also by competition. The established price not only has to cover costs and promise a profit. It must also be competitive with similar tours, or provide some features which make it seem worth the difference to a client.

INCENTIVE TOURS

Incentive tours are another matter, and the markup here could be as high as 25–30 percent. That's because these tours take more time, often require a site inspection, may have to be more individualized (rather than follow an established route), and may involve more costs to the travel agency in terms of printed materials, gifts, phone calls, meetings, and other expenses. There are tour operators who specialize in incentive travel and are expert in all phases of this travel area, from promotion to personalized programs. The travel agency may work through one of these suppliers, could use a standard tour operator, or might make all arrangements on its own. Regardless of the method, the same costing logic applies. You add up all the expenses and you add in your profit.

INDIVIDUALLY GENERATED TOUR

Let's look at one last example—the individual who organizes his or her own tour, probably with the services of a travel agent. Ordinarily, an educator, cleric, or local personality may be recruited by a tour operator or travel agency to escort or manage a tour. But sometimes this individual may build a special tour: a playhouse director may want to take a group to New York to see a sampling of Broadway's offerings; or a pastor may decide to take parishoners to some European shrines during the parish's 50th anniversary year; or an English professor may want to set up a student or adult tour of literary sites in Britain.

A sensible way for the professor to proceed, for example, would be to first determine the best time for his schedule, and then to jot down the places he would like to visit and the things he would like to do. The next step might be the travel agency, where these plans would be discussed and refined. A tour operator might be contacted to cost out the basic tour. Meanwhile, the travel agency is checking on air travel. When these figures are in hand, the professor must then decide what other costs will be involved. Will he hire a few guest lecturers while en route? Will he present each tour member with special materials, like literary guidebooks or anthologies? How much will be built in for his own expenses?

Let's cost out a two-week literary tour of Britain, assuming an adult tour membership of approximately thirty persons:

Land costs (This figure, from a tour operator, includes luxury coach transportation, porterage, all first class hotels, breakfasts, most dinners, two plays, cabaret, local guides, transfers, and the services throughout of a driver/guide)	$ 1,000.00
RT Air	$ 800.00
Tour manager's pro-rated costs	$ 45.00
Cost of guest lecturers (per person)	$ 20.00
Text and printed materials	$ 30.00
Expenses	$ 30.00
Miscellaneous and contingency fund	$ 25.00
Agency (and, perhaps, tour manager) profit	$ 200.00
TOTAL COST OF TOUR PACKAGE TO CLIENT	$ 2,150.00

These three sets of simulated figures barely scratch the surface. A bus tour originating in the tour members' home town might involve nothing more than a markup of the net figure from the coach company. There are Fly/Drive packages, in which the round trip air may be combined with car rental and vouchers for stays in a select list of hotels. There are also Fly/Cruise packages which may use air to and from the port of embarkation, and those which supply air one way with return by cruise ship. There are small group tours involving bed and breakfast accommodations, and, on the other extreme there are castle or manor house stays, with both offering car rental rates. There are also student tours, where accommodations may be dormitory-like and meals less appetizing.

Costing a tour, then, requires careful projections of potential expenses, along with the list of known expenses (like group air fares), plus sufficient funding to cover things like the tour manager's costs, preparation and organization time, extra activities and fees, and enough to handle emergencies. To this must be added profit, either in the form of markups, commissions, or add ons. If you estimate incorrectly, you could be like the painter who bids too low on a home decorating job. You lose money.

And the object of the tour, from the planner's viewpoint, is to make money.

❏ CHAPTER HIGHLIGHTS

❏ Costing principles are simple: you must cover expenses and you should make a profit.

❏ Each segment of the travel industry approaches costing in a slightly different way.

❏ In costing, the details are important.

❏ Basic costing elements include transportation, accommodations, meals, entertainment, porterage, entry fees, tour management or guide expenses, miscellaneous costs, an emergency fund, and profit.

❏ Independent tour operators normally build a 10 percent profit on top of the net costs.

❏ Land costs include all of the tour operator's expenses, except for air or other major transportation to the departure point, plus profit.

❏ Travel agencies build their costs and profits on top of the tour operator's net cost to them. The travel agency also earns commissions from large tour operators, from air and cruise lines, and from other sources.

❏ Incentive tours take more time and money, so the markup is generally higher.

❏ Individuals who build and lead tours, with the help of a travel agency and tour operator, must include their own expenses in the price of the tour.

❏ CASE PROBLEMS

1. As a group travel representative for a local travel agency, you are discussing with a local business executive the possibility of his firm providing a tour as an incentive for the large sales force. This executive asks what you get out of it, and you tell him that, in addition to commissions from the airlines, you also add 20 percent to the cost of the overall package. At this, the executive asks why he shouldn't deal directly with the airlines and the hotels himself and save the firm some money. How do you respond? How do you convince him of the value of your services?

2. Using the Group Tour Pricing Sheet *as a guide, cost out a tour of your selection. Secure what information you can, then estimate the costs of the other items—like entertainment. Include your expenses (if you are involved) and profit.*

PROMOTING THE TOUR

LEARNING OBJECTIVES

After reading this chapter you will be able to:

- ❏ Understand the value of word-of-mouth and personal contact in selling tours
- ❏ Know what news is and how to write a news release
- ❏ Determine how advertising fits into the marketing picture and why print advertising is the primary method of promoting tours
- ❏ Understand how a tour brochure is produced
- ❏ Appreciate the role of other promotional tools

KEY CONCEPTS

Advertising	Itinerary	Promotion
Attractions	News	Proofreading
Brochure	News release	Publicity
Conditions	Out-of-home advertising	Shell
Design	Page proofs	Telemarketing
Dummy	Paper stock	Typography
Electronic media	Presentations	Videocassette
Galley proofs	Print advertising	Word-of-mouth advertising

Once the tour is planned, it must be promoted. The tour manager may or may not be involved in this phase, although this person's cooperation will be expected. There are a few tours which have waiting lists from year to year, and **promotion** for these is simple. Others have to be marketed. The goal of all promotional efforts is to inform, interest, and involve. In terms of tour promotion, the obvious objective is to fill space on the plane, ship, or coach with travelers who can afford and enjoy the trip.

WORD OF MOUTH

This inexpensive method works well for tours that are periodically repeated. Previous tour members tell their friends and inquiries are directed to the travel agency, tour operator, or tour manager. **Personal testimonials** are among the strongest ways to convince others about a product or service.

The promoters must, however, have a system for taking advantage of word-of-mouth success. Contacts must be followed up, printed materials supplied, perhaps even personal visits made or encouraged. Getting the lead is a big step, but you want to turn this expressed interest into a sale.

PRESENTATIONS

Besides the one-on-one approach to sales, and the over-the-counter sales a travel agency may make, the tour sponsor tries to get the message to larger groups. These groups may be assembled for the express purpose of hearing about the tour, as in the case of a travel club, incentive group, or a travel program hosted by a tour operator, carrier or travel agency. There are formal occasions that may include slides or a film, an orientation by a spokesperson, and an opportunity to ask questions. The setting may be strictly business, or there could be food, drink, door prizes, and other items. Some meetings are organized with the express intention of convincing interested persons to sign up for the trip, while others are more introductory, **providing information** rather than soliciting membership.

Even informal meetings may result in potential tour customers. Travel agency personnel and occasional tour leaders may be part of a luncheon program or book club meeting where their remarks foster inquiries about trips.

Results from such gatherings—and from word-of-mouth—are not easy to analyze. The decision to travel may come months later. Still, such oral presentations are very important and their value cannot be discounted. That's one reason tour operators and travel agencies like to have tour managers and other personnel whose interpersonal skills are an asset.

PUBLICITY

There are many forms of **publicity,** but the most common is the reporting or creation of **news** which will be picked up by the media. Editors and news directors are wary of any unsolicited information which appears to be a not-so-subtle plug for a tour or a tour company. Yet travel is news, and the adept publicist can often find ways to present material that has a legitimate editorial basis. Besides the travel pages, which serve as an outlet for features on destinations and attractions, there may be room elsewhere in newspapers or newscasts for tour-related news. Updated information on newsworthy regions of the world makes good copy, as do current data on exchange rates, travel tips, political observations, and other themes. You can't try to palm off puffery as news; that sort of material belongs in an ad. However, with a little thought, news value may be created from a routine tour story.

Complete details on travel **news releases** and features can be found in two books from Delmar's travel series: *Effective Communication in the Travel Industry* and *Travel and Tourism Marketing Techniques.* Although this chapter will address these topics much more superficially, it does provide a glimpse at what news is and how it is communicated.

News is really any information that interests a segment of the population at any one time. News can be built around details individuals need to know, around timely stories, around personalities, around unusual or humorous happenings, even around a fresh approach to an old situation.

If the travel staff member is inexperienced in writing news releases, a call to the media about the story idea might result in coverage by a reporter—if the news is significant, and if the reporter isn't tied up with other assignments. If possible, it's best to learn how to recognize news and how to write it in a professional manner.

The News Release

In preparing to write the news release, the writer must first try to think like an editor. Why should this story be published or aired? Does it have any real information for prospective readers, listeners, or viewers? The news release writer should also make certain the technical and mechanical aspects of the news story are correct, that the details are accurate and complete, and that other media needs and deadlines are observed.

The news release should be typed, double-spaced (so the editor can edit), on white paper, and with adequate margins—usually about 1½″ on each side. Paragraphs should be short and indented about seven spaces. If possible, the story should be confined to a single page, but take more space if needed.

News stories may take other forms, but the tried-and-true method calls for the important information to be at the beginning of the release, probably in the lead paragraph. This graph answers the who, what, where, when, why, and how questions characteristic of journalists.

The source of the story should be identified, along with the date and place of origin, and the information on when this story may b released. Normally, this latter designation calls for IMMEDIATE RELEASE.

Besides the books mentioned earlier, there are numerous newswriting and public relations texts which provide other details on the news release. A sample release follows.

```
Jeffrey Smith
Monmouth Travel Agency
Clarinda, MN  55111
(612) 573-9094 (O)
(612) 357-4909 (H)
```

FOR IMMEDIATE RELEASE

    CLARINDA, MN (April 22, 1991) -- Officials of the Minnesota and Pacific Railroad leave today on a special tour of European railway systems.

    Twenty-two MPR executives, including President Wilbur Tibbs, are part of an exclusive tour arranged by Monmouth Travel Agency of Clarinda. After landing in London, the group will board "The Flying Scotsman" for the trip to Edinburgh. Three days by rail through the Scottish Highlands will follow. The railroad execs will cross the Channel by ferry and spend ten days on the Eurail network, visiting France, Belgium, German, Austria, Italy and Spain.

    "It's not strictly relaxation," explained Tibbs. "We want to compare service, schedules, and equipment."

    The special tour returns June 10.

--30--

Fig. 4-1. One acceptable format for a news release

    News releases for radio and television are written for the ear. They are normally shorter, geared to the abilities of the average station announcer or anchorperson, and contain phonetic pronunciations of unfamiliar or difficult words. "Edinburgh" could be followed by (ED -N - BUH -RUH).

    Feature stories also help promote a tour. These may appear in a newspaper travel section or consumer magazine, and are generally written by staffers or free-lance writers. The agency, operator, or tour manager may have nothing to do with these, but reading about the locale may help the prospect make a decision.

Fig. 4-2. Print advertising is the primary form of communication about tours.
(Courtesy of KLR International)

Advertising

This is also a specialized field, and is covered in a number of **advertising** texts, as well as in Delmar books like *Hospitality and Travel Marketing* and *Travel and Tourism Marketing Techniques*. These books go into detail on the principles of advertising as part of the marketing mix; they also provide tips and examples of copywriting, illustrations, layout, placement, and other mechanical elements.

The sponsoring agency or tour operator would normally be responsible for the advertising, rather than the tour manager; with larger firms, an advertising agency would be employed.

While tours are advertised on radio and television (especially when the tour manager may be a local on-air personality), the **electronic media** are normally utilized for more generic travel advertising. Perhaps bowl game packages or destinations like Hawaii could appear with some regularity on television, but most tours favor the print media.

Fig. 4-3. Local travel agencies may combine many tours among their advertised offerings. (Courtesy of AAA Travel Agency)

Part of the secret of advertising is placing the message where prospects are most likely to see or hear it. Consequently, the travel pages of daily papers or the pages of travel magazines are prime print candidates. People turn to these media when they are travel-minded. Telephone book yellow pages are used for travel agency identification for the same reason.

There are always arguments about whether it is better to focus on a single tour in a print ad or whether the sponsor should combine several tours. Most go for the latter approach. Although a very popular tour, with a popular leader, might be singled out for a few exclusive ads.

When advertising is employed as a promotional tool, its cost must be figured in pricing the tour. These costs are spread over the target number of tour members. Some costs can also be assumed by the sponsoring agency, since any form of advertising also helps their general image and recognition.

Fig. 4-4. Tour companies also package a number of tours together. (Courtesy of InterPacific Tours International)

Rarely does a tour ad spell out many details of the tour. The destination, number of days, and price may be the only items in a combination ad. Sometimes the price is omitted. What the ad seeks to do is have the reader inquire—by phone, coupon, or personal visit. Single-purpose ads may contain a few more details, but only enough to whet the prospect's interest.

Other forms of advertising—like the **out-of-home** or outdoor board media—are almost never used to promote tours. Window cards and billboard posters might be part of the tour campaign, but the major tools, outside of **print advertising,** are the **itinerary** and the **brochure.**

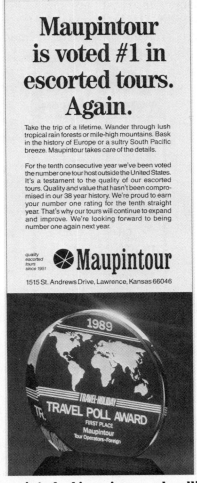

Fig. 4-5. Sometimes the printed ad is an image ad, selling the firm instead of a specific product or service. (Courtesy of Maupintour)

Best of Morocco   15 Days

CASABLANCA RABAT TANGIER FEZ VOLUBILIS MOULAY IDRISS
MEKNES ERFOUD RISSANI TINERHIR OUARZAZATE MARRAKECH

From Caravan, all the mystery and magic of Morocco, in air-conditioned comfort and style. Follow ancient camel caravan routes to Saharan outposts, thrill to exotic native entertainment, marvel at Erfoud, remote Rissani, Ouarzazate, Marrakech and more. A fascinating, unique and unforgettable travel experience presented with Caravan care.

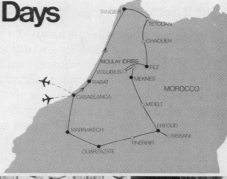

1st day—U.S.A. Overnight by jet to Morocco.

2nd day—Casablanca, Morocco Morning arrival at Casablanca airport, then to your hotel, with rest of the day free. Tonight, Caravan's welcoming cocktail party. Then a welcoming dinner with wine and entertainment at El Andalous. (D)
Hotel: Sheraton DL

3rd day—Casablanca Morning sightseeing of all the highlights of Casablanca. Lunch at La Reserve. Afternoon free to enjoy as you please. (B,L)

4th day—Casablanca-Rabat A short drive takes you to Rabat, capital of Morocco. On sightseeing you'll see the Royal Palace and visit the Chellah fortress. Afternoon free to shop, enjoy the hotel's pool. (B,D)
Hotel: Hyatt Regency DL

5th day—Rabat-Tangier Stop at Souk-el-Arba-du-Rharb en route along the Atlantic coast road to Tangier. Afternoon sightseeing includes the Kasbah and the Forbes museum. Caravan Moroccan dinner party tonight, with wine and entertainment. (B,D)
Hotel: El Minzah DL

6th day—Tetouan-Chaouen-Fez This morning, to Tetouan. Then into the mountainous Rif area to Chaouen. Lunch at the Parador Hotel Chaouen and walk through the Kasbah and Medina. Then to Fez. (B,L,D)
Hotel: Palais Jamai DL

7th day—Fez John Gunther called Fez the most romantic city on earth. You'll see it all in morning sightseeing, then the rest of the day is free. (B,D)

8th day—Volubilis-Moulay Idriss-Meknes This morning to Volubilis, visit the Roman ruins. Then a photo stop at the holy town of Moulay Idriss. Continue to Meknes, home of the Sultan of Morocco. Afternoon sightseeing. (B,L,D)
Hotel: Transatlantique DL

9th day—Meknes-Erfoud Follow ancient camel caravan routes, this morning, into the Middle Atlas mountains to Midelt for lunch. This afternoon, cross the High Atlas over the Camel Pass (6,300 feet) and descend to the oasis of Erfoud, gateway to the Sahara. (B,L,D)
Hotel: Riad Salam FC

10th day—Erfoud and Rissani Morning excursion to the great sand dunes of the true Sahara. You visit the oasis of Rissani, with its nomad encampment. Then return for a free afternoon in Erfoud. Tonight, Caravan party with drinks and entertainment by Berber villagers. (B,D)

11th day—Tinerhir-Ouarzazate Fabulously scenic day! See remote oases, sandstone fortresses and more as you drive to Tinerhir for lunch. This afternoon, you visit the "Grand Canyon" of the Sahara. Continue, then, through desert landscape featured in many movies, including "Lawrence of Arabia," to Ouarzazate. (B,L,D)
Hotel: Belere FC

12th day—Ouarzazate-Marrakech This morning, through mountain passes to the walled oasis-city of Marrakech. Afternoon free. Tonight, out with Caravan to a Moroccan dinner with wine and show at the Casino. (B,D)
Hotel: Es Saadi DL

If you go shopping in the souks in your free time, be prepared to bargain.

13th day—Marrakech Morning sightseeing features the best of Marrakech. Ride a camel, too! Leisure time until late this afternoon, when you visit the great Djemaa El Fna Square, with its magicians and snake charmers, and sip refreshments. Dine with wine tonight, Moroccan style, under Caida tents and witness a Fantasia, with rifle-firing horsemen on Arabian steeds. (B,L,D)

14th day—Marrakech-Casablanca Morning drive to Casablanca. Afternoon free. Tonight, Caravan's farewell dinner party with wine, for a festive finale. (B,D)
Hotel: Sheraton DL

15th day—Casablanca Off by jet for a same-day arrival in the U.S.A. (B)

CARAVAN DEPARTURES 1990		
No.	Leave New York Saturday	Leave Casablanca Saturday
6402 B *	Mar. 3	Mar. 17
6406 B *	May 5	May 19
6408 B	Sept. 22	Oct. 6
6410 B	Oct. 13	Oct. 27
6412 B	Nov. 3	Nov. 17

CARAVAN DEPARTURES 1991		
6401 B	Feb. 2	Feb. 16
6403 B	Mar 2	Mar. 16
6407 B	May 4	May 18

LAND PRICE	$2498
SINGLE ROOM SUPPLEMENT	$495
* LAND PRICE	$2198
* SINGLE ROOM SUPPLEMENT	$375

To obtain total price, add the land price to the air fare from your departure city, which your Travel Agent can provide.

SAMPLE APEX AIR FARES

	Low	Shoulder
New York	$582	$682

Shoulder: May, Sept. and Oct. departures.
Low: Feb., March and Nov. departures.
Air fares are correct as of Sept. 1, 1989 and are subject to change. For more air fare information, see back cover.

ROYAL AIR MAROC	IT0AT1CA09

Fig. 4-6. A lot of information can be found on a single brochure page—dates, itinerary, cost, and even a map. (Courtesy of Caravan Tours)

The Itinerary

The purpose and concerns about the itinerary are discussed in earlier chapters. Here we are interested in getting everything down on paper. Keep in mind that, with many tour operators, itineraries are repeated year-after-year, with minor alterations. Consequently, there is no need to start from scratch each time. However, at one time this sort of original planning had to be done, and, for a new journey, it still has to be accomplished.

Planners may have their own methods of proceeding. On occasion, some special event, like an athletic contest, grand opening, or political happening might be the focus, and other activities are tailored to this event. Most tours, though, insert events once they have established the route.

One sensible way to order the information would be to select dates, then decide on places to be visited and length of stay in each, then select and confirm hotels (usually through the on-site tour operator), and then add in the **attractions,** meals, and other extras. When this data is firm, you organize it into a day-by-day itinerary. Prospects might be furnished a preliminary itinerary, even before the final details are set; but, if so, this should be clearly labeled as "preliminary."

The final itinerary could take several forms. The tour manager may have the most detailed copy, complete with hotel contacts, information on ticket pickup, times of special meals or attractions, and other data of use to the director. Less detailed, less businesslike information on the tour may be made part of a brochure. While this is day-by-day, it is concise and intended to sell the trip rather than remind the tour member where he or she should be during a certain day. That sort of specific data is reserved for another version of the itinerary, the one the tour manager or travel agency or tour operator supplies to the committed traveler. This version stays with the tour member en route, and copies may be left behind with relatives, business associates, or friends who need to know the location of the individual.

Copies of the latter two itinerary forms are shown in Figures 4-6 and 2-4.

The Brochure

As a primary sales tool, the brochure is more than the itinerary. It contains information on the tour managers or escorts, on the items covered by the tour price, on various costs and tour **conditions,** and may also include details on hotels, events, and even tour tips.

Some tour brochures are large, like the Caravan/Europe book which contains 116 pages and provides information on forty-five different tours, along with maps, color photographs, many details on Caravan and its guides, hotel specifics, and more. Smaller tour operators may take sixteen to twenty-four

IRISH BOOKS AND MEDIA, INC.

TENTATIVE ITINERARY: 1990 Program

March 8: Departure. Dinner on flight to Ireland. Light breakfast snack before arrival at Shannon (March 9).

March 9-10: Two nights at the Breaffy Hotel, Castlebar, Co. Mayo. Castlebar is in the shadow of St. Patrick's pilgrimage mountain. Details of the history of this pilgrimage will be given--as well as information about the recent controversy about a gold find there. Castlebar also played an important part in modern Irish history. A day tour is planned for the second day here.

March 11: We leave Castlebar for the town of Monaghan (Co. Monaghan). This is the county that juts upward into the "soft belly" of Northern Ireland. Today we hope to visit with Bishop Duffy and, along the way, to pass through Frenchpart (Co. Roscommon), the birthplace of Dr. Douglas Hyde, one of the shapers of modern Ireland. Monaghan itself is an important town. Hillgrove Hotel.

March 12-13: Two nights at the Glendevlin Hotel, Dundalk (Co. Louth). This city has extensive connections with Saints Patrick and Brigid. She was born nearby, at Faugart where Edward Bruce, the Scot, was crowned King of Ireland by the Irish. Dundalk is also the death place of Cuchulain, the great mythical hero of Ireland.

March 14-15: Two nights in the recently refurbished, well located Mont Clair Hotel. You may think you know Dublin but Eamon Mac Thomais will open your eyes!

March 16-17: Two nights in the Blarney Park Hotel in the town of Blarney (Co. Cork, the "Irish Texas"). We have a tentative personal reception with the Lord Mayor as well as a viewing spot for Cork's St. Patrick Day's parade. Great shopping in Blarney!

March 18-19: Two nights in the Royal Hotel in Killarney. (Co. Kerry). There's more to Killarney than the beauty of its lakes and mountains. "History" has given birth to many fables about St. Patrick, The O'Donoghue, and the Colleen Bawn but there is plenty of real history and literature here.

March 20: Unfortunately, it's time to return home from fabled Ireland. We'll drive through Tralee and Listowel (well-known authors in both towns), crossing the Shannon by ferry in Co. Clare and driving along the Shannon to the Airport. We would expect to arrive in Kennedy Airport, New York, about 3:45 pm.

1433 FRANKLIN AVENUE EAST • MINNEAPOLIS, MINNESOTA 55404-2135 • (612) 871-3505

Fig. 4-7. Even without slick paper and photos, a printed itinerary can be appealing. (Courtesy of Irish Books & Media)

pages to explain their wares, and the most common format would be a two-or-three-fold single sheet which would fit inside a #10 envelope or slide nicely into a travel agency rack.

The types and quality are diverse, with some sponsors opting for a simple, inexpensive, one-color brochure and others producing the massive four-color tomes with multiple offerings. Part of the format decision would depend on purpose and scope, and part on cost and competition. For a single tour, the #10 version may suffice, but multiple choices would require additional space—and cost.

Fig. 4-8. Most brochures rely on scenic photos to attract the reader. (Courtesy of Swiss National Tourist Office)

   Local travel agencies often take a tour operator's brochure and personalize it with their name and address, or they employ a brochure **"shell"** supplied by an operator or carrier and imprint their own information. This shell would be comprised of a flat sheet with color photographs. Little or no copy would be included. The agency or sponsoring group writes its own copy and has this set by a local printer, or may use its own desktop printer. The result is a combination of the supplier's artwork and the local sponsor's prose.

Creating Your Own Brochure   If you must **design** and produce your own brochure, you will probably need help with the technical aspects, like design and **typography.** Reviewing existing brochures may give you some ideas. Printers and advertising agencies are sources of production assistance.

   You normally begin by writing the copy, keeping in mind the approximate space you have to fill. If you've already decided that your brochure will fit into a regular envelope, you might even start by folding paper, taking an $8\frac{1}{2}'' \times 11''$ sheet, or an $8\frac{1}{4}'' \times 14''$ sheet, and folding it to meet your needs, Figure 4-9. Then you can rough out the space for copy and pictures before turning this over to someone with design talent.

   The copy will consist of introductory material about the tour, the tour company, the tour leader, and the places to be visited. A semi-detailed itinerary would follow. Added to this would be information on tour costs and conditions, plus other details which the potential traveler might need to know. Once hard copy is typed or the data placed on a disk, it must be set in type. Before it gets to the printer, however, every effort should be made to see that the material is complete, accurate, free of typographical errors and misspellings, and ready to be printed. Changes made after this initial copy stage get increasingly expensive.

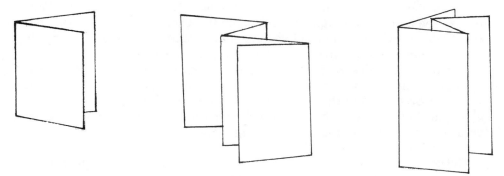

Fig. 4-9. Planning brochures starts with folding paper. Shown here are a simple one-fold brochure, with four panels for copy or photos; an accordion-fold brochure, with eight panels for material; and a two-fold brochure with eight available panels.

Printers and typographers can be helpful in selecting an appropriate type face. The chief consideration is readability, but there are other facets of type selection, such as attractiveness, appropriateness to the message, and flexibility.

By the time the **"galley proofs"** (long sheets of typed copy) are supplied by the printer, the design should be well in hand. These galley proofs are read for accuracy, then approved. They may then be set into **"page proofs,"** occupying the same space they will in the finished book or brochure. These page proofs are also checked, just in case some error has crept in or some new information has surfaced.

At this point, it depends a lot on how much help the individual or company producing the brochure has. If the whole project can be turned over to an art department or studio, or to an advertising agency, that's great. All the tour operator or travel agency has to do is supervise the accuracy and quality.

If, however, this is a bare bones effort, the tour planners may have to fashion their own design, locate their own art, paste the type carefully on a **"dummy"** (a mock-up of the final brochure), and supply all of this to the printer. Since this is a specialized set of skills, and since this brochure is your contact with the public, every effort must be made to keep the result professional, Figure 4-8.

Design Very few travel brochures attempt anything revolutionary. They are standard printed pieces, heavy with attractive photos (showing tourists enjoying exotic offerings) arranged in a pleasing way. The copy should be both informative and alluring and, when set in type, it, too, becomes part of the design. Even a person with a modest flair for layout can envision a brochure that succeeds graphically.

Good photography is the key. Photos can be procured from carriers, tourist boards, free lance photographers, and photo libraries. Caravan Tours employs photographers to take photos of various tour groups in foreign settings, thus allowing ample choice when they assemble the annual tour book.

Good color and design, plus striking headlines, enable certain brochures to stand out from others in travel agency racks. The larger tour operators also mail their brochures to those who have traveled with them in the past.

Reviewing the steps that go into the creation of a simple brochure, produced from scratch, we find the following steps:

1. Gathering of all pertinent information—dates, route, hotels, features, costs, conditions, tour leader biography.
2. General decision on size and design of brochure, with, perhaps, the folding of paper and creation of a rough dummy.
3. Writing and checking of copy, also calculating how the copy will fit the brochure. Headlines and subheads should also be written at this point.

Tour conditions – please read carefully

HOW TO MAKE YOUR RESERVATION?

See your travel agent. Your agent will handle your reservation free of charge and help you make your other travel arrangements.

DEPOSIT AND FINAL PAYMENT

A non-refundable deposit of $100 per tour and person is required for us to hold seats for you. This deposit forms part of your final payment which is due 45 days prior to departure. Acceptance on the tour is subject to presentation at departure of the Tour Membership Certificate evidencing receipt of full payment by Globus-Gateway.

Please make checks or money orders payable to your travel agent.

CANCELLATION FEES

If cancellation in writing is received by Globus-Gateway more than 45 days prior to departure, the non-refundable deposit will be retained (maximum 20% of total price). For cancellations received within 45 days of departure, the following per person cancellation fees apply:

45-16 days prior to departure: 20% of total price (maximum $200)

15-1 days prior to departure: 35% of total price

On departure day and later: 100% of total price.

Cancellation charges also apply to additional accommodations reserved prior to and after the tour.

REVISION FEES

A handling fee of $20 per transaction will be charged for any alteration or revision made to a booking.

REFUNDS FOR UNUSED SERVICES

All claims for refunds must be made through the travel agent from whom the tour has been purchased WITHIN 45 DAYS after termination of the tour. The claim must be accompanied by a STATEMENT FROM THE TOUR DIRECTOR, certifying exactly the services not taken.

No refund can be made for unused transportation where group tickets are involved. No refund can be made for services not taken in Europe unless the services omitted cover 48 consecutive hours or longer. Refunds for missing occasional sightseeing or meals, etc. are not granted.

Refunds are made on the basis of savings recovered from non-use of hotels, etc.

MEMBERSHIP

In order to ensure congenial membership, Globus-Gateway reserves the right to accept or reject any person as a tour participant and to expel from the tour any participant whose conduct is deemed incompatible with the interest of the tour group.

Each handicapped participant who requires special assistance must be accompanied by a qualified helper who assumes total responsibility for the handicapped participant's well-being. Globus-Gateway reserves the right to exclude from the tour any handicapped participant whose physical condition impairs customary operation of the tour.

YOUNG TOUR PARTICIPANTS

We grant 10% discount on the tour price of young tour participants up to the age of 18 years, provided they are accompanied by at least one adult. On escorted tours we do not accept children under 8 years because we have found that they are too young to enjoy touring.

The land arrangements for infants of up to 2 years are free of charge, provided the parents pay directly to the hotel(s) for food, crib, etc. On inter-European flights infants are allowed to travel for 10% of the regular air fare if they do not occupy a seat. This air fare is payable directly to the airline.

SMOKING

Please note that smoking is not allowed on Globus-Gateway motorcoaches.

TOUR PRICES

All tour prices for land arrangements are based on rates (including foreign exchange rates) known August 1988 and expected to be in effect at the time of departure. They are subject to increase without notice if such rates change prior to departure. For our price guarantee see page 7.

PASSPORTS

A valid passport is required of all tour participants. A U.S. passport is valid for 10 years. Passports are issued for individuals, husband and wife, or for a family.

To apply for passports you can contact either your local passport office, designated federal or state clerk of court, or selected post offices. Of course, your local travel agent will help you to obtain the necessary forms for passport application.

VISAS

At the time of printing, visas for France and Eastern European countries are required of all tour members. U.S. citizens do not require visas for any other country.

Detailed visa information will be mailed to your travel agent with our invoice and tour confirmation. Non-U.S. citizens must consult with the appropriate consulates to determine if any visas are needed.

FOREIGN CURRENCY

Carry a small amount of cash in each nation's currency before entering the country (except for Eastern Europe, where currency must be purchased within each country). It is always advisable to carry the bulk of your money in Travelers Checks. For convenience you should have some Travelers Checks in $10 or $20 denominations.

MAIL

Please advise friends and relatives to allow seven days or longer when writing to you in Europe. Your tour number and arrival date at the hotel should be clearly written on the front of the envelope. A list of your hotels and their addresses will be sent to you prior to departure.

TRANSATLANTIC FLIGHTS

Air fares quoted in this brochure are subject to change without notice.

Cancellation charges are imposed (at time of printing) only after the ticket is issued: $50 per person or 10% of air fare, whichever is higher.

Participating carriers: See page 18; effective dates of operation of tours: January through December 1989.

HOTEL ACCOMMODATION

The hotels listed on page 15 will be used on almost all departures. If a change becomes necessary for any reason, hotels substituted will be the equivalent of those shown.

While every effort is made to reserve only twin-bedded rooms, it may occasionally happen that a hotel provides some double-bedded rooms instead. These rooms will be allocated to couples.

Please note that throughout Europe it is standard policy that hotel rooms are not available for check-in before 1:00 p.m.

PRIVATE BATH AND SINGLE ROOMS

In exceptional cases, particularly in Scandinavia, provincial Britain, Russia and Eastern European countries where private bath or single rooms may sometimes not be available as reserved by us, refund will be made by the tour director. Claims made in this respect cannot be accepted after the tour.

CABINS ON NIGHT FERRIES

Cabins with private facilities cannot be provided on the overnight ferries Brindisi-Patras and Palermo-Naples. Single cabins cannot be provided on any of the overnight ferries featured in this brochure. Single tour members will usually be asked to share a cabin.

BAGGAGE

Free **airline** baggage allowance is two bags per person with combined maximum linear dimensions (length plus width plus depth) of 106″. Neither bag may exceed 62″ in length.

However, due to limited motorcoach capacity we urge our tour members to carry only **one** bag per person with dimensions not to exceed 30″ x 18″ x 10″.

Porterage for this bag is included in the tour price. If a second piece of luggage is carried, a fee of US$10 for tours of up to 19 days and US$20 for tours of 20 and more days will be collected by the tour director in Europe.

Globus-Gateway will furnish each client with a complimentary **travel bag,** which we recommend taking on the trip and which should be taken care of by the owner at all times. Should you prefer to take along another travel bag, the standard measurement of 17″ x 14″ x 8″ should not be exceeded.

No responsibility is accepted for loss of or damage to baggage or any of the passengers' belongings. Baggage insurance is recommended. See the facing page for our all-inclusive travel insurance.

NOT INCLUDED IN THE TOUR PRICE

Federal Inspection Fees for the U.S. Customs and Immigration ($10) and the $3 International Air Transportation Tax; passports; visas where required; tips to your tour director, tour driver and local city guides; gratuities on cruise ships. Laundry, beverages and food not on the regular table d'hôte menu (these items will be billed to you before leaving the hotel or restaurant), as well as all other items of a personal nature.

146 US

Fig. 4-10. In short or long form, conditions relating to each tour should be spelled out, so that tour members know what to expect, and so the tour company and agent are protected from subsequent complaints. (Courtesy of Globus-Gateway)

4. Photos should be assembled almost as soon as the tour is approved and should be on hand now.
5. Copy goes to the typesetter, then proofs are returned for **proofreading,** and the final set copy is approved.
6. Final layout is set, pictures placed and indicated on dummy, copy either pasted up or supplied to printshop for pasteup.
7. Instructions are provided to printer as to color(s), folding, numbers to be printed, and expected date of delivery. **Paper stock** is selected at this time, or, in all probability, earlier.
8. After delivery of brochures from printer, they are distributed. Envelopes for mailing to clients can be addressed in advance, perhaps using personal computers for labels. Other copies may be circulated among the travel agencies involved.
9. The metal plates used in printing will be saved by the printer in the event that additional copies might be needed.

Those are the general steps, but many other details could intrude. Other forms of illustrations—like line drawings—might be planned, requiring the work of an artist. Special paper stock could be specified, resulting in delays. (It's wise to check with the printer to see what paper stock is on hand or readily available before committing to the printing surface.) Special treatment, like die cutting, extra folds, or offsize formats may also present problems.

For the larger books from major tour operators, the principles are the same but, because of the complications of the larger size and multitude of illustrations, and the amount of type needed, a much longer time frame must be used. Every color photo, for example, has to be "separated," meaning that the original is divided into four plates for printing—yellow, red, blue, and black—printed one on top of the other, in perfect register. This gives the full color effect, but it takes time and is not inexpensive.

Direct Mail Offers Selectivity

Newsletters, individual letters, brochures and other printed pieces may all be part of a travel firm's direct mail campaign.

The obvious advantage of direct mail is the ability to reach select prospects with an advertising message. If you can isolate those recipients who are most likely to respond positively, you have achieved the highest form of promotional impact. You have eliminated a lot of "waste advertising," narrowing the readership to those who should have an interest in what you are selling.

Travel agencies and tour operators maintain their own lists composed of regular clients or good prospects. They may also purchase lists and experiment with "cold" mailings, mailings to those with whom they have no previous experience. Picking the right lists is a science. Are subscribers to travel maga-

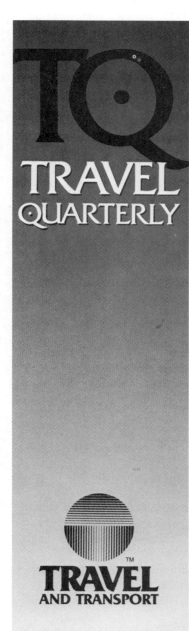

WINTER 1989
Volume No. 6

Oberammergau: don't miss the chance of your lifetime.

Discover the age-old spectacle of the Oberammergau Passion Play this year-- or wait another ten years. Tucked amid the glory of a 14-day European tour, Oberammergau is the opportunity of a lifetime to see an historic reenactment of Christ's Passion.

Together, Travel and Transport and TWA bring you two unique tour packages with tickets to Oberammergau '89.

The Heart of Europe

Experience a brilliant sampler of cultures and customs! Your travels, from London through France and on into Switzerland, Austria, Liechtenstein, Germany and Amsterdam, are highlighted by tickets to the full-day Oberammergau performance. This two-week adventure starts at $1,228 plus air fare. Departures available May through September.

The Promenade

Explore the natural beauties of Germany's Rhineland and Austria's Alps while gaining a special perspective on the medieval pageantry of Oberammergau. Stops at Westminster Abbey in London, St. Mark's in Venice, St. Peter's Basilica and the tiny church of St. Francis of Assisi, plus guaranteed seats at the Passion Play, make the Promenade a vacation to be enjoyed--and remembered. Fourteen days from $1,318 plus air fare. Departures available May through September.

Contact your nearest Travel and Transport office for details and a color brochure about Oberammergau. Remember, it's the opportunity of a lifetime that only occurs once in a decade!

Fig. 4-11. Company newsletters are used to inform staff as well as to encourage bookings by clients. (Courtesy of Travel & Transport)

zines better prospects than subscribers to business publications? How important is income? Age? If you buy a list of car owners, are Cadillac owners more likely to travel to Hawaii than Volkswagen owners?

For special tours, the list may already be compiled. Universities can supply alumni lists, and clubs and organizations planning a tour can provide their rosters.

Even with an intelligent list, the mailing package must still sell the tour or the tour company. This requires the ability to write prose that evokes interest, and both the trip and the price must be right. This isn't as easy as it may sound. Some commercial writers make a good living just by composing successful mailing pieces. Designers augment their efforts by organizing the material into an attractive, comprehensive whole.

Other Promotional Tools

Dozens of other items may be used in promoting tours: from a personal letter to **videocassettes;** slide shows are common; **telemarketing;** and even giveaway items, like maps.

It's well to remember that all of these sales aids normally rely on some personal contact to tie down the prospect. This is likely to be a travel consultant, but could be an active tour manager.

❏ *CHAPTER HIGHLIGHTS*

❏ Effective ways to market tours include word-of-mouth and personal contacts, one-on-one or in small groups.

❏ While much of the publicity in the travel industry is written by professional travel writers, the tour operator or travel agent should have someone capable of composing a news release, at the very least.

❏ The news release contains news, no puffery, and answers the basic "who, what, where, when, why, and how" questions.

❏ Major players in the travel industry utilize advertising agents to write, design, and place their advertising. Smaller agencies may have to struggle with the production of their own print ads. Some ads focus on single tours; most promote a variety of trips.

❏ The tour itinerary may appear as a working agenda for the tour manager, as part of a brochure, or as a personal guide for tour members.

❏ Brochures are commonly small enough to fit a #10 envelope, but some issued by large tour operators run to well over one hundred pages.

❏ While many tours use prepared brochures or brochure shells, some build the printed piece from the ground up. This requires knowing all the steps from creation of the idea to the finished printed product.

❏ Although travel brochure design is rarely unusual, it does take technical skills and should employ the services of a professional.

❏ Other promotional tools also exist, but some effective personal contact is needed to close the sale.

❏ *CASE PROBLEMS*

1. Select a tour from any brochure at a local travel agency, and assume you have the job of promoting it. Write a news release about this tour, trying to give it some news angle that will help with its editorial acceptance. This story is for your local newspaper. Check the format in this chapter before committing the release to paper.

2. Assume that a football team in your region has been invited to play in the Sugar Bowl in New Orleans on New Year's Day. Build a seven-day trip around this event, making tickets to the game part of the package. Put together a small brochure (8½" × 11" sheet, folded twice to give you six panels), writing the copy, preparing the itinerary, selecting or indicating the photos you want, and making a rough dummy to show the printer what you want. The week does not have to be spent entirely in New Orleans. What are you going to offer? How are you going to enthuse a potential tour member? The copy, dummy rough, and picture selection should be submitted to the instructor. It is not necessary to write down costs or tour conditions, and you may use yourself as tour manager for any biographical data you need to supply.

THE TOUR MANAGER

LEARNING OBJECTIVES

After reading this chapter you will be able to:

❏ Differentiate among the three principal types of tour managers
❏ List the duties of the tour manager
❏ Explain the source of tour leaders
❏ List the seven skills and fifteen personality traits common to good tour managers
❏ Discuss compensation for the tour manager, along with that individual's on-tour authority
❏ List some general sources for training and education

KEY CONCEPTS

Anticipation	Escort	Local guide
Assertiveness	First Aid	Occasional tour escort
Attention to details	Flexibility	Patience
Authority	Forcefulness	Personality traits
Company manual	Freelance escorts	Professional tour leader
Compensation	Geographic knowledge	Prospects
Continuing education	Good health	Sensitivity
CTC	IATM	Tact
Diligence	ICTA	
Enthusiasm	Language skills	

Tour managers (or escorts) make or break a tour. A bright, positive well-organized individual can turn a potential disaster into an experience; while an inept person can dampen a sunny day. As in any profession, there are those who perform admirably and those who just try to get by, but, overall, the caliber of tour leader has improved. Agencies are more conscious of their responsibilities, tour operators are more demanding of their personnel, and the availability of both books and training helps standardize tour management.

WHAT IS A TOUR MANAGER?

Regardless of the title you bestow on this person, the duties are somewhat consistent. They amount to overseeing a group of tourists, making certain their expectations are realized to the fullest. Often, the tour manager accompanies the group and serves as the liaison between the paying customers and the tour operator, helping with personal problems, seeing that the itinerary is followed, keeping tabs on the business end of things. In this role, the tour manager is like the home owner who hires a painter to touch up the interior walls. You plan, check, assess—but you don't handle a brush. Some tour managers may do much more—like the home owner who shares some of the painting chores.

Because of the overlapping of duties, it's difficult to draw a fine line between the terms **"escort"** and "tour leader" and even "tour manager." They should represent different functions, but the distinctions are rarely that neat.

There are **professional tour leaders,** men and women who make their living, or a significant part of it, from escorting travelers. Often they are based in destination countries and work familiar territory year after year. While this occupation offers an excellent opportunity to travel and to meet new people, it's not as glamorous as it looks or sounds. For one thing, it's hard work; for another, the typical pay is nothing to get excited about. There is also the chance of disagreeable passengers, hitches in the itinerary, boredom with the routine, and the impediments such a lifestyle places on relationships. A significant percentage of the full-time tour leaders are single.

Pros are usually tied in with specific tour operators. They are often multilingual and conversant with the customs and culture of their specialty areas. They receive individualized training for the job, frequently serve an apprenticeship, and periodically attend refresher courses. They may also possess a disproportionate share of the traits covered later in this chapter.

Freelance escorts may serve a number of companies and their commitment may be as complete as the full-time leaders', or as short as they can afford to make it. Free-lancing is less secure, but does allow for a certain amount of freedom and variety, plus the possibility of negotiating terms. The freelancer may be every bit as educated and knowledgeable as the full-time professional, and usually has some language skills.

Then there is the **occasional tour escort,** the person who takes a trip or two a year, the individual for whom this book will be most valuable. Their duties could be more organizational and managerial, and less informative.

They may not have a second language or the complete command of alien **geography** and culture. Perhaps their host duties will be supplemented by the commentary of a local or regional guide.

The occasional escort may be a member of a travel agency staff. Some like this duty—but not too often. Old timers get quite expert, and their trips fill up regardless of the destination. Tourists know they'll be taken care of, and that they'll have fun.

Non-travel-agency people may also escort. Their interests, expertise, or visibility may lead them to this undertaking. The trip may be their annual or semi-annual vacation or, if they have considerable free time, it may be an adjunct to their regular travel.

Duties of the Tour Manager

There is no set roster of duties for the tour manager, although some responsibilities are fairly common. It depends somewhat on the individuals involved and the tasks which must be performed. The more things a leader is able to do, the more valuable this person becomes, regardless of the number of support personnel involved.

Generally, the tour manager (or tour leader) must be prepared to handle emergencies as well as routine chores, much like a scoutmaster, infantry platoon leader, or office manager.

Depending on talent and experience, the manager may also assume some or all of the local guide duties. If he or she knows the country, commentary may be shared with a local person. A theater tour to New York, escorted by the director of a community playhouse or a college drama instructor, may not require another local guide—unless tourists want a city tour. Weekend football excursions would not normally add personnel for travelogue remarks. A cruise usually eliminates the need for more than an escort.

Even when the tour includes an experienced **local guide,** it helps if the escort can share some microphone time. Passengers expect a certain amount of this, and it also frees up the professional guides somewhat. Exchanging comments, stories, jokes, and songs makes for a pleasant combination.

Prior to embarking, the manager should also be active in helping to publicize the tour.

Where Do Tour Leaders Come From?

Excluding the professional or freelancer, occasional leaders may come from the ranks of educators, religious leaders, entertainment figures, political personalities, retired military personnel, individuals in business or the professions, and others. Some are travel agency staff members.

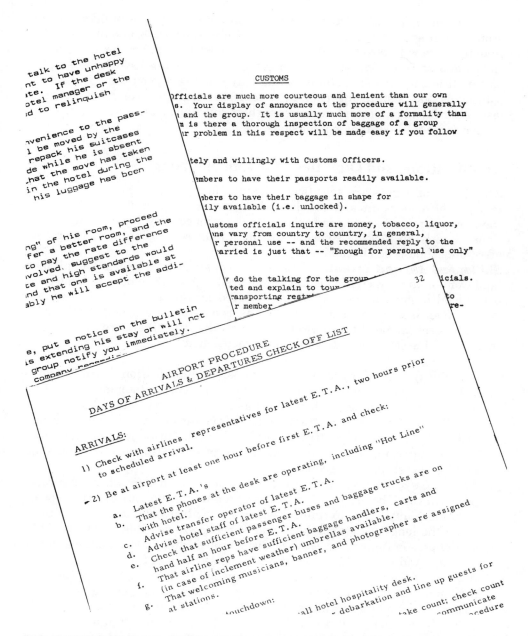

talk to the hotel
nt to have unhappy
ste. If the desk
otel manager or the
d to relinquish

nvenience to the pass-
l be moved by the
repack his suitcases
de while he is absent
hat the move has taken
in the hotel during the
his luggage has been

ng" of his room, proceed
fer a better room, and the
to pay the rate difference
volved. suggest to the
te and high standards would
nd that one is available at
ably he will accept the addi-

e, put a notice on the bulletin
is extending his stay or will not
group notify you immediately.
company renardi

CUSTOMS

fficials are much more courteous and lenient than our own
s. Your display of annoyance at the procedure will generally
and the group. It is usually much more of a formality than
n is there a thorough inspection of baggage of a group
r problem in this respect will be made easy if you follow

tely and willingly with Customs Officers.

mbers to have their passports readily available.

bers to have their baggage in shape for
ily available (i.e. unlocked).

ustoms officials inquire are money, tobacco, liquor,
ns vary from country to country, in general,
r personal use -- and the recommended reply to the
arried is just that -- "Enough for personal use only"

y do the talking for the group   32   icials.
ted and explain to tour
ransporting rest
r member

AIRPORT PROCEDURE
DAYS OF ARRIVALS & DEPARTURES CHECK OFF LIST

ARRIVALS:

1) Check with airlines representatives for latest E.T.A., two hours prior
to scheduled arrival.

2) Be at airport at least one hour before first E.T.A. and check:

　　a.　Latest E.T.A.'s
　　b.　That the phones at the desk are operating, including "Hot Line"
　　　　with hotel.
　　c.　Advise transfer operator of latest E.T.A.
　　d.　Advise hotel staff of latest E.T.A.
　　e.　Check that sufficient passenger buses and baggage trucks are on
　　　　hand half an hour before E.T.A.
　　f.　That airline reps have sufficient baggage handlers, carts and
　　　　(in case of inclement weather) umbrellas available.
　　g.　That welcoming musicians, banner, and photographer are assigned
　　　　at stations.

touchdown: all hotel hospitality desk.
　　　　　　　　　　　　－ debarkation and line up guests for
　　　　　　　　　　　　take count; check count
　　　　　　　　　　　　　　communicate
　　　　　　　　　　　　　　　　cedure

Fig. 5-1. Many tour operators and travel agencies prepare their own informal manuals for tour managers.

Teachers may take a study group to a foreign country, or build a package around their specialty, or may merely use their group skills and blocks of free time to see new landscapes. Ministers are featured as leaders for tours to the Holy Land or European shrines. Entertainers, including local radio and TV personalities, have their adherents and may promise a good time. Incumbent politicians, like a state governor, offer tourists a little prestige. Farmers may lead other farmers, doctors may escort their colleagues, and ski fanatics may gather those with similar persuasions.

Qualifications and Qualities of a Tour Manager

Some tour managers are specifically trained for this role; most are not. The majority of leaders must make do with a few sheets of written suggestions, their own common sense, and whatever experience they have accumulated. Consequently, in seeking someone to lead a tour, some general and personal attributes should be checked out.

Skills, Assets, and Talents   Despite our constitutional guarantee, all men (and women) are not created equal. Some are brighter than others; some have better health; some are gifted with more varied backgrounds. What you want in a tour leader is a mix of as many strengths as possible, along with a minimum of weaknesses. Some of these assets are learned, while others are inherent. Of the acquired assets, these few might be mentioned:

❏ *The ability to attract prospects*   Obviously, the professional tour leader, or the tour escort, may have little to do with securing tour members. The occasional tour manager, however, has to be able to command a following. The tour company or travel agency is counting on the name or reputation of this person to attract clients. This reputation may be from another occupation, or may be merely result of word-of-mouth comments on managerial skills or personality.

❏ *Knowledge of the area*   Everyone has to start fresh somewhere, but having been there before is a definite asset, enabling the tour escort to speak with more authority, to counsel wisely on facilities and attractions, to judge the length of travel days, and to recognize possible problems. This sort of person figures out ways to avoid crowds at Windsor Castle and the Vatican, and knows the reputation of restaurants in Suva.

❏ *A grasp of the destination language*   Such skills are required of the professional, but most occasional leaders would be without conversational speech. They end up in places where they must rely totally on the local guide. Nevertheless, if a working knowledge of the **language** is part of the tools of even the amateur leader, that's a plus—particularly in places like Russia and China. Not only the more common languages, like

Europe's finest team of tourism experts

Globus-Gateway has assembled Europe's top tourism professionals into a tightly knit, superbly functioning travel organization. We can show only a few faces, mention only a few names. Names are not so important, they change – even at Globus-Gateway, where lifetime careers are the rule rather than the exception. What matters is the spirit, the commitment to quality at all levels, the will to serve at a time when service is considered an endangered species.

"The tour director makes or breaks the tour"

This travel industry saying is very true. Therefore we dedicate more time and effort to selecting and training tour directors than to any other facet of our escorted tours.

To become a Globus-Gateway tour director a candidate must be at least 25, have an excellent educational background and extensive travel experience. Above all, we look for reliable people with friendly, outgoing personalities. Obviously, excellent command of English is a prerequisite, and candidates who will direct tours on the Continent must also speak at least two other major European languages.

After thorough theoretical training and severe oral and written tests, candidates are assigned to our top tour directors for on-the-job training.

This rigorous course equips every Globus-Gateway tour director to organize your days intelligently, smooth the way for you everywhere, and deliver an interesting running commentary.

A wealth of experience

An elite corps of 260 senior European tour directors is one of Globus-Gateway's most precious assets. Together these experts have clocked about 2'500 seasons on the road, successfully conducting more than 20'000 tours!

This represents an unbelievable wealth of first-hand touring experience on which we eagerly draw to refine our product. Globus-Gateway tours are carefully updated for each new season, and if necessary even during the season, to respond to changing conditions and the emergence of new opportunities. Our senior tour directors have a major say in this process – and you benefit!

Friendly hosts take care of you in London, Paris and Amsterdam

If your Globus-Gateway arrangements include a stay in the British capital, you'll enjoy the efficiency and friendliness of our team of uniformed London hosts. On independent tours, local hosts will also take good care of you in Paris and Amsterdam.

We select and train our hosts every bit as carefully as our tour directors. Their ambition is to make your stay as pleasant and interesting as possible.

Uniformed hosts are based at every Globus-Gateway hotel in London. In Paris and Amsterdam a local host will visit your hotel every day at a pre-arranged time.

Local guides provide deeper insight

Globus-Gateway invites local experts to join you in major European cities and places of historical interest. They know their way around and offer perspectives that a non-resident could hardly provide – history and culture, of course, but today's life, too, described with wit and humor.

A look behind the scenes

If you have a good time and your tour lives up to your high expectations, a lot of credit goes to the Globus-Gateway people you don't meet – the men and women behind the scenes.

The planners shape future programs; the negotiators contract for the right ingredients; the operators carefully look after tours in progress; area representatives at major crossroads throughout Europe give our tour directors local support.

All key positions are held by people who have honed their skills in many years of dedication to quality touring. Careers of 20, 30, and even 40 years are nothing unusual at Globus-Gateway. Our success is built on experience.

The highly motivated, highly efficient Globus-Gateway crew is the envy of the European travel industry.

Fig. 5-2. Besides selling hotels, sightseeing and attractions, tour operators can also sell prospects on the firm's experienced tour directors. (Courtesy of Globus-Gateway)

French, German and Italian, may be helpful but also, in certain circumstances, a fundamental grasp of sign language.

❑ *Education and intelligence*   Although these two attributes should coincide, they may not. Some educated individuals are not models of intelligence, and many intelligent people may not have much formal education beyond high school. Still, you want someone as a leader who is bright, who is quick to absorb and retain information, who speaks well, and who has somehow acquired good taste and good manners. The leader, however, should not be an intellectual who overpowers or bores the traveler. The best escorts are those who are only slightly smarter (but a lot more experienced) than the people they serve.

❑ *Experience and age*   Again, these factors should coalesce, but sometimes they don't. Some elders never seem to learn from experience, and some youngsters seem born mature. Age isn't everything, but a few gray hairs help in commanding attention and respect. However, it's better to have a competent youngster than an incompetent veteran. While direct travel experience is best, other experiences in leadership roles may transfer. The trick is to mold this alternate background in tourist terms. A financial tycoon, used to ordering his minions around, might produce a profitable balance sheet but he'd make a poor escort.

❑ *First aid skills*   As we'll see later, the leader must be cautious about assuming any medical burdens. But skills like artificial respiration, CPR, water safety, and first echelon **first aid** are valuable leadership adjuncts. Having someone competent in these areas provides a lot of comfort to tourists.

❑ *A penchant for details*   **Organizational skills** are often undervalued, particularly in areas like tour leadership where the emphasis is on charisma. You still want someone who thinks ahead, looks ahead, and calls ahead; someone who plots the itinerary in advance and monitors it daily; someone who is able to keep clear, complete, and accurate records. Leaders who slough off these duties are the curse of tour operators and agency managers. The good tour manager is always alert, always calculating, and always making notes.

Personality Traits   When you list **desirable traits** in any job description, you invariably create a perfect specimen. No human being measures up to these models. There are gaps in all our psyches. Still, this occupational litany sets forth characteristics one would hope to find in an employee, including the demanding role of tour escort. Given below are the assets most often mentioned in a survey of tour leaders or operators:

❑ *Forcefulness, decisiveness*   Regardless of other qualities, the leader has to **be able to lead,** has to have the ability to manage people, has to be able to make a decision. This is no job for an uncertain, timid personality.

❏ *A positive outlook*   The tour leader is an optimist, at least externally. And this optimism must be made contagious. Negative or cynical leaders are a drag. While rose-colored glasses shouldn't be in the leader's carry-on bag, a certain maturity is essential, enabling him or her to maintain a perspective and to communicate this confidence.

❏ *Tact*   Escorts must be **diplomats,** both with their tour members and with the suppliers of services. Gossip must be ignored; confidences have to be honored; feelings must be considered. Tour leadership can be exhausting and exasperating, but the tour leader must remain above the petty elements. He or she deals with each situation as firmly and pleasantly as possible.

❏ *Honesty and loyalty*   These virtues must be practiced on behalf of the escort's own integrity, the people he or she is leading, and the company that is paying the bills. Everything must be above board. There should be no hidden expenses, no cheating of clients. The leader shouldn't knock the firm for which he or she works. This is both unfair and unwise, and ultimately reflects back on the escort. In crises, the tour manager levels with passengers and employers. And reports and expenses are scrupulously handled.

❏ *Assertiveness*   This term has become a buzzword in today's society, and thousands of individuals pay high fees to gain this sort of presence. The tour leader had better possess self-assurance, self-pride, and a certain amount of ego. When a desk clerk insists there are no single rooms as promised by the vouchers, the leader must be **adamant.** "Get me a supervisor." This doesn't mean being loud and abusive, or acting tough; it means exhibiting inner strength and resolution. It means insisting on the rights of your tour members.

❏ *A calm demeanor*   Sweaty palms, maybe, but always a reassuring smile. The best leaders don't panic, even internally. They are cool in crises and respond immediately to emergencies. They are able to think clearly when chaos threatens. They seem at ease in the midst of trouble, and this soothes their charges. Experience helps in developing this trait, but some individuals possess it instinctively.

❏ *A warm personality*   The previous qualities seem almost militaristic in their application. And there must be a bit of the commanding officer in the tour escort. The difference is that this is a group of independent revelers and not a platoon. The tour leader, while establishing leadership credentials, must still communicate a sunny disposition, flash that ready smile, and reveal an **enthusiastic bonhomie.** Tourists expect their escorts to be lively, gifted with attractive voices, and to have that essential sense of humor. It doesn't pay to be officious, cold, or imperious with tourists or with hotel and restaurant personnel. Your reputation spreads, and you may be traveling this way again.

❑ *A clean and neat appearance*   Tour members can afford to look casual or disheveled, but the tour manager presents a perpetually scrubbed appearance. Travelers wonder how he or she can keep looking so fresh. Neatness adds to authority and it sets an example for others. An unkept escort reflects poorly on himself or herself, on the sponsoring company, and on the caliber of the tour.

❑ *Good health*   Not every tour manager has to be a dawn jogger or an isometrics fanatic, but each one should be in reasonably **good health,** free from debilitating complaints, and blessed with a reserve of stamina. The leader must always be "up" and stay ahead of his or her passengers. First up and sometimes the last to bed. Even when the escort is not feeling in top form, the illusion of vitality has to be there. There must also be resiliency, an ability to bounce back from the head cold or upset stomach, along with the will power to persevere, though ailing. Escorts, like mothers, can't really afford to get sick.

❑ *Sensitivity*   In addition to plotting routes and meeting emergencies, the tour leader studies his or her passengers, anticipating personality conflicts, massaging egos, tuning in on complaints, assessing the degree of fatigue, comforting the frightened or the lonely. The escort also notices things—the new hairdo, the special dress, the newly purchased sweater, the treasured souvenir. The leader has to be part psychologist, alert to people and their moods. At the same time, the tour manager can't be too **sensitive** personally. The occasional griper can't get under the leader's skin. He or she must ride with the punches.

❑ *Flexibility*   Some people panic when their routine is threatened. This often occurs with solid planners, who like things neat and orderly. The old Murphy's Law certainly applies to tours: "If anything can go wrong, it will." Planning minimizes catastrophe, but some changes are inevitable. There are equipment breakdowns, failures in communication, disagreeable and troublesome passengers, illnesses, natural disasters, transportation delays, and so on. Tour leaders **think on their feet.** They have the ability to change directions when the situation dictates.

❑ *Diligence*   Some tour leaders coast. They sit out the cruise alone. They get their people to a destination and disappear. Perhaps they are holed up with local buddies or merely incommunicado in their own rooms. They do a minimum of work. The real leader isn't afraid of hard work. He or she is **on top of things,** handling any reasonable task that needs to be done. This sort of escort is interested in everything working well, including making sure that each tourist enjoys his or her free time.

❑ *Sacrifice*   As with any leadership role, the escort must be willing to forego his or her own comfort for the good of the traveler. This may mean a swap of accommodations, or the interruption of some personal plan. The leader must be willing to **eat last, drink last, relax last.** This attitude persists from takeoff until the last bags leave the Stateside carousel.

❏ *Anticipation*   While flexibility is a necessary virtue, the wise escort figures out in advance everything that might go wrong and tries to ensure against these occurrences. This means frequent conversations with the bus driver or cruise personnel, advance phone calls, a survey of facilities before leading in the group. Nothing is taken for granted; **all items are checked and rechecked.**

❏ *Ability to create lasting friendships*   An experienced escort is able to bring people together, to seek out the lonely and integrate them, to make quartets of couples. The diverse group of individuals is made to think like a family, like men and women who enjoy each other and who want a minimum of friction. At the end of a good tour, the members are almost unwilling to part. They frequently stay in touch with each other and often travel together on subsequent trips.

Negative Qualities   No one has all the positive qualities listed above, at least not in perfection. Every tour leader is partially flawed. What tour operators want to avoid, however, are those potential leaders who are cursed with major defects. You don't want tour managers or escorts who are dishonest, lecherous, unstable, suffer from substance abuse, are lazy, timid, or abrasive, or who have no talent for managing others. These qualities are a liability in any job, but they spell disaster if inflicted on a group of people living in close proximity for weeks. When the leader loses respect or credibility, the tour falls apart.

COMPENSATION

As mentioned earlier, escorting tours is not a highly paid profession, although some veterans make a comfortable living for it. Most tour managers pursue more psychic rewards—the love of travel, a second income, the enjoyment of sharing one's knowledge with others. Even while these inducements are present, the job remains hard work and is **rarely adequately compensated.**

The escort may draw an annual or seasonal salary, may receive a stipend for each trip, or may take the tour for expenses. His or her hotel, food, and regular entertainment will be paid, and there should be a fund in the leader's possession for phone calls, buying occasional drinks for tour members, supplying an occasional modest surprise, for tipping, and for emergencies. If the escort is unsalaried, and if the tour makes money, many operators will share some of this largesse with the leader, particularly if this person helped with promotion and recruitment. This seems only fair.

The tour escort never solicits tips from passengers. If the subject arises, he or she should opt out of the conversation. Advice may be given, if requested, on gratuities to drivers, local guides, and others, but the leader should be indifferent to personal tips. If the tour members take up a collection for the escort, this may be accepted, but it's a good idea to blunt such fund-raising in advance. Many times a tour group will buy a gift for the leader and this may be acknowledged, particularly if it would be awkward to refuse. *But, to repeat, the escort should do nothing to encourage such gifts, especially those of a monetary nature.*

AUTHORITY OF THE TOUR LEADER

A tour leader's lines of authority aren't absolute, but they are substantial. Most tour operators spell them out in their manuals. In general, the escort is expected to maintain discipline and to meet emergencies with responsibility. This means the tour leader may dismiss from the tour individuals who are making others uncomfortable or who are making the leader's job impossible. The escort may also suggest itinerary changes for the convenience or safety of passengers, and he or she may allocate portions of the emergency fund when reason dictates. The leader is in charge and calls the shots.

Fig. 5-3. The tour manager must always be aware of the group, counting heads frequently.

Even within the broad responsibility, the leader has to be aware that such jurisdiction is limited. Nothing should be done that will later provoke unnecessary criticism of the escort or the company, or that may result in a lawsuit, or the withholding of payment by a supplier. Thoughtless personal attacks, unwarranted accusations, unauthorized medical advice, poor solutions in time of danger, reckless disregard for the published itinerary, arbitrary handling of personal conflicts—these and other lapses make both the leader and the operator vulnerable.

The escort should not demand alterations in the programmed itinerary. Such changes may be requested if the escort feels tour members are tired or would be otherwise inconvenienced, but this should be handled carefully.

The best course is a blend of diplomacy with **authority**. Perform those duties you have an obligation to perform, but keep all things in perspective. Tour leadership is not democratic, but neither is it autocratic. It revolves around good judgment and common sense. You lead, but you never seem to dictate. Leaders should review their responsibilities with their employers so there can be no misunderstandings. Many companies have their own guidelines, regulations, and limitations, in addition to the general terms governing group leadership.

TRAINING

Nothing beats experience, but experience takes time. Fortunately, there are some resources available to beginners.

Company manuals are useful tools. They can be brief folders capsulizing primary escort duties, or detailed brochures covering everything from lost passport to typical gratuities. Conversations with experienced escorts are another possibility. In these discussions, the newcomer should take notes and should have a list of questions to be answered. If the veteran has been to the specific locale the beginner plans to visit, so much the better.

Courses and Organizations

There are travel schools which include sessions on tour escorting, and college curricula which also touch on this specialty. Some offer a complete course in tour managing and guiding, to provide competent tour escorts for visitors to America, inculcating all of the skills found in the best of foreign escorts.

The International Association of Tour Managers, a professional worldwide organization begun in 1961 in London to upgrade and standardize tour management, defines its objectives as "the maintenance of an accepted code of

"Country Pursuits"
in England, Ireland and France

Escorted Programs

For travellers who prefer the companionship and convenience of a scheduled group tour, Abercrombie & Kent offers escorted programs in Britain, Ireland and France. These itineraries, which have been compared to "a travelling house party,"

At top: British Guides Gillian Gibbons and Ann Montgomery. Bottom row: Irish Guides Helen Cole and Eileen Connellan.

feature travel in comfortable luxury transport, stays at the finest country house and châteaux hotels and unique sightseeing excursions with the professional English-speaking guide which accompanies the tour throughout. Travellers dine at in-hotel restaurants often listed by Egon Ronay, Michelin or Gault-Millau. Some lunches are included but we have also planned for some to be taken on your own, as we know you will want to try the excellent and often surprisingly inexpensive fare offered by the local pubs, sidewalk cafés and bistros which dot your path.

Group Size

Our escorted programs are planned for a maximum of 12 to 15 passengers, an ideal number which enhances the feeling of a "travelling house party."

Itineraries And Points Of Departure

We have designed a wide variety of escorted programs, each highlighting a specific region of Britain, Ireland and France. In England, our popular 6-day **Legends of Sarum** travels in the south and west; **A Romantic's England** includes the North and the Lake District on a 6-day tour; and **The Grand Tour** traverses the island

from Edinburgh to Bath for a total of 12 exciting days. These programs depart from London's Savoy Hotel.

New this year, our 7-day **Scottish Sampler** offers an introduction to the beauties of Scotland's countryside.

Our **Irish Idyll** spends 10 days exploring the highlights of Britain's neighbor across the Irish Sea, on a tour which begins with an overnight stay at the Shelbourne Hotel in Dublin.

In France we offer two very special escorted itineraries: the 8-day **Le Cœur de la France** concentrates on the Ile de France, Val de Loire and Burgundy regions near Paris, and **Le Grand Tour de France** spends 12 days exploring near the capital and south to Provence and the Riviera. Both of these programs depart from the Hôtel Lutétia-Concorde in Paris.

London and Paris Stopovers

Please note that escorted "Country Pursuits" programs in England and France **do not** include London or Paris hotel arrangements. We have purposely left these plans to your discretion, allowing you to stay in the hotel of your choice for as long as you choose, before or after your tour. In making your plans, we suggest that you consider one of the London or Paris hotels described on pages 8 and 9 of this brochure.

Guaranteed Departures

We are pleased to again offer guaranteed departures for all "Country Pursuits" programs in Britain, Ireland and France. Once your deposit has been received and your date confirmed, Abercrombie & Kent guarantees that your program will depart as scheduled.

Fig. 5-4. Guides are featured in this brochure page. (Courtesy of Abercrombie & Kent International, Inc.)

conduct amongst professional Tour Managers, thereby enlisting the confidence of the travel trade and public." Not a union but an association, **IATM** screens all membership applications carefully, requiring five years of tour management experience, references from members and employers, personal interviews, and confidential general membership approval. Members wear a small oval gold badge and meet annually in different international locations. Allied memberships are allocated to tourism-related firms and individuals, such as hotels, restaurants, carriers, travel agents, shopping centers, entertainment centers, and other organizations.

IATM officers point out that tourists to the United States now outnumber those from the United States and emphasize that there are not enough experienced tour managers to handle this influx. They stress the importance of the tour manager as an ambassador who can soften cultural shock for visitors to our shores. For information on IATM membership, or on the NYU six-week course, interested persons should write to: International Association of Tour Managers, North American Region, 100 Bank Street, Suite 3J, New York, NY 10014.

Tour management skills are also taught at the International Tour Management Institute, 625 Market Street, San Francisco, CA 94105 and at the American Tour Management Institute, 271 Madison Avenue, Suite 1403, New York, NY 10016. Other travel organizations (ASTA, ARTA, ICTA) periodically offer programs that deal with tour management. Some helpful books and periodicals are also available.

In its series of books to help travel agents prepare for their **CTC** (Certified Travel Consultant) exam, **ICTA** (The Institute of Certified Travel Agents) includes a volume entitled *Tourism for the Travel Agent* (ICTA, Wellesley, MA 02181). *The Tourism System: An Introductory Text* (Mill & Morrison, Prentice-Hall, Englewood Cliffs, NJ 07632) came out in 1985. There are also some relevant ideas in *The Psychology of Leisure Travel: Effective Marketing and Selling of Travel Services* (Mayo & Jarvis, CBI Publishing Co., Boston, MA, 1981).

It's worth mentioning that many travel companies provide their own tour management training, along with their own printed materials. These are very specific and practical.

For general information on the tour management profession, you can write to: US Tour Operators Association (USTOA), 211 East 51st St., New York, NY 10022.

❏ *CHAPTER HIGHLIGHTS*

❏ Tour managers may be full-time professionals, free lance escorts, or occasional tour leaders. They make or break a tour.

- ❏ Tour leaders, who may come from a variety of backgrounds and professions, also have a variety of duties, ranging from business functions to commentary.
- ❏ Tour managers should be knowledgeable, intelligent, experienced, organized, and might also possess linguistic and first aid skills. Personally, they should be assertive, decisive, positive, tactful, honest, warm, calm, neat, healthy, sensitive, flexible, diligent, and outgoing.
- ❏ Although some tour managers and escorts do well financially, most find their rewards in travel, added income, and the chance to share knowledge. While their authority has its limits, they must always remain in charge of the group.
- ❏ Experience may be the best teacher, but tour management courses and books can help.
- ❏ Individual travel agents, tour operators, and carriers provide their own short courses in tour management, along with their own manuals. This training is generally very pragmatic.

❏ *CASE STUDIES*

1. A local cleric comes to you, the president of a medium-sized travel agency, and says he's been thinking about leading a tour to the cathedrals of Europe. He tells you that as a very young boy he went to France with his parents, and he's always wanted to go back. His church has about eight hundred parishioners and he thinks he may be able to get some of them to sign up for the tour. What questions would you ask him? What would you tell him?

2. If you were writing a tour manager's brochure for those in your firm who might lead future tours, how would you express the firm's policy on the authority of the tour manager? Write a short paragraph covering this, keeping in mind the responsibilities and limitations.

6

PREPARING FOR THE TOUR

LEARNING OBJECTIVES

After reading this chapter you will:

❑ Know what information a tour manager needs and where to get it
❑ Understand what items are part of the tour manager's notebook and how each item is used
❑ See what materials are normally supplied to tour members
❑ Be familiar with passport and visa regulations, understand something about health concerns while traveling, and learn more about photography tips
❑ Appreciate the need for caution with money, travelers checks, and credit cards, along with the need to brief tour members on foreign currency
❑ Know how to pack more efficiently, and in accord with carrier and tour operator restrictions
❑ Understand the value of travel insurance and of tour member meetings

KEY CONCEPTS

Accident insurance
ARTA
Baby sitter cards
Baggage list
Baggage tags
Brochures
Cancellation insurance
Checklists
Commentary
Confirmations
Contacts
Credit cards
Electrical appliances

FAM trips
Foreign currency
Guidebooks
Handicapped tours
Health cards
Hotel lists
ICTA
Itinerary
Luggage insurance
Luggage limitations
Mail information
Money belts
Motion sickness

Packing
Passenger lists
Passports
Photography
Prescription medicines
Report forms
Rooming lists
Safety
Tour member meetings
Travelers checks
Vaccinations
Visas

The more you prepare, the less likelihood of something going wrong, or of something being left behind. Tour members (aided, perhaps, by the agency) have to get their acts together, and so do tour operators, travel agencies, and tour managers. **Checklists** are essential. Too many items are involved to trust to memory. Well in advance of the hectic final days before a trip, the tour manager should have a complete roster of things to be accomplished, and should tick these off as completed. A few of these chores take minutes; others take weeks.

GATHERING FURTHER INFORMATION

Even though some tour managers merely accompany the group, looking after routine details, it always helps to have some knowledge of the places to be visited. Tourists expect this. They'll ask questions about monetary exchange, or good restaurants, or prominent landmarks, or distances. They may query you on flora and fauna and history. "What is that yellow bush we keep seeing?" "How many francs in a dollar?" "Where's a good place to get fish?" While the local guide may field many of these, it increases the stature of the tour manager if some useful responses are made.

If this is a regular beat for the manager, the problem is largely solved, although it helps to keep current and to review new material. For those unfamiliar with the destination, various educational aids exist. They help the leader first to learn, and then to learn to share.

As a first priority, the escort must become familiar with maps of the countries to be visited. Get good maps—detailed maps—not sketchy ones that show only major cities. Travel the entire trip mentally, considering distance and terrain, familiarizing yourself with place-names and key highways. Refer to the map when studying the itinerary or perusing **guidebooks.** City maps are also helpful, particularly for places like London, Paris, Rome, Tokyo, New York, and other major population centers.

Most libraries are well stocked with guidebooks. Fodor and Fielding are the big names, but there are Blue Guides, Mobil Guides, and dozens of others. In these pages the escort will find information on mileage, day tours, famous landmarks, history, culture, hotels and restaurants, even average temperatures, clothing recommendations, and foreign phrases. Details on the areas to be visited should be studied closely and committed to memory, if possible. Most guides are very portable and can be carried on tour for instant reference.

In addition to tour guides, there are many travel books that provide a more relaxed look at these nations, often including helpful photos and interesting anecdotes. Depending on how deeply the escort plans to get into the subject, volumes on history, art, sociology, and anthropology may also prove useful.

Fig. 6-1. Basic volumes like the *Official Airline Guides* and the *Hotel and Travel Index* are indispensable tools. (From Reilly, *Effective Communication in the Travel Industry,* copyright 1990 by Delmar Publishers Inc.)

The United States Passport Service prepares material on most foreign countries. While its prose is terse, each brochure does focus on specific items of concern to traveling Americans. Consulates are also rich sources of information, as are the tourist bureaus in most countries. From the latter, you get not only maps and the typical brochures, but also regional booklets, schedules of events for the year, and items as specific as subway and train timetables.

The International Association of Tour Managers provides courses and a newsletter. **ARTA** and **ICTA** offer both seminars and printed materials, including, from ICTA, such publications as *Marketing Travel to Music Groups,* by William Wardell and *Travel and Stay Healthy,* by Joan Ehrenfeld. Eric Olson, a tour manager in Hollywood, publishes a magazine called *The Tourmaker.* The International Travel Library publishes a series of books covering hotels and resorts, international steamship schedules, a *World Travel Directory,* a *Travel Market Yearbook,* and other volumes. From the Brigham Young University Language and Intercultural Research Center come "Culturgrams." These are four-page pamphlets capsulizing the history, customs, lifestyles, and language of sixty-nine different countries. *Traveling Times,* another California-based tabloid, carries articles of a general and professional nature.

Then there are consumer publications like *Travel/Holiday, Travel Leisure,* and trade journals like *Travel Weekly, Travel Agent,* and *Travel Trade.* Many other magazines carry travel details, as do local and national newspapers. The tour manager should keep files of clippings from these sources on destinations he or she is likely to visit.

Travel Source Book Match makes the task even easier. For a fee of approximately $15, *Book Match* will provide you with a bibliography to fit both destination and interests, along with mini-reviews and other helpful hints. You tell them, for example, that you plan to conduct a tour of France, Germany, and Italy, specializing in visits to cathedrals; they'll provide the list of books that specifically cover this topic. Their address: Travel Source, 20103 LaRoda Court, Cupertino, CA 95014.

FAMILIARIZATION TOURS

Familiarization trips **(FAM trips),** mentioned earlier in this text, are another great asset. These packages are offered to travel consultants at a considerably reduced rate by carriers, tour operators, tourism bureaus, even destinations, hotels, and attractions. The aim of the sponsors is to showcase their offerings. For the travel agent or tour operator, the benefit is the opportunity to make an on-site inspection of the properties and events.

As an example of these familiarization trips, a fifteen-day tour of Bali, Bangkok, Singapore, and Kuala Lumpur was available to travel personnel for under $1,000. Eleven days in the Balkans was priced at $650. A Rose Bowl package, including RT air, hotel, game tickets, parade seats, transfers, and a New Year's Eve dinner came to $475 for the travel professional. There are weekend packages in resort cities, cruises, visits to Disney World and hundreds of other opportunities. Lists of these are contained in travel trade publications.

Travel agency managers encourage personnel to take these trips, often picking up part or all of the cost, and distributing these opportunities fairly with the firm. Those who take FAM trips are expected to file detailed reports on their experiences as an aid to other consultants and tour managers.

Besides making the trip personally, the tour manager can talk with others who have been in that locale, picking their brains for tips on hotels, restaurants, and things to see and do, along with things to avoid.

Some fundamental knowledge of the language is a big plus. Short of being proficient in the native tongue, the escort may still take a crash course in a language, or cram with a self-teaching record or book. Knowing how to read common signs, menu notations, and hotel information is very helpful; and even

---

MANY VIDEOS AVAILABLE

Travel agencies and libraries, as well as carrier and tourism bureaus are sources of travel videos. These may be used by the tour manager as a personal educational adjunct and can also be shown to prospects interested in a special area. Hundreds are available, including:

Glimpses of China	Greece and the Greek Islands
American Hawaii Cruise	Sunline—Amazon and Rio Cruise
Holland America-Spectacular Alaska	South Africa
Eurail	Journey to Adventure
TWA Getaway to Europe	Ireland—Bird's Eye View
The Other Britain	Hong Kong Tempo
Scandinavia in Short	New Zealand
Welcome to India	Las Vegas
The Bahamas: A Self Portrait	Delta River Cruise
Mexico: The Amigo Country	Maupintour's New England
Iberia—Spain, Portugal	Rhine Impressions

Fig. 6-2. Travel videos help create tourist enthusiasm.

the stylized phrases for standard conversations can assist one out of a difficult spot. Besides its emergency value, this basic language skill is a good way to establish group authority.

The tour manager must also be aware of local customs (especially the taboos and the unusual laws), the local currency, and rate of exchange. Tour members will undoubtedly query the tour manager on what to expect for their dollars.

Besides FAM trips, tour managers may also make "site inspection" trips to an area targeted for a specific future tour.

CHECKLISTS

Some travel checklists are available in booklet form. Magazines periodically include their suggestions for a quick review of preparations. These are handy ways to battle the tendency to forget something in the hectic days before a trip. If you can't find a handy checklist, make your own.

In *Travel/Holiday* there is a regular feature called "The Travel Advisor," in which tips are provided in a wide range of travel areas. Periodically, some of these tips are assembled into a checklist, as in the magazine's September 1986 issue. Larger travel agencies may offer booklets for travelers, reviewing with them a multitude of travel considerations. "Travel Planners" are available from tourist bureaus. AT&T co-sponsors a travel planner with the European Travel Commission, covering everything from **passport** and **visa** details to a weather summary. There is also information on clothing sizes, the metric system, value-added taxes, electrical current, appropriate dress, and even tipping and bicycle rental.

THE ITINERARY

Tour managers must mentally tour the entire route before the trip takes off. Think through possible hitches. If you drive from Kendal to Stratford, will you have time for supper before the Shakesperian performance? Does the excursion boat to the islands leave on a Tuesday? Are the shops open on the Monday afternoon you've scheduled for shopping? Can you reach the crystal factory before it closes for the day? Have you allowed enough time at the pyramids? Should you book a big banquet the night of your arrival?

Even though the hotels are set as part of the **itinerary,** you must think through this aspect of the tour, too. Here's where having been on the premises is a big help. How far is it to the shopping areas? Are there certain rooms to avoid because they are located next to the all-night subway, or right over a noisy bar? Is there a new and old section? How long does it take to get to the airport? How is the restaurant and how far are other restaurants? The hotel may have changed hands; or it is being remodeled; or the place is understaffed; or there is no elevator. Although the tour manager cannot always change these conditions, it is prudent to know about them so that, when appropriate, tour members can be alerted.

All planned events should be nailed down. Perhaps you intend to have a chamber music recital at the hotel. The group and hotel have both responded affirmatively, but somehow the interaction between both never comes off. Don't assume that anything will go right automatically. Check these details out. If you are attending the medieval banquet, are you making the first or second sitting? Does the cruise ship have the amenities you've promised clients? What's playing at the Palladium?

Seat assignments on airplanes and cabin assignments on ships should be known. Cruise ships supply stateroom charts, and there are diagrams of the different aircraft configurations. Tourists will want to know these things, so having the details in advance is an advantage.

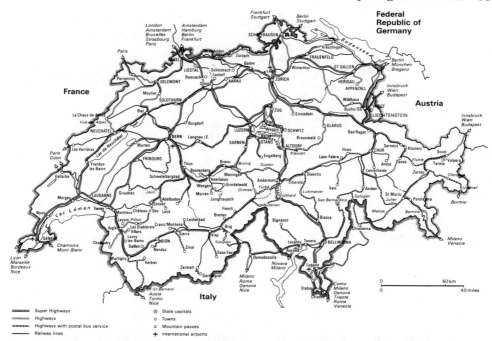

═══════ Super Highways	⊙ State capitals
────── Highways	○ Towns
∎∎∎∎∎∎ Highways with postal bus service	✕ Mountain passes
────── Railway lines	✈ International airports

Fig. 6-3. Tour planners work with maps, ascertaining the best routes and the time to be allotted to travel. (Courtesy of Swiss National Tourist Office)

ORGANIZE COMMENTARY MATERIALS

Assuming the escort is going to have something to say, even if he or she isn't doing the bulk of the descriptive work on the tour, it pays to gather material well in advance of the trip, and to collect it in some readily usable form.

A three-ring notebook with flexible binder works well. Two or three of these fit handily into any luggage. Perhaps one contains the itinerary, addresses of foreign contacts, national and city maps, maps of the underground systems, charts on monetary exchange, names of restaurants, list of optional tour choices, facts about entertainment selections, hotel **rooming lists,** mail information, several passenger lists, pages from the agency's tour manual, tipping suggestions, and other items directly pertinent to the trip.

The second (and third) book can be filled with historical and cultural facts, jokes and anecdotes, songs, appropriate poetic and literary selections, and other materials. The first notebook helps the escort accomplish the required duties, while the second or third gives this person something to say en route.

```
June 3      Ayr          Burns dates — 1759-1796
                         Suppers celebrate his birthday every January 25
                         Jean Armour
                         SONG SHEETS FOR LOCH LOMOND
                         Bring Burns poetry book. Use A Red, Red Rose and
                         The Banks O' Doon and some of The Cotter's Saturday
                         Night
                         Hours of the Burns Museum??

                         Tell them about the Glencoe Massacre. (2/13/1692)
                         Campbells/MacDonalds    Glen of the Weeping

                         Balloch Castle  1800    Wallace/Bruce took refuge

                         Glasgow   shipbuilding  12th century cathedral
                                   university over 500 years old



June 4      Windermere   Lunch at Gretna Green? What about bride & groom?

                         Carlisle   Romans    Castle/ Queen Mary's Tower museum
                                    Sir Walter Scott's marriage

                         Read from some of Scott's works. Also Wordsworth.

                         Cruise schedule? Beatrix Potter.  Oldest mountains?
```

Fig. 6-4. Tour managers often prepare their own commentary notes. These may be part of a notebook, on cards, or on scraps of paper inserted into a guidebook. It depends a lot on preference and experience.

The First Notebook

Here, in more detail, are some of the items to be found in the working notebook.

❏ *Passenger list*   The basic **passenger list** gives the traveler's name and address, plus the first name of the spouse. The escort must get to know this list thoroughly, along with the preferred method of addressing each passenger. To this fundamental information might be added: passport number; notes on general health; allergies, if any; special diet, birthdays and anniversaries; next of kin; people to be notified in case of problems; blood type; physician's name and address; any other helpful details.

❏ *Rooming lists*   The roster of names can also be used for a rooming list. Merely type the name of each hotel on separate passenger list sheets. As you get to the hotels you can write the appropriate rooms by each name. You can also make special sheets for each hotel if you wish. In either case, take some extra sheets along in case you mess one up.

❏ *Baggage lists*   A few sheets for the **listing of baggage** should suffice for most trips. Again the roster of names appears, with a space beside each

Pleasant Prospect Tours
ORIENT DISCOVERY TOUR
October 6-22, 1991

TOUR MEMBERS

BYERS, Mr. and Mrs. Allan (Wilma)
2536 N. 61st Ave.
Wheaton, IL 60186

MONTINI, Ms. Loretta
3319 Spring St.
Itasca, IL 60143

COWDIN, Mrs. Justine
2222 Boniface Dr. #7
Shorewood, WI 53212

MONTINI, Ms. Sabrina
2391 Lakeshore Dr. #309
Chicago, IL 60605

FRANCKE, Mr. and Mrs. Steven (Bev)
9110 Wethersfield Lane
Winfield, IL 60190

PRICE, Mr. and Mrs. Harry (Donna)
1175 Congress Blvd.
Adams, IL 61101

HOLT, Mr. and Mrs. Arthur (Alice)
164 Phoenix St.
Wheaton, IL 60186

SCHERER, Mr. Thomas L.
414 Buffalo St.
Chicago, IL 60606

JAMES, Mr. and Mrs. Kevin (Mary)
5141 Calvert Ave.
Montello, WI 53948

THOMAS, Mr. and Mrs. Lester
11915 Appleton Court
Skokie, IL 60017

PHILBIN, Ted (Tour Manager)
Pleasant Prospect Tours
99 Grive Place
Wheaton, IL 60185

Home Address:
2525 Alameda Lane
Wheaton, IL 60186

Fig. 6-5. Tour member lists are provided to all tour members—primarily as a means of getting to know one another. But the list also helps the tour manager—who may want to add emergency phone numbers to his/her list.

name to record the number of bags. The bags are noted at departure time and modified if tour members add or subtract from their initial count.

❑ *List of persons at destination stops* You'll want the names of people in gateway cities, airline or cruise personnel, names of the tour operator contacts, motor coach company personnel, individuals in charge of special events, tourist bureau contacts, overseas representatives of your company, embassy staffs, perhaps even physicians, hotel managers, business representatives for some incentive tours, and the like. Each name should be accompanied by a title, address, and most importantly, a phone number. The more phone numbers, the better. If a telex number is desirable, add this. Try to consider all the individuals and types of individuals who would be useful in an emergency, and jot these names down.

❏ *Hotel confirmations* Bind into this folder all hotel confirmations, letters from hotel managers, and **confirmations** from restaurants, theaters, or other suppliers en route. In case of discrepancies or disputes, you have the documents with you. Include, also, all travel arrangements.

❏ *Detailed itinerary* This is particularly important for bus trips and less so for cruises and train tours, where stops are less frequent and scenic attractions fewer. The basic itinerary supplied by the tour operator is a start, but the escort should have an hour-by-hour docket, much more complete than the itinerary handed to tour members. This is a good place to make marginal notes about people to see or calls that should be made ahead.

❏ *Report forms* The escort needs space to **record daily happenings**— problems with passengers, missed connections, altered itinerary, hotel and restaurant assessments, and other matters. In addition, there should be an expense sheet for the recording of all monies expended by the tour manager. Since there is often little time for record keeping on tour, the more accessible and efficient these forms are, the easier the escort's task.

❏ *Trip brochures* A few copies of the tour **brochure** should be kept. The escort may need to check this en route, or the local guide or driver may want one, or suppliers may ask for a copy. Tour members may lose theirs and ask for another. Sometimes you recruit people from other, less satisfactory tours by supplying them with a copy; next time, they may book with you.

❏ *Miscellaneous* Many tour managers keep extra copies of everything, from passenger lists to itineraries. They also bind in maps and informative articles, along with fact sheets, addresses of friends, and checklists of other things to do.

MATERIALS FOR TOUR MEMBERS

Tour operators and/or travel agencies regularly supply some materials to travelers. The kind and number of these gifts vary from place to place, but the idea behind the items is to provide more comfort and interest on the trip. Some

R O O M I N G   L I S T

HOTEL: Mandarin Hotel   October 11-12

Mr. and Mrs. Allan Byers   24

Mrs. Justine Cowdin   11

Mr. and Mrs. Steve Francke 21

Mr. and Mrs. Arthur Holt   20

Mr. and Mrs. Kevin James   25

Ms. Loretta Montini   23

Ms. Sabrina Montini   23

Mr. and Mrs. Harry Price   28

Mr. Tom Scherer   19

Mr. and Mrs. Lester Thomas 27

Ted Philbin (Tour manager) 18   KEYS?

Escort   40   MEALTIMES?

Driver   41   DEPARTURE?

Fig. 6-6. The tour manager writes the room numbers next to the tour members' names; also checks on the location of the room keys, time of meals, sets up departure times, and checks for mail. A separate sheet is prepared for each hotel.

allow the tourist to stay in communication with his or her relatives. The tour manager must be able to answer queries on these items. Some of the things frequently supplied are:

❑   *"Baby sitter" cards*   These cards or sheets contain information on how the traveler can be reached en route, giving hotels (with addresses, phone numbers, and telex info), plus dates and destinations. Several of these would be supplied to each tour member.

❑ *Mail information* This could be part of the "baby sitter" card or a separate sheet that would include the average number of days to be allowed for mail from the United States to various parts of the world; the cost of airmail postage to these same destinations; the correct manner to address air mail envelopes; details on sending cables; and other pertinent data. The travel agency is usually listed below in case relatives seek further advice.

❑ *Hotel listings* All hotels are listed, together with addresses and phone numbers. These sheets, too, are for relatives and friends of the tour members.

❑ *Passenger list* Each tour member should get a couple of these. This makes the group more congenial, and aids those with short memories.

❑ *Preliminary itinerary* The final itinerary is usually given to tour members at departure time. Prior to that, perhaps all they have is the advertising brochure. However, some agencies also supply what is clearly labelled as a preliminary itinerary, giving the traveler some idea of the proposed trip.

❑ *Flight bags* These are an expense item for the agency and not all travel companies supply them. Those that do generally label the bags with their name, providing both identification and advertising. These should be a distinctive color and of serviceable quality. One to a client is the custom.

❑ *Baggage tags* Each tour member is given at least two of these, and the tour escort takes along a dozen or more to replace lost tags. A unique color and shape help with instant identification. Many companies seem to use red and green, and when several tours are in one hotel, the sorting of the bags can get confusing. A variant shape (a kiosk, a triangle, an ellipse) helps differentiate. Old tags should be removed when the new ones are applied, and many veteran travelers also stuff a business card inside each case, in the event the bag is lost and the tag torn away.

❑ *Maps* Some sort of map is a nice gift. Occasionally, these maps will be premarked with the route, or the escort and/or driver may mark them at the conclusion of the journey—if the passenger approves. The tour operator or tourist board may supply these and they are usually not in great detail. Passengers should be encouraged to purchase their own more complete maps.

TRAVEL TIPS

The travel agency may also pass along various tips on everything from **packing** and **photography** to insurance and foreign customs. Some of this informa-

CLOTHING SUGGESTIONS (cont. from page 5)

Ladies

1 or 2 light or medium weight three-piece suits (knits are excellent)
2 extra blouses (1 dressy and 1 casual)
1 sweater or cardigan
1 medium weight rain-repellent coat (all purpose)
3 basic dresses (including a dressier type outfit for cocktail parties, etc.)
3 pairs of shoes (2 comfortable walking shoes and 1 dressy)
1 robe, slippers
nightgown or pajamas
2 handbags (1 large and 1 smaller for dress, large enough to carry passport)
4 sets lingerie. Nylon takes less room and dries fast. Be sure to take enough stockings, all the same color, for the entire trip.
1 or 2 sports outfits and swim attire if resort areas are on your itinerary.
Pantsuits - are "in" around the world. You might prefer to substitute pantsuits for one of your regular suits or for one of your basic dresses.
Don't forget scarves, jewelry and accessories, cosmetics, facial tissues.

Gentlemen

1 or 2 suits (one preferably dark for evenings in the big cities)
1 or 2 extra pair of slacks
1 sport jacket
1 sweater
1 light or medium weight rain-repellent topcoat
2 pairs of shoes (wear one pair, pack the other)
3 dress shirts and 3 sport shirts (preferably the wash-and-wear variety)
3 sets of wash-and-wear undershirts and shorts
1 robe, slippers (optional)
Pajamas, socks, neckties (2 or 3 are enough), handkerchiefs. Bring your favorite toilet articles, although you can usually purchase these items abroad.

Miscellaneous

Extremely useful items are: small pocket or pen flashlight, small first-aid kit, sunglasses, spot remover, shoe cleaner, sewing kit (with a few extra buttons and safety pins), a bar of your favorite soap (soap is not always supplied in hotels), sanitary products, cold-water/hard-water detergent, extra pair eyeglasses or your prescription, sufficient quantity of any regularly used medication, shower cap, several soft washcloths, alarm clock, address book, instant coffee, instant juice mix.

6

AVERAGE TEMPERATURES*

The weather is no more predictable when traveling than at home. As you travel, be prepared for a few days of unseasonally hot and/or cold weather. The Fahrenheit Temperature guide "layer" your clothing as the needs undertaken perspiration.

*Celsius

.2
42
50
67
61
à 55
31 81
58 54

7

HANDBOOK for TRAVELERS

Compliments of TRAVEL AND TRANSPORT

Fig. 6-7. Some travel agencies supply handbooks to travelers, listing tips on everything from packing to tipping. (Courtesy of Travel & Transport)

tion may be given at **tour group meetings** before departure, but it's helpful to the participants to have it all in writing.

PASSPORTS

Remind travelers that everyone (even children) touring in a foreign country must have a passport. Give the tour members ample time to apply or re-apply for the passport, filling them in on what is necessary in order to obtain this document: proof of citizenship (a notarized birth certificate, affidavit of birth, baptismal certificate, or naturalization papers), proof of identity (e.g., a driver's license with photo and signature), and two recent portrait-like photos (2″ × 2″, color or black and white, dull finish, front view of face). Many travel agencies use a special polaroid camera to take such passport photos, but most travelers go to a studio specializing in this service. Vending machine pictures are **not** acceptable. The photo must be signed just as the tourist signed the passport application—which may be supplied by the travel agency.

Along with the items mentioned above, the passport applicant must bring to the passport agency (typically located in selective post offices in larger cities) the passport and execution fee ($35 for the passport and $7 for processing the application, except for travelers under the age of eighteen who pay only $20 for the passport). Cash is not acceptable for this transaction. Use check, money order, **traveler's check,** bank draft, or similar instrument.

Passports are good for ten years and may be renewed by mail. The old passport serves as proof of citizenship and identification, and should be mailed, together with two new photos (signed), the fee, and the Application for Passport by Mail form.

Visas, which constitute permission from a foreign country to visit, are not universally required. Most European countries, for example, do not require them. Since the rules on visas, tourist cards, and **health certificates** often change, and differ, even for adjacent nations, in terms of length of stay and other particulars, it's best to check with a knowledgeable travel agent or tour operator about the current requirements. They should have the information in their computer reservations systems or in their Official Airline Guide Travel Planners.

HEALTH TIPS

The tour manager should not try to replace the family physician, but there are some things in the health area that are important to know, both for the manager and for general advice to tour members. The tour manager should be wary about suggesting particular medicines or remedies, since bad advice could lead to a law suit. (Chapter 9 covers emergency health matters.)

The destination affects health concerns, as does the age and general condition of the traveler. Some foreign areas call for special shots or **vaccinations,** everything from smallpox to typhus injections. The United States Passport Service can supply this information, as can most travel agencies. Check early, since the potential for diseases like malaria requires the taking of pills two weeks before departure. When shots are mandated, the traveler is issued a health card which must be shown once the person returns to this country. Keep in mind that a country which may not require health certificates from a person traveling directly from the United States may insist on one if there is an en route stop at an "infected area."

Before leaving, tour members should check with their physicians, discussing what medicines, if any, should be taken along; reviewing their shot record; and getting a checkup while there.

If you're taking the group to areas where English is not routinely spoken, you may want a list of English-speaking doctors. Write to IAMAT (417 Center St., Lewiston, NY 14092) for a list of such physicians in 125 different countries. Other helpful agencies are Global Assist, the Intermedic Inc. network of English-speaking physicians, the fee-based membership in International SOS Assistance Inc. and the International Travelers Association (ITA).

Tour members should bring with them any **prescription medicines** (like heart and blood pressure pills), keeping them in their original bottles so they are not confiscated by customs officials. It's also prudent to carry on one's person a list of the generic names of all his/her prescriptions, plus a list of one's allergies. If available in tablet form, medicines are easier to carry this way. Medicines taken regularly should be with the traveler, in a carryon bag or purse. Some experts advise taking along twice as much medicine as needed, packing the extras in another bag. If the first is lost, the traveler is still covered.

An extra pair of glasses and the optometrist's prescription should be brought along, as well as extra false teeth, hearing aid batteries, and the like. Some people also like to carry an antacid, aspirin, Tylenol, antihistamines, decongestants, sunblock, throat lozenges, and a variety of other common medications. The tour manager may want to have a supply of these, too, along with bandaids and some first aid items; but should dispense these items with caution.

Travel can be tiring. People may be sitting for long periods on planes and buses, getting less oxygen, losing sleep, eating irregularly, drinking more, changing time zones. These factors affect health, and stress the fact that people should moderate their habits, get all the rest they can before the trip and, en route, carry all necessary medicines, and watch the food and drink intake. (See Chapter 7 for further en route suggestions.)

Alcohol reaches the bloodstream faster on airplanes, because of the decrease in atmospheric pressure. The effects of alcohol are heightened by the use of medicines like antihistamines, tranquilizers, sleeping pills, and **motion sickness** medicine. Moderation in eating, drinking, and the intake of medicine is advisable.

Ninety percent of travelers experience motion sickness at some time. Finding a seat in the center of the plane, a cabin amidships, or a seat nearer the front of the motorcoach helps. Many tourists take an antihistamine pill up to an hour before departure. A modern treatment is the Scopolamine patch that is tucked behind an ear to provide time-release protection.

People with chronic medical problems may also experience discomfort when flying. Head colds, sinusitis, asthma, pregnancy, recent surgery, heart problems, eye injuries, anemia, malaria—these are some of the conditions that should warrant a visit to the doctor's office before taking off.

When traveling outside the normal tourist routes, the United States Public Health Service recommends that tourists take gamma globulin shots to prevent the onset of hepatitis. They add that this process should be repeated every three months during extended stays in tropical areas or developing countries.

The United States Center for Disease Control in Atlanta, Georgia publishes a weekly chart of countries where there have been outbreaks of quarantinable diseases. People traveling to these countries despite the warnings are usually required to sign cards indicating they are aware of this potential danger. Remember that requirements for children may be different than those for adults, and that some shots must be taken several weeks before the trip in order to be effective.

For the **handicapped traveler,** the United States Travel Service, Department of Commerce, issues a brochure of travel tips, and Chatham Square Press, New York, published a book by Louise Weiss called *Access to the World,* which also treats this subject. A number of tour groups specialize in travel for the handicapped, including Evergreen Travel Service (Lynnwood, Washington), Flying Wheel Tours (Owatonna, Minnesota), Rambling Tours (Hallandale, Florida), and Vagabond Tours for the Deaf (Margate, Florida).

The tour manager must also be conscious of health problems that could occur at the destinations (e.g., altitude sickness, allergic reactions, the effects of imbibing contaminated food or water). In some locales, it is prudent to not only refrain from drinking the water, but to also refrain from using it in ice cube form, for brushing your teeth, or rinsing out your mouth. Bottled water should be opened at your table, and the seal checked. Be cautious about uncooked vegetables, about foods left out too long in tropical heat, and even airline food on planes originating in countries where these warnings apply.

There are some helpful books available on this topic. *A Physician's Guide for Travelers* (Dr. Edward Orzac, E.S.O., Inc., P.O. Box 149, Hewlett, NY 11559) sells for $2.95; *The Healthy Traveler* (Beth Weinhouse, Pocket Books, 1230 Avenue of the Americas, New York, NY 10020) goes for $6.95; and *Health Information for International Travel* is free to travel agents who write to Travelers' Health Activity, Centers for Disease Control, Division of Quarantine, CPS-DQ Mail Stop E03, 1600 Clifton Rd., N.E., Atlanta, GA 30333.

PHOTOGRAPHY

Just as the tour manager should be timid about prescribing medical treatments, he or she should also step lightly when it comes to providing photographic advice. Even poor photographers may resent someone telling them what they should be doing. However, for those who may request assistance, or as part of a general mailer or instruction to tour members, it's handy for the tour manager to know something about the use of a camera.

Remind tourists to check their cameras to be sure they're in good shape. If they've purchased a new camera, they should experiment with it before departure, to iron out any problems. If the camera is a foreign make, they should register it with the customs authorities before leaving, to avoid the possibility of paying duty on the camera on the return trip. This goes for any foreign-made item—watch, field glasses, radio, lenses, and the like. The traveler should carry a Certificate of Registration for each of these things taken abroad.

Film is invariably cheaper in the United States, so the tour member should get plenty before departure. Because film is really the least expensive part of photography, it's a shame to run out. Experts advise that travelers not try to take both still and movie cameras, because they become burdensome and enough time can't be devoted to either, resulting in poor pictures. They also advise taking along several lenses, and are especially high on zoom lenses, since these replace several other lenses.

Other recommendations of the pro's are: insure the equipment, and take several speeds of films, anywhere from ASA 64 to ASA 400. Flash attachments, filters, cleaning equipment, and other items are good to have along. Some countries limit the amount of film which can be taken in, so this should also be checked.

There are college and technical school courses on photography, hundreds of photography workshops, and plenty of books on the subject. People using still cameras or video cameras will find these an excellent investment. Barring those, camera buffs should at least chat with someone familiar with the equipment, and should experiment while still at home.

For those concerned about possible x-ray damage to film at airports, a hand inspection may be requested; or a lead-lined protective bag could be purchased at a photo shop. Professionals seem nervous about *any* form of x-ray, even though airline representatives insist that their equipment is a threat to only the very fast film. The tour manager should be conservative on this issue!

On cruises, camera bugs find they can take more equipment along, since they can leave some in the cabin rather than having to tote it everywhere. The cabin is also a smart place to keep film, since it's cooler. Outside, the camera lens should be protected.

Most travelers carry their equipment rather than pack it in their luggage, where it could get damaged. And the wise photographer brings the film home to be processed—because it costs much less.

In some countries there may be restrictions on the use of video cameras, along with prohibitions on shooting certain locations.

Remember that heat can damage film, including heat inside vehicles. In these conditions, film may warp, lose color, or fog over. If the camera gets wet (in a light rain, for example), it should be dried off as soon as possible. That's why camera covers help; so do camera bags, or even plastic bags which can be wrapped around the camera. A lens tissue or soft, dry cloth, not any chemicals used to clean glasses, should be used to dry or clean a lens.

Other tips about photography appear in the next two chapters.

MONEY

Tourists should be advised to carry only a small amount of cash, including only a small amount of **foreign currency,** if they bring that with them. There are also limitations on the amount of currency one can bring into foreign countries, or back into the United States.

Travelers checks are still the best and safest way to carry funds. They can be supplemented by personal checks (which can be used with varying success) and **credit cards,** preferably the credit cards most acceptable in the destination countries.

The major credit cards have strengths and weaknesses. Visa and Master-Card, for example, provide a high degree of acceptance, a chance to spread payments over several months, plus bank-backed credit. However, they come with a high interest rate, something American Express and Diners Club assess only on airline tickets on extended payment plans. These latter two cards, however, require that charges be paid in full when the bill is received. But their offices may have far more convenient hours than the typical bank card.

Card holders should be aware of other benefits available to them, like **accident insurance and even luggage insurance** on some cards; the ability to guarantee a room reservation; the opportunity to cash a personal check or access an automated-teller machine; discounts on car rental, hotels, and other services; even medical and legal referral services.

Travelers should keep a running tab of their expenses, to save a surprise bill later. They should also check their statements for error. Since credit card fraud is growing, tourists should never give a caller their credit card number over the telephone, should save their receipts, make certain they get their card back at places of purchase, and should immediately destroy all out-dated cards. A list of credit card numbers, along with a list of travelers check numbers, should be carried in a couple of places by the tour member, and an additional

Foreign Exchange	Currency	Value in U.S. Dollars (January, 1990)
Argentina	Peso	.0006
Australia	Dollar	.7670
Austria	Schilling	.0843
Belgium	Franc	.0284
Brazil	Cruzado	.06468
Britain	Pound	1.6585
Canada	Dollar	.8498
Chile	Peso	.003875
Colombia	Peso	.002314
Denmark	Krone	.1531
Egypt	Pound	.3856
Finland	Markka	.2516
France	Franc	.1747
Greece	Drachma	.006369
Hong Kong	Dollar	.1280
India	Rupee	.0586
Indonesia	Rupiah	.000557
Ireland	Punt	1.5703
Israel	Shekel	.5263
Italy	Lira	.000798
Japan	Yen	.006893
Jordan	Dinar	1.5399
Kuwait	Dinar	3.4335
Lebanon	Pound	.01808
Malaysia	Ringgit	.3699
Mexico	Peso	.000370
Netherlands	Guilder/Florin	.5270
New Zealand	Dollar	.6010
Norway	Krone	.1533
Pakistan	Rupee	.0471
Peru	Sol	.000124
Philippines	Peso	.0452
Portugal	Escudo	.006745
Saudi Arabia	Rial	.2667
Singapore	Dollar	.5329
South Korea	Won	.001455
South Africa	Rand	.3922
Spain	Peseta	.009153
Sweden	Krona	.1624
Switzerland	Franc/Franken	.6698
Taiwan	Dollar	.0386
Thailand	Baht	.03883
Turkey	Lira	.000431
Uruguay	Peso	.001248
Venezuela	Bolivar	.0230
West Germany	Deutsche Mark	.5893
Yugoslavia	Dinar	.08326

Fig. 6-8. Examples of some foreign currencies and their exchange rates. Tour managers should check these regularly when planning tours.

copy should be left at the traveler's home. Carbons of credit card purchases should always be destroyed.

If the tour is a lengthy one, some tourists have their local bank dispatch funds to them at certain key cities. Tour managers who want to avoid carrying around too much paper can do the same.

Money belts are recommended as safe places to keep funds. A shirt or breast pocket for men, and the bottom of the pocketbook for women, are the safest places for wallets. "Joggers' belts" are also popular. When in areas that have a reputation for pickpockets and thieves, the tour manager should advise tour members to be especially careful. The tour manager may also remind them of the wisdom of stashing valuables in the hotel safe.

You can often get a small amount of foreign currency at a local bank, in tip packs, but carrying this overseas isn't usually necessary. International airports have banks on the premises, so you can exchange currency, or cash travelers checks right away.

It helps to inform the tour members of the exchange rate and about the monetary system of the nations they'll visit. Since many of them will forget this, or will panic when faced with a transaction, it's better to have something printed up, even with illustrations of the foreign coinage and bills.

ELECTRICAL APPLIANCES

Hair dryers, traveling irons, electrical razors, and other appliances will not work in foreign countries without special attachments (which can be purchased in this country) and adaptor plugs. Even with these devices, some outlets work and some are balky. It's better to leave these appliances at home, if you can, remembering that most hotels and cities can handle your needs. Travelers carrying butane hair curlers in their luggage have had them confiscated, so it's best to check in advance.

The Franzus Company publishes a brochure on foreign electrical currents, and also sells a line of converters and adaptors. Other makes are also on the market. The OAG (Official Airline Guide) *Travel Planner* lists details on electrical currents in specific countries, too.

PACKING

The secret to packing is to take as little as possible and to plan items intelligently. The tour manager must let tour members know what the **luggage limitations** are. These may be set by the international carrier (and detailed in their brochures), and could be further restricted by the tour manager or tour operator. After all, even if the airlines would allow every passenger to take four bags, where would these fit in the touring coach?

If possible, it's advisable to pack everything except carryon items into one bag whose total weight does not exceed forty-four pounds. Some tour conditions vary, permitting a couple of bags, and specifying certain linear dimensions for luggage, so this information should be passed along to tour members.

When measuring luggage to stay within the total 106 inches required by some international airlines, keep in mind that no single bag may exceed sixty-two inches (length plus width plus depth). If one bag is fifty-eight inches, the second can be no more than forty-eight inches in total dimensions. However, if the forty-four pound weight limit applies, both bags cannot exceed this limit.

Often the airlines will ignore this weight, or they may just weigh the total baggage of a tour and not worry if it adds up to a few more pounds than would be allotted per person. But the tour manager should not promise this latitude to passengers. It's better to advise them to stay within limits. The single bag under forty-four pounds remains the safest alternative. (First Class passengers are allowed sixty-six pounds and 124 inches total.)

Regulations regarding baggage on cruise ships, planes, and domestic buses and airlines should be checked out in advance.

Carryon luggage, which is not normally reckoned in the weight, may include purses, camera equipment, umbrella, books, usually the flight bag and similar items which may be stored under the seat. The common dimensions for such storage is figured at forty-five inches. Suit bags, which can be hung in the plane's closet, are often allowed, but not guaranteed. Hat boxes or wig boxes are checked as luggage. Exceptions are noted in the worldwide OAG volume.

Because travelers have been ignoring the regulations about carryon baggage or have been stretching the rules to the limit, many airlines have tightened their restrictions. People trying to carry oversized luggage aboard will be sent back to the airline counter to check the item in as regular baggage. Carryon luggage that exceeds the stated limits may be a hazard, can cause delays when late arrivals can find no compartment space, and may be dangerous for other passengers in the event of turbulence.

Since airlines and aircraft differ, the tour manager should call the airline well in advance to learn their restrictions and policies regarding weight, size, and types of items. Knowing the configuration of the particular aircraft also helps when considering space underneath the seats.

The important thing to remember is that you should learn the specific airline policies and obey these policies. That's how you and your passengers stay out of trouble and avoid what may be a considerable excess baggage charge.

Besides tagging each item, including carryon items, many veteran travelers identify their bags for ready retrieval by using decals, colored twine, a wraparound strap, or other marking. Since much luggage is similar, this makes good sense. It's also smart to put some identification—like a business card—*inside* the luggage, just in case the exterior tags are ripped off and you need to identify the contents.

Any traveler should keep an eye out for new, convenient pieces of luggage, especially if the old units are getting threadbare. There are compact carryons with many pockets and compartments which open out into a garment bag. There are expandable bags, lightweight bags made of sturdy new synthetics, ones with recessed wheels, luggage with combination locks, and a variety of other models.

Packing Sensibly.

Sensibly filling these bags is nearly an art. ASTA (American Society of Travel Agents) provides brochures titled "Packing Tips for Her" and "Packing Tips for Him" which condense a great deal of information into a few pages. So does the *European Travel Planner* mentioned earlier in this chapter. ASTA's packing objectives are:

"To protect clothes in transit; to make them easily available when you arrive; and to make them easy to repack."

Light, durable luggage is preferred, with ample room. They should have locks that work and the tourist should retain a couple of sets of keys.

And now the contents!

Some planning must go into packing. Consider the climate and season of the destination, the customs of the country (are shorts and halter tops allowed?), and the specific activities in your itinerary. Then try to economize as much as possible on selections, making each item in the wardrobe do double duty in combination with other items. Anticipating what you'll need for each occasion and organizing your clothes around one basic color is sound advice. Plan accessories, eliminating duplications and nonessential pieces. Avoid clothing that requires special care or that can be worn only once. Polyesters, wash-and-wear outfits, and other convenience clothing are the best. Mix and match outfits provide a fresh look. Knit clothes also travel well.

Clothing should be comfortable—particularly shoes. One pair of shoes for walking and another for dress should suffice; a sweater, an all-weather topcoat, permanent press shirts, a crushable hat, cocktail dress or long skirt, bathing suit, at least three sets of underwear (one for wearing, one for washing, and one in reserve), quick-drying nylons and panty hose, a couple of pairs of pajamas or nightgowns (permanent press), bathing cap, a few neckties, scarf, lightweight jacket, slacks and suits, and a minimum of jewelry. The ASTA pamphlets and many travel agency brochures contain specific lists of clothing items to pack. Some are more generous in terms of shoes, underwear, socks, and even slippers, but the goal should still be to travel as light as possible.

Avoid carrying heavy appliances, but do take along cosmetics, medicines, soap (including a small packet of detergent), sewing kit, suntan lotion (if appropriate), toilet articles, sunglasses, travel alarm, towelettes, plastic bags, safety pins, spot remover, foot powder, shoehorn, sanitary napkins, pocket flashlight, home keys, and, perhaps, insect repellent and water purifying tablets. It's also a good idea to carry along a short rope and clothespins for bathroom drying. Some of these items—the ones that may be used en route—should be in the carryon flight bag or tote bag. These could include toothbrush and toothpaste, razor, slippers, change of stockings, washcloth, medication, and the like.

Again, minimizing the load remains the objective. Porters are no longer universal, and you may end up carrying your own bags at times. To help you cut down, picture yourself struggling through customs laden with excess baggage.

Odd-shaped items, like shoes and gloves, belong at the bottom of the suitcase, and items which can be packed flat should not be folded. Extra plastic bags, plus bags for shoes, are a good idea. Some travelers recommend shoe mittens rather than plastic bags, which can scratch the shoes.

Dresses and slacks can be layered, folding overhanging edges into each other. Put tissue paper on the inside fold of garments that might wrinkle. Level out layers of clothing to prevent shifting. Tuck socks into spare spaces. Belts should be placed, unrolled, along the sides of the cases. Underwear and pajamas should be folded lengthwise in thirds and rolled, sometimes with socks in the center. Pants and jackets are sometimes interlocked in folding, with the coat folded with sleeves back. The ASTA *Tips* even shows packing diagrams.

Do not pack things like tickets, passports, and medications. These should be with your carryon luggage. In fact, the flight bag or tote bag should be packed with the thought in mind that you might not see your other luggage for twenty-four hours. Can you survive on what you have with you? There are other miscellaneous tips:

- ❏ Buy sturdy, good quality luggage to begin with.
- ❏ Allow time for packing. Don't throw things in in a hurry.
- ❏ Place liquids in plastic bottles, only two-thirds full.
- ❏ Carry plastic skirt hangers.
- ❏ Bring a collapsible bag to carry gifts you buy.
- ❏ When you get to a destination, take out your clothes and hang them up. (Maids may also press things for you, if necessary on short stays.)
- ❏ Roommates may divide clothes, in case one bag is lost.

Added Packing Tips for the Tour Manager

Even though the tour manager has to carry more items than most travelers, the rule about minimizing effects applies here as well. Experienced leaders soon realize they have been bringing things they never used or wore, and they discard these on subsequent trips.

The tour manager should have an accordion envelope to hold tickets and baggage stubs, plus a handy wallet-like holder for travelers checks and vouchers and other important papers. These should be kept with the leader or placed in the hotel safe.

In addition to the items suggested above for all tourists, the tour manager *may* also want to take along extra baggage tags, itineraries, and passenger lists; playing cards; bottle opener; extension cord; alarm clock; rubber bands; needle and thread; motion sickness pills, laxatives, aspirin, and other common medicines; electrician's tape; maps and guide books; scissors; paper clips; ball-point pens; notepads; face cloth; plastic sandwich bags; perhaps a traveling iron, hair dryer and converter; perhaps a tip pack of foreign money, or liquor, or candy, or gifts.

The tour manager has to be even more careful than other tourists to avoid packing in suitcases any item he or she will need en route. Leaders must keep in mind their responsibility to others, and pack for the tour members as well as for themselves.

SAFETY

Tourists should be reminded to cancel their home deliveries (like newspapers and milk), and to have friends or neighbors check the vacant home periodically. Local police should also be notified and given the return date. All of this should be done close to departure so that details of your absence are not passed along. The milkman and newsboy shouldn't be given your precise schedule.

The house should be securely locked, appliances disconnected, except for a couple of lamps which should be fitted with timers to come on at set intervals.

Pay bills in advance and ask your post office to hold your mail until further notice.

Arrangements should be made for the care of plants and pets.

Using a business address instead of a home address on your luggage tabs is a deterrrent to those who hang around airports checking these tags, just to see who might be out of town.

Don't take anything on the trip that you'd hate to lose. Expensive jewelry and credit cards (ones you don't need) fall in that category, but so might photos, rare books, and other keepsakes. Camera, binoculars, expensive watches, and other items should be registered with Customs before departure, to avoid questions about purchase on the return trip.

For more safety tips, invest $1 in the U.S. State Department's *A Safe Trip Abroad* (Dept. 153R, Consumer Information Center, Pueblo, CO 81009).

INSURANCE

Promoting travel insurance is ticklish. The travel agency doesn't want the traveler to think this is a plot to build up agency profit. and yet, various forms of travel insurance are considered a good idea by almost everyone in the travel business.

There are all sorts of policies, covering accidental death and dismemberment, medical and dental care, **trip cancellation** or interruption, lost luggage, emergency medical evacuation, and even the repatriation of a person's remains following death while abroad. All of these possibilities are unpleasant to think about when contemplating a pleasure trip, but they happen all the time. Those considering the purchase of this insurance should read the policies closely, to make certain what they cover and to determine what exclusions apply. The traveler should also review his or her own policies to avoid overlap.

Even with insurance, a person who becomes ill while traveling may be required to pay the physician or hospital and then file a claim for reimbursement. The insurance company could contest a claim if it is proven that the illness or condition existed prior to departure.

Insurance for lost luggage gives you some funds to replace missing items until the claim is settled. Trip cancellation insurance helps take the sting out of ruined vacation plans or an illness that arrives after it's too late to cancel.

Premiums for all forms of travel insurance start as low as $5 or $10. Increases depend largely on the amount of coverage you want. For trip cancellation, for example, it may be necessary to cover only that amount you would forfeit in the event of cancellation and not the entire cost of the tour package. Your own accident or home owners policies may cover you and some of your possessions while traveling, so you could exclude that expense.

Half a dozen major companies (Travel Guard, Mutual of Omaha, HealthCare Abroad, Access America, ARM's Carefree, and Travel Insurance Pak) specialize in travel insurance. Other companies may provide some of this coverage.

As far as the tour manager is concerned, the travel agency or tour operator may pay for this person's insurance, or it could be treated as one of the expenses a tour manager should build into the cost of the trip.

MEETINGS WITH TOUR MEMBERS

Pretour meetings serve a variety of purposes. They introduce people to one another, help iron out details and answer questions, establish the authority of the tour manager, whet the appetites of the passengers, and may serve to entice others to book.

Letters should be sent in the name under which guests will be registered. Also mention date of expected arrival of addressee, exactly as indicated in sample below.

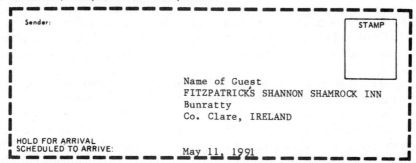

Sender:

STAMP

Name of Guest
FITZPATRICK'S SHANNON SHAMROCK INN
Bunratty
Co. Clare, IRELAND

HOLD FOR ARRIVAL
SCHEDULED TO ARRIVE: May 11, 1991

CABLE INFORMATION

Cables should be sent to the hotels "Letter Telegram." This is comparable to a Night Letter; delivered on the morning after the telegram is dispatched in the U.S.A. If faster delivery is desired, send "Straight Cable." Use first and last name of addressee. Unless full name is preferred, sign cables with only first name. The minimum cable charge includes 21 words, counting name, address, message and signature, except that name of country does not count as a word.

The schedule below indicates the number of days required for AIRMAIL DELIVERY from various points in USA to your friends or relatives abroad

Letters TO Mailed FROM	Europe	Middle-East	Far-East	Pacific Islands Australia New Zealand	Hawaii	Central America	Latin America	Africa	Russia
East Coast	6	7	9	8	6	6	7	8	7
West Coast	7	8	8	8	5	6	7	8	9
Midwest	7	8	8	8	6	6	7	8	7
South	7	8	9	8	6	5	6	9	8

IMPORTANT: This applies to mail between key cities only (New York—Copenhagen, Chicago—Paris, or San Francisco—Tokyo, etc.).
A day or two longer should be allowed for mail to smaller, off-the-beaten-path places. If you mail from a small town in the USA an additional one or two days should be added.

EXTRA TIME SHOULD BE ALLOWED FOR LETTERS TO ARRIVE AT DESTINATION PRIOR TO THE WEEKEND WHEN DEPARTURE OF ADDRESSEE IS BETWEEN SATURDAY NOON AND MONDAY NOON.

Fig. 6-9. Tour members should be provided with information on the way friends may write to them overseas. A hotel list may also be supplied, giving addresses and overseas phone numbers.

The number of pretour meetings may be as few as one or as many as four or five. One or two would be the norm. The travel agency would be the likely sponsor, arranging for a place (perhaps a private home or a convenient hotel suite) and for any refreshments. There could be some simple decorations to match the theme of the trip: appropriate travel posters, maps, and artifacts; the food, too, could have a harmonious flavor—tea and scones for Ireland and the

British Isles, baklava for a Grecian cruise, fortune cookies for an excursion to China.

All those who are signed on for the tour should be urged to attend, including those who live too far away to come. Invited along with them might be others who have expressed real interest, plus friends of the tour members who might consider joining up. At least one representative of the travel agency should be on hand, plus the tour manager, and perhaps representatives of the carrier or the tour operator. Sometimes the latter two agencies may help with meeting costs.

Name tags should be issued to all attendees and an informal atmosphere should prevail. Give people a chance to know one another. Often at these meetings tourists booking single rooms but seeking a roommate may pair up. Others may discover kinships they didn't know existed. For all of them, a certain amount of anxiety is removed.

The program should be simple. The representative of the travel agency may introduce everyone, saving the professional personnel and carrier/tour operator guests until last. This representative may cover some aspects of the tour and make some suggestions for preparations. The tour manager may then take over, or share the platform with the agency representative.

The itinerary will be reviewed and ground rules established. Any anticipated problems, like the stricter surveillance in some countries, will be covered. Travelers should be told what to expect and what unexpected things could sometimes occur. Team members then field questions, pass out materials, and review any matters left hanging. A checklist of topics helps here. The program may also include a slide show or film. When the evening (or afternoon) is winding down, the tour manager inquires if any of the non-booked guests wishes more information or wishes to sign up.

It usually works better to have the refreshments before the meeting, so that individuals can get acquainted first, and so that the questions are handled in a more organized manner. However, it's also well to have drinks or something after the more formal session, to allow further mingling, individual questions, and the opportunity for new tour members to enlist.

These pretour meetings should be well-planned and well-executed, since they set the tone for the subsequent journey, and they help in signing up those still wavering.

❏ *CHAPTER HIGHLIGHTS*

❏ Prior to embarking on a tour, the tour manager should secure as much information as possible, studying maps, reading guidebooks, consulting some travel services, visiting the area (perhaps on a familiarization tour), and talking to people who know that tour area.

GROUP TOUR SET-UP FORM

Operating
Branch _____   *Tour Number _____

Dates of Tour _____ _____ _____   _____ _____ _____

Description_____   Destination_____ (3 letter code)

City Origin #1_____ (3 letter code)   City Origin #2 _____

Air Carrier Name _____   Flight Number _____

Departure Time_____ (AM, PM)   Return Time _____ (AM, PM)

Flight Capacity _____

Print
Home Address?_____ (Y or N)

Air-Only Price _____   Commission Rates
                                                    External _____
*Supplied by Accounting Department   Internal_____

		Room Prices			
Hotel Name	Capacity	Single	Double	Triple	Quad
_____	_____	_____	_____	_____	____
_____	_____	_____	_____	_____	____
_____	_____	_____	_____	_____	____
_____	_____	_____	_____	_____	____
_____	_____	_____	_____	_____	____
_____	_____	_____	_____	_____	____

_____ Domestic

_____ Foreign

	Date	By
Prepared		
Approved		
Keyed		

Net Cost of Tour
   Per Person $_____
   Mark-up on Gross_____%
   Mark-up (Dollars) $_____
   Gross Selling Price $_____

Outside Wholesalers: _____

Comments: _____

APPROVED BY:
   Regional V.P. _____   Submitted By _____

   Operations V.P. _____

TT-AG-11

Fig. 6-10. This form and the two forms that follow help the travel agency set up a tour, record details for their files, and list the tour members. (Courtesy of Travel & Transport)

THE Group Department

DATE _____

BRANCH _____

AGENT _____

NAME OF GROUP _____

KEY CONTACT _____

PHONE NUMBER _____

ADDRESS _____

TRAVEL DATES: DEPARTURE _____ RETURN _____

DESTINATION(S) _____

_____

NUMBER IN GROUP _____

SPECIAL REQUESTS: _____

_____

_____

_____

PREVIOUS GROUP DESTINATIONS/HISTORY: _____

_____

_____

TYPE OF GROUP: ⧄ Social   ⧄ Special Interest   ⧄ Incentive

COMMENTS: _____ ⧄ Meeting

_____

_____

_____

_____

_____

MANAGER'S SIGNATURE _____ DATE _____

Fig. 6-11.

GROUP NAME:

GROUP# TG

DATES:

RESERVATION MANIFEST

PAX #	NAME	PAYMENTS	GENERAL REMARKS

Fig. 6-12.

❏ The tour manager should mentally review the itinerary, checking each move and each event against the planning required.

❏ If the tour manager is to handle some of the commentary, he or she will need to assemble printed materials to help with this.

❏ The tour manager also keeps a notebook containing passenger and rooming lists, baggage lists, contacts, confirmations, extra itineraries and brochures, report forms, and other letters and documents.

❏ Tour members are often supplied with "baby sitter cards," information on hotels and mailing addresses, lists of fellow passengers, baggage tags, maps, and even flight bags.

❏ Passports, good for ten years, are required for all foreign travel, but visas are not as universal.

❏ The tour manager should be wary about involving himself in medical problems, but should be familiar with medical matters as they involve travelers. He/she should know procedures for dealing with serious illness of a tour member while abroad.

❏ While unsolicited advice about photography should be issued sparingly, the tour manager should know enough to help those shutterbugs who request assistance.

❏ Travelers checks are the safest way to carry funds, and the tour manager should recommend this, along with general advice on credit cards and the local currency.

❏ Electrical appliances must be converted to the local current, but the fewer appliances carried, the better.

❏ Packing is an art, but it has a practical side, too. The size and weight of luggage must conform to airline and tour operator standards. Tour members are advised to pack efficiently and to travel light.

❏ Various forms of travel insurance (accident, luggage, cancellation, etc.) are recommended, but travelers should check their own policies as well as the benefits of those being offered.

❏ Tour member meetings are a good idea for socialization, communicating information, and recruiting uncertain prospects.

❏ *CASE PROBLEMS*

1. As tour manager you note that, half way through a two-week trip, one of the tour members has been unable to shake a persistent cold and hacking cough he's had almost since arrival aboard. He's been taking cough drops with little effect. Other tour members are obviously annoyed, and a couple of them seem to have picked up the cold. What action should you take, if any?

2. In your role as tour manager, you've informed everyone by mail and at a pre-tour meeting that luggage will be restricted to one bag per person, weighing no more than forty-four pounds. Everyone conforms to that regulation except for one couple who arrives with five cases between them. How do you handle this? Keep in mind the departure schedule, the attitude of other passengers, the potential embarrassment of the offending couple, possible airline disapproval, and the space on the touring coach.

3. You are leading a tour of Rome for a group of fifty college students. One develops appendicitis and requires emergency surgery. As tour manager, what actions do you take?

GETTING AWAY AND GETTING THERE

LEARNING OBJECTIVES

After reading this chapter you will:

- ❑ Know how to check in tour members and their luggage at the departure airport
- ❑ Understand more about the characteristics of the different types of carriers and the problems each may present
- ❑ Realize there are ways to minimize illness, boredom, and jet lag while traveling
- ❑ Know about checking into a foreign country, clearing their customs, and changing dollars into their currency
- ❑ Appreciate the need to keep track of travelers and luggage throughout

KEY CONCEPTS

Airline seating	Customs	Lost luggage
Airport check-in	Delays	Motorcoach
Baggage count	Early boarding	Motorcoach seating
Boarding pass	Eurail	Safety
Carriers	FAA	Ship's officers
Carryon luggage	Health tips	Smoking regulations
Cruise meals	Intermediate stops	Trains
Cruise ships	International lounge	
Currency exchange	Jet lag	

Like Aristotle's formula for a well-made play, each tour must have a beginning, a middle, and an end. More attention must be paid to the middle, perhaps, but the extremities are also important. First and last days are remembered.

Although some tours may originate with local transfers to an airport, most begin in airports, even those which eventually become cruise or bus trips. Consequently, the tour manager must have an effective routine for checking people in. The tour manager and a representative of the travel agency should arrive at the local airport about two hours before departure time—and this time should be checked in advance, to avoid unnecessary waiting. The airline should provide a separate check-in area, preferably at the end of the counter, and this should be identified by a sign (provided by the travel agency or airline) identifying the **check-in location** for tour members.

CHECKING IN

Travel agency personnel, working with the airline staff, should handle check-in procedures. This leaves the escort free to mingle with tour members, to meet their families, and to respond to last-minute questions. The escort may also pass out materials: final itineraries, maps, baggage tags, and other items. (Some agencies have more elaborate handouts at departure time. For example, Green Carpet Tours issues an "Almanac" to each traveler, containing tips on traveling, maps, and facts on places to be visited, with room for notes.) At this time, the tour escort should also note arrivals of tour members, counting those on deck and those yet to show.

While the escort socializes and tabulates, the travel agency staff member(s) tag baggage, help the airline passenger agent process tickets, count the number of pieces of luggage forwarded by each tour member, and record the appropriate number opposite each tourist's name on the **Baggage Count Sheet.** This sheet, plus the ticket envelopes and **boarding passes,** will then be turned over to the tour manager. Sometimes identifying stickers will be issued by the travel agency. They may also be attached to baggage by the agents or tour members. **Carryon luggage** should also be tagged and identified.

Once the passengers have assembled, the tour manager should make an effort to keep them together. If an airline lounge is available, that's perfect for small to medium-sized groups. Short of that, all tour members should be alerted as to the flight time and told to be at the departure gate (or other assembly area) at a time well in advance of departure. The tour manager should also know where everyone is, particularly if there are delays and the temptation to stray is strong. Before heading for the departure gate, the tour manager must check the coffee shops, bars, gift stores, game rooms, and other airport facilities. Travel agency staff members may help with this. You can never count heads too often. Just when you think everyone is on hand, some tour member decides to buy travel insurance or a paperback, or revisit the restroom. It's much safer to follow the military routine and have the group "in formation" long before they absolutely must be there. Of course, a solid pre-tour orientation helps eliminate much of this confusion.

Pleasant Prospect Tours   Orient Discovery   October, 1991

B A G C A G E   C O U N T

NAME	JOIN IN	# OF PIECES	WEIGHT
Mr. and Mrs. Allan Byers	CHI	3	
Mrs. Justine Cowdin	(NY)	3 2	
Mr. and Mrs. Steve Francke	CHI	3	
Mr. and Mrs. Arthur Holt	CHI	2	
Mr. and Mrs. Kevin James	CHI	2	
Ms. Loretta Montini	(NY)	2	
Ms. Sabrina Montini	(NY)	1	
Mr. and Mrs. Harry Price	CHI	2	
Mr. Tom Scherer	CHI	1	
Mr. and Mrs. Lester Thomas	CHI	3	

Fig. 7-1. The tour manager checks off the total number of bags per person at departure, and updates the list as changes are made. Often, the individual baggage weights are not recorded.

KNOW YOUR AIRPORTS

Airports vary considerably in size and convenience. In a 1988 *Travel Weekly*, futurist John Naisbitt, a prototype frequent flyer, rated airports, giving high marks to San Francisco's "most civilized airport in the world" and calling Washington's National Airport a "disgrace." He finds other terminals "beautifully organized" and still others are panned for the long distances between gates and the absence of enough carts. Anyone who travels a lot appreciates the fact that, in some cities the time spent getting from point A to point B can be a pedestrian challenge, especially when time between flights is tight. Consequently, the tour manager should be familiar with the layout of home and intermediate airports. Airlines have copies of the airport layouts they utilize and these are often reproduced in their in-flight magazines. Rand McNally publishes a magazine-size atlas that includes airport diagrams for many major cities. The OAG Travel Planners also include such graphics.

Another handy book is the pocket edition of Crampton's International Airport Transit Guide which tells you "How to Get from the Airport to the City

All Around the World." This is valuable when you have a long layover in some airport and tour members wonder if they have time to visit the nearby metropolis. Transportation choices are listed, along with fares.

Incidentally, another booklet worth having is the Department of Transportation's *Fly Rights* publication, available for $1 from the Consumer Information Center, Box 100, Pueblo, CO 81002. This small document gives information regarding airline obligations for overbooking, late or cancelled flights, and other passenger concerns. The tour manager should certainly be familiar with these rules.

Airports may not make the tour manager's job any too easy. Few have facilities for gathering tour members in a single quiet spot. Instead, the tour manager has to assemble people in some corner, hopefully out of the heavy traffic. Instructions may have to be yelled to confused tour members. Sometimes, too, the facilities for loading and unloading coaches are too crowded, too distant, too hard to find. Directional signs are often lacking, especially for those travelers who don't speak the local language. Some tour managers also complain about the shortage of **currency exchange** services and of porters.

A word of caution about airports. Since they are crowded, and since travelers are presumed to have money, this is a ripe arena for thieves, especially in unattended rest rooms. Travelers should not hang purses or travel bags on the door hooks of public rest rooms. Particularly after a person has made a purchase, the professional pickpocket may be watching to see where the wallet or coin purse is stashed. Tour leaders should warn tour members to be wary. They should also be told to guard against the pairs of thieves who work in tandem. One may deliberately drop a bill where the "mark" will find it and place it in his wallet. Then the other man moves in and lifts the wallet. Being conscious of these possibilities is a prime safeguard—there is no need to spoil a vacation before it starts.

In addition to materials, like the notebooks, that the tour manager has prepared in advance, he or she now assumes responsibility for the tickets and baggage receipts. Some tour operators suggest returning these to each passenger, making them responsible, but it works more smoothly if the tour manager never lets these items out of sight.

SMOKING RULES

Although the regulations may not be to the liking of every tourist, the current rules on smoking aboard domestic flights simplifies this aspect of the tour manager's duties. There's no need to separate tour members for this leg of the journey. Charter and international flights by U.S. airlines permit smoking but there has to be a no-smoking section as well. Foreign airlines are not covered by these rules, although they may invoke regulations of their own.

For the international flight, it is necessary to determine the smoking preference of travelers and to seat them accordingly. Normally, all of this is accomplished in advance, so that **seating assignments** are set before the tour begins. However, some carriers have restrictions on pre-flight seat selection for passengers traveling on heavily-discounted airfares.

Then the tour members get boarding passes, if these haven't been issued earlier. It's not possible to please everyone with seating, but the leader should make certain smokers and nonsmokers are properly sectionalized, and that spouses and others traveling together get adjacent accommodations. The airline's passenger agent will also help group tour members so they're not scattered throughout the plane. This makes it easier for the tour manager to keep things under control.

Veteran travelers are familiar with the configuration of aircraft, and they try to select seats on that basis. The quietest area is in front of the engines, the bumpiest nearest the tail, and the noisiest near the galleys and restrooms. The roomiest seats in the Coach class are behind bulkheads and by emergency exits. They may offer ten or more inches more leg room, even more than available in First Class. Charter flights, which add extra seats, may be over six inches less comfortable than normal airplane seating. Of course, from the tour manager's point of view, this information shouldn't be broadcast, but these seats could be allocated to taller persons or potential gripers.

Nonsmokers have to be seated in a nonsmoking area, even if this means reducing the size of the smoking area. If there aren't enough smoking seats, however, the smoker cannot demand expansion, and this situation will probably require tactful handling. With the domestic smoking bans now in force, this is more of a concern for foreign flights.

Few seating arrangements are perfect since configurations of aircraft differ. If they are window seats, perhaps they are at an odd angle for the in-flight movie. If they are aisle seats, they could be too close to the restrooms (where people congregate) or the smoking section, for nonsmokers. The tour manager should try to be considerate and equitable, and that's about all that can be done. A person cramped on an outward bound flight might be given a choice seat on the return trip. The tour manager might want to make notes of such situations, but the unhappy passenger is likely to remind the escort anyway. Tour managers should request seats at the front of the group for themselves, making for ease of checking and earlier deplaning.

CARRYON LUGGAGE

Hopefully, the tour manager or travel agent has detected any potential problem with carryon luggage. If not, this is the point where an alert person at the gate may send an offending traveler back to the ticket counter. Keep in mind that the **FAA** spot checks airlines to see that they are enforcing the stricter carryon regulations which went into effect on January 1, 1988.

Signs are generally posted where tourists can see them. "CARRYON BAGGAGE MUST FIT UNDER THE SEAT. OVERSIZED ITEMS MUST BE CHECKED." That's the way Eastern's gate counter sign spells it out. The tour manager also cautions tour members.

Despite this, passenger agents cite stories of people carrying aboard large musical instruments, valuable crockery, framed posters, rugs, automobile tires, and huge stuffed animals.

Often the airlines will let tour members board as a group. This makes it easier for the tour manager to check them aboard and to note if anyone is missing. The tour manager then boards last and, once aboard, counts again.

INTERMEDIATE DOMESTIC STOPS

If the plane stops within the United States, the tour manager must again note who gets off (if this is permitted) and then make certain these individuals get back on again. If there are absentees, the flight attendant or passenger agent must be notified. If additional tour members join the group en route, the tour manager locates them and helps them with their tickets and baggage, doing the job done by the travel agent(s) at the original departure city. These newcomers should be introduced to the other tour members at the earliest convenient time.

Many tour leaders are identified by special name tags or badges, and these command more attention from service personnel. (On a selfish note, such badges may also earn tour managers discounts in shops or preferential treatment in restaurants, but the manager must be careful about accepting such favors. Tour members could be resentful, or could suspect a fix.)

CHECKING THROUGH INTERNATIONAL

Except for tour members, joining the tour at the international airline desk, baggage should have been checked through from departure city to destination city and need not be hand-carried to the international carrier. However, the bags may still be weighed here, individually, or in a group. Since baggage routines vary among airlines and destinations, the tour manager should try to find out in advance what the drill will be. It's best to try to stay under the weight or measurement limits. In a sticky situation, where airline staffers demand extra money for individual overweight luggage, the offending passenger must pay this difference.

Once the tour arrives at the international airport, the tour manager must again remember to keep them together. Sometimes this means walking to the international wing; sometimes it means taking an intra-airport bus or limousine (for which the tour manager generally pays). Get everyone together, remind them where they are headed, and try to get them all on one vehicle. For large groups which must be split, assign a responsible person to see that they get off at the proper stop. No one should be allowed to stray from the group until it is checked in at international.

Once the tour members are reassembled in the **international lounge,** the tour manager collects the passports from tour members and brings them and the tickets to the carrier desk. Arriving at this desk early makes things much easier. The agents are not as likely to be busy and can handle the tour more efficiently, matching passports to tickets, pulling the appropriate coupons (the tour manager should monitor this), and returning tickets and passports to the tour manager, along with boarding passes. The passports and boarding passes are given to tour members, but the ticket packets are retained by the tour manager. Again, seating should be as sensible and equitable as possible.

Tour members now wait in the general international lounge, or, if the group is small and lucky enough, in the private lounge of the airline. If there is considerable time before departure, they may be allowed to go off to visit friends, or take a cab into town. In these cases, the tour manager sets an early return time, and finds out where everyone will be. This information might include a phone number where various members can be reached. Getting such numbers enables the tour manager to place a call if the plane's departure is delayed, or if the traveler fails to show at the appointed time.

The tour manager should also get as much information as possible on the flight, including the kind of plane, meal service, movie schedule, flight time, and time of arrival. Making these details available to the passengers enhances the manager's status.

At the agreed-upon assembly time, the head count starts again. If persons are missing they should be paged, or the previously-submitted phone numbers called. Once everyone is together, they should be kept together, even if the plane doesn't leave for half an hour. **Early boarding,** if permitted, should be requested, and the boarding procedure is the same as on domestic flights.

Only those who have led tours can appreciate how many things can go wrong at this juncture. A tour member leaves a raincoat in the lounge, goes back to retrieve it, forgets the boarding pass, and can't get back in . Someone follows a crowd through an adjoining gate and boards the wrong aircraft. A husband goes to the restroom and his wife takes both passes aboard. So the escort must remain alert, keeping sergeant-like track of the passengers, and must stay calm. After all, this is just the beginning of the trip!

CARRIERS

Each method of transportation has plus and minus features. Choices must be made, based on scheduling, speed, comfort, and expense.

Airlines

While travelers think of airlines in terms of service, the airlines also concentrate on their function as businesses. The emphasis in recent years has been on maintaining or improving service and safety standards, both of which require financial commitment. The average major airline has a payroll of approximately thirty-six thousand employees, and must maintain a fleet of about 275 airplanes. When things are good, profits may exceed $250 million, but a bad year can make that a minus figure. In 1986, Pan Am, hit hardest by European unrest and terrorism, showed losses of almost $470 million. So, while safety cannot be compromised, there may be cutbacks in personnel or services which affect tour groups.

Service, **safety,** and performance do not go unnoticed, however. Various magazines and associations periodically survey readers and members for their opinions on airlines. Items generally checked are convenience of schedules, ease of ticketing, on-time record, overbooking, baggage handling, cleanliness of equipment, attitudes of personnel, seating configurations, safety procedures, frequent flier programs, and food and drink service. In *Advertising Age's* 1987 survey, for example, the overall leaders were American Air Lines, Delta, and United Air Lines. Schedule, convenience, and cost may be major factors in a travel agency's, tour operator's, or tour organizer's choice of carrier, but the general reputation also figures in.

The tour escort and travel agent can minimize some flying concerns by a little passenger indoctrination beforehand. For a start, passengers may need to be sold on some of the less familiar but equally competent airlines. They know TWA and United, but they've never heard of SAA or Air-India. A few reassuring words help, and the airlines can do the rest.

Some travelers have a phobia about flying. They may never have flown before, or may have been frightened on their few routine flights, or they may have had a bad experience and quit flying. A preflight discussion of the construction and maintenance of planes, their safety features, the lengthy hours of pilot training, the preparation of flight plans, the existence of alternate landing strips, the automated back-up systems, the use of radar, and the constant links with ground control should dispel much apprehension. There are also courses which are designed to help travelers conquer such concerns.

When there is an emergency, such as a storm or malfunctioning equipment, the tour manager has to mask any personal fears. The stomach may be churning but the face must be calm and comforting. This minimizes the chance of hysteria or panic—or illness. Many people react wide-eyed to the slightest turbulence. While pilots frequently inform and cheer such timid travelers, the escort can also help. A smile, a wink, a shrug may communicate that all is well.

Tour Managers Set an Example   Since tour members tend to emulate their leader, it's important that the escort display interest in the routine instructions of the flight crew, including the familiar seat belt, oxygen, and flotation explanations. This way, the passengers also listen. One tour manager recalls an incident when the oxygen masks dropped down, not because of any emergency, but because a switch had inadvertently been hit. "Funny thing," he said. "Even though many of us had heard the lecture dozens of times, nobody reached for the masks. We sat stunned for a few moments until the captain told us it was a mistake."

Recent studies made in the wake of airline disasters as widely separated as Lockerbie, Scotland and Sioux City, Iowa, reveal that passengers can do a great deal to increase their chance of survival by listening to the commentary of the cabin attendants or paying attention to the video display on safety. The ability to evacuate the plane quickly is a major asset, so knowing where the nearest exit and an alternate exit are located is a must.

On long flights the tour manager should periodically patrol the aisles, checking to see that tour members are feeling reasonably well, that they are comfortable, and that their questions get answered. This is also a good time to get to know people better and to provide special attention to first time travelers.

Some travelers feel they can't be happy except on a wide-bodied plane. The big ones, like the 747 and the DC-10, can be very comfortable, but they also have their claustrophobic inside seats, and they can be a pain when everyone funnels through **customs** at once. Coach passengers may also resent being barred from the First Class lounge on such a plane.

Comfort can be enhanced by doing a few exercises en route, or at least getting up and walking, or stretching. Even in one's seat, it's possible to fight fatigue and stiffness by rotating the head, breathing deeply, putting pressure on the arm rests, jogging the legs up and down, rowing or apple-picking with the arms, flexing arms and shoulders, and similar exercises. Some European airlines show in-flight films of cabin exercises, or pass out literature with similar suggestions.

Another way to avoid the in-flight blahs is to eat and drink sensibly. Airline food varies. Some is prepared hurriedly, or too early, and is dry before it is served. This is further complicated by the drying action of the on-board ovens and the dehydration caused by high altitudes. Steak and fish are particularly affected by this. Some cooks also claim that foods which taste proper on land often taste bland in the air, so this calls for additional seasoning. Eating moderate amounts more often is the best idea. Special diets should be arranged before departure. Airline personnel try to discourage excessive drinking to some degree, but the escort must also be alert for tour members who tend to over-imbibe.

Some Health and Comfort Tips   The tour manager can't mother a whole group of adults, but knowing some things about in-flight comfort and discomfort adds to his/her stature. There are helps in the form of booklets and brochures, including those mentioned in the previous chapter. Some are quite specific. There are even wallet-size cards of tips for pregnant travelers (available from St. John's Hospital and Health Center, Maternity Services Department, 1328 22nd Street, Los Angeles, CA 90404).

More common tourist conditions would certainly include the common cold, a minor irritation that can be very painful at a cabin altitude of eight thousand feet. The problems seem to occur more during the descent than at any other time, so the tour manager might be alert to this. Physicians may advise those with colds not to fly at all, but it's unlikely a cold-ridden passenger will put off a tour that has been in the works for months—especially if he or she is going to lose part or all of the payment. Taking appropriate pills in advance, or drops or spray before the descent can help. Swallowing helps open the nasal and aural passages, as does holding the nose and blowing gently. Staying clear of the smoking section is beneficial, as is sitting up instead of leaning back. Airline personnel have their own tactics, like putting warm paper cups over ears that hurt. Dryness of the skin can be helped by application of a lotion. Dehydration can be eased by drinking water, fruit juice, or pop. Coffee and alcohol are diuretics and may have the traveler heading back and forth in a crowded plane.

Then there is **jet lag,** that tiring interruption of our internal biological rhythms. There are as many suggestions for conquering this malady as there are country home remedies. Some are just good sense: taking it easy the day before departure, eating lightly en route, avoiding alcoholic beverages, and adjusting as soon as possible to local time. Alternating heavy and light meals a few days before departure makes adjustment simpler. Physicians may also prescribe a pill to get the traveler through the first day or two—products like Halcion or Restoril, or their prescription equivalent.

There are other tricks, too. Some east/west travelers (jet lag is not really a problem on north/south flights) prepare a week ahead, varying their meal and sleep schedules to slowly creep up on the destination time. Aboard the plane, as well, they eat on destination time, even if it means carrying a sandwich on board; they sleep on destination time, perhaps right through the meal or movie.

Government Periodicals and Subscription Services

Price List 36

Edition 215
Fall 1989

Superintendent of Documents
U.S. Government Printing Office
Washington, D.C. 20402

Settling Down. Basic financial advice for the two-income family just starting out on how to manage money and plan for the future. 6 pp. (1988, USDA) **464V. 50¢.**

What You Should Know About the Pension Law. Explains your rights on pension benefits, payment schedules, and protections. 60 pp. (1987, DOL) **441V. 50¢.**

Your Insured Deposit. How your money is protected if your bank or savings institution is insured by the Federal Deposit Insurance Corporation. 11 pp. (1987, FDIC) **584V. Free.**

Credit

Building a Better Credit Record. Explains what credit bureaus are and how they can help you, how to read your credit report and improve your credit record. 14 pp. (1988, FTC) **442V. 50¢.**

Buying and Borrowing: Cash In On the Facts. Useful advice on solving credit problems, co-signing loans, buying on credit or by layaway, comparing warranties, and shopping by mail and phone. 16 pp. (1986, FTC) **443V. 50¢.**

Consumer Credit Handbook. How to apply for credit, what to do if it is denied, how to correct credit mistakes, and how consumer credit laws can help you. 44 pp. (1986, FRB) **444V. 50¢.**

Equal Credit Opportunity and Age: Your Rights. What a creditor may and may not consider when determining your credit worthiness. What to do if credit is denied. 4 pp. (1987, FDIC) **445V. 50¢.**

Fair Credit Reporting Act. How to check the data in your credit file. What to do if credit is denied because of incorrect information. Spanish version included. 7 pp. (1980, FTC) **447V. 50¢.**

Home Equity Credit Lines. Pros and cons of using your home as collateral for a loan. Answers questions on interest rates, closing costs, and repayment terms. 4 pp. (1987, FTC) **449V. 50¢.**

Investment

A Consumer's Guide to Coin Investment. Different types of coin investments and their growth potential, grading standards, selecting a dealer, and scams to beware of. 39 pp. (1987, USPS) **567V. Free.**

● *If you invest in jewelry, see "About Fine Jewelry" on page 12.*

Financial Institutions: Important Consumer Information. Discusses the laws governing bank accounts, credit cards, loans, mortgages and more. How and where to complain if you have credit problems. 13 pp. (1987, FFIEC) **450V. 50¢.**

Investment Swindles: How They Work and How to Avoid Them. How to spot illegal investment schemes and to protect yourself against legitimate sounding telemarketing and direct mail offers. 20 pp. (1987, CFTC) **568V. Free.**

Investors' Bill of Rights. Tips to help you make an informed decision on investment risks and costs. 6 pp. (1987, CFTC/USPS) **569V. Free.**

The Savings Bonds Question and Answer Book. Explains everything about the savings bond program, including information on purchase, interest, maturity, replacement, redemption, exchange, and taxes. 12 pp. (1987, TREA) **451V. 50¢.**

Understanding Opportunities and Risks in Futures Trading. For the novice investor, explains the commodities market, the risks involved, and regulations governing it. 45 pp. (1986, CFTC) **452V. 50¢.**

What Every Investor Should Know. Basic information on choosing and safe-guarding investments, trading securities, and protections guaranteed by law. 35 pp. (1985, SEC) **146V. $1.25.**

TRAVEL & HOBBIES

Access Travel. Design features, facilities, and services for the handicapped at 519 airport terminals in 62 countries. 39 pp. (1985, OCA) **570V. Free.**

Family Folklore. How to record family stories and traditions for genealogical research. 7 pp. (1986, SI) **147V. $1.00.**

Foreign Visa Requirements. Before you can travel to most countries, you need a visa. Here are requirements for 212 countries and the addresses of embassies and consulates where visas may be obtained. 12 pp. (1989) **454V. 50¢.**

11

Fig. 7-2. A number of government publications relate to travel and are available free or at a modest cost. (Courtesy of the U.S. Government Printing Office)

Some other tips:

- ❏ Set watches to destination time once on board the plane.
- ❏ Eat high-protein breakfasts and lunches and high-carbohydrate dinners.
- ❏ Drink coffee in the morning if traveling east and in the afternoon if traveling west. That helps adjust to the fatigue factor.

If a person just can't sleep on planes and has seen the movie before, the lucky traveler might be on one of those planes experimenting with back-of-the-seat entertainment centers which offer a choice of video terminals right at your station, plus video games, even computers, fax machines, and satellite hookups for the first class business traveler. Flights of the future will make films passé.

Other Considerations   The best advice to give travelers who want to take photos from the plane is to sit on the shady side of the plane, in front of the wing, and shoot with their lens perpendicular to the window, and close but not touching it (to prevent vibration). Fast shutter speeds (at least 250) work better and the focus should be at infinity. If you want to establish perspective, include part of the wing in the shot. Some nations forbid photography in planes or airports, so this should be cleared with the flight crew.

During the flight, debarkation cards will be circulated. The escort may have to help some people fill these out, particularly such entries on the place where passports were issued or the address abroad. The former information should be on the individual passport; the latter may be listed as a specific place or just "touring."

When there are **delays** at airports, the tour manager must be a model of patience. The waiting must be made as painless as possible, and all information on departure communicated to tour members quickly and honestly. Sometimes meals may have to be arranged (normally at the airline's expense, in case of mechanical delays) or overnight accommodations booked. The leader should know or find out who is responsible for paying for these items, since the rules vary. If the delay is a long one, the tour manager may suggest chartering a bus to the nearest town for shopping or entertainment, may arrange for a lounge in a nearby hotel, may book in a film or a few TV sets, or can start card or other games. People should be kept together, since delays can be suddenly corrected and the flight ready to embark.

Cruise Ships

The important people to know on a cruise are the chief purser and chief steward. Despite the lifestyle shown in *Love Boat,* the captain doesn't have unlim-

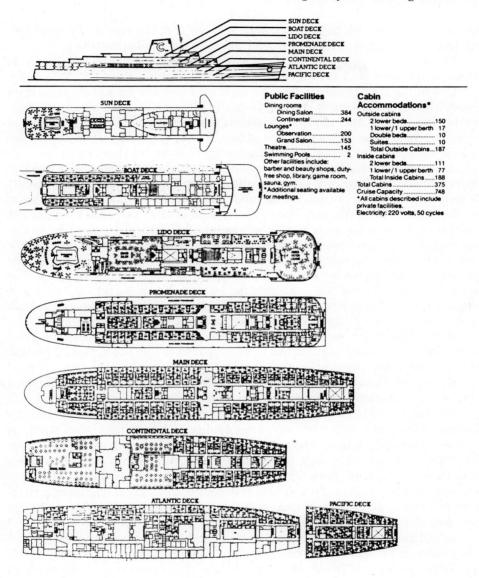

Fig. 7-3. Tour managers should know the configurations of planes, coaches, and cruise ships. (Courtesy of Costa Cruise Lines)

ited time to spend with passengers, and he doesn't get involved in the mechanical details of tourism. The purser and the steward are better contacts.

The chief steward will work out the meal arrangements and the chief purser helps with land arrangements after debarking.

One of the first things to be done is to **arrange for meals** for the entire group. The second sitting is later and usually preferable. Since all dining room seating is arranged during the first few hours aboard ship, getting this handled immediately is wise. If some of the group members would rather attend another sitting, or dine alone, or join nongroup friends, let them do so.

Another important personage is the ship's baggage master who handles the luggage. One of the nice things about a cruise, from the viewpoint of escort as well as passenger, is that the baggage doesn't have to move in and out of hotels; it stays put. When the baggage is unloaded at the customs pier, the usual procedure is for each bag to be tagged alphabetically according to the passenger's name and passage class. They could also be tagged numerically or color coded. The tour manager can ask that all bags of the tour members be tagged with the same letter sticker, so they'll be together on the pier. The letters "X" and "Z" are the most popular letters; they are also used by many tours. "W" or "J" might be better. If a bag is missing, the escort should look in the customs section under the tour member's initial.

Heavy baggage is usually taken from the cabins the night before docking, so tour members should be warned to be prepared to live out of their ovenight bags for that final night.

As with any accommodations, there can be complaints about the cabins on cruises, even though passengers should know they get what they pay for. If there is substance to the complaint, the escort should try for an adjustment. Some tour leaders may offer to exchange cabins with the dissatisfied party, or let the passenger see that others are similarly situated, or try to make up for this lapse in some other way. A number of cruise directors suggest waiting until the second day to check on tour members' comfort. At first some travelers are surprised at the size of a cabin on board ship, but after a day these spatial concerns abate, and the tourist accepts this new way of living. This saves the tour manager at least one headache.

In addition to the chief steward, purser, and baggage master cited earlier, other individuals aboard ship can be helpful to both tour manager and passenger. Various **ship's officers** have duties that may interest the tourist, from nagivation to communication. While they have their routine duties and may not be ready available, a polite introduction by the tour manager may provide the traveler with an opportunity to see how things run aboard.

Ship's officers may also join passengers at dinner, the bar, or at a dance. However, most ships have the regulation that they must be invited. Since there are always many more single women on cruises than single men, the ship's officers offer the only possibility of escorts. To facilitate some of this companionship, there are often "ladies' choice" dances.

In many ways, leading a cruise is much easier than conducting a land tour. Except at ports of call, passengers are contained and countable. They can't get lost, and there is no anxious waiting for them to board a bus. Since they are virtually on their own for meals and activities, there is little chaperoning or commentary required. There is also a ship's doctor to attend to illnesses, a recreation coordinator to oversee entertainment, and plenty of time for relaxing and visiting.

However, the tour manager shouldn't coast, totally ignoring the tour members. He or she should be in evidence, should be available, and should be aware of illnesses, disputes, and questions about shipboard procedures. Tour members should know how to reach their leader, and the leader must know where they are located and what sitting they attend.

Two out of three cruises are tied into jet packages, so this means scheduling must be coordinated to arrive at the dock early, but not too early. Leone von Weis of the Hamilton Travel and Incentive Corporation recalls a time when the plane arrived late and the ship had departed. Solution? Two yachts were chartered and they caught up with the cruise ship at the first port of call. An expensive remedy, but one that certainly enhanced that company's reputation.

Motorcoach

When there are extra seats on a bus, the situation is more comfortable. Circulation of passengers is easier, and there is room to place bundles, or even stretch out a bit. Where conditions are more crowded, rotating seats is a good idea. This ensures that some individuals don't monopolize the more desirable seats—those toward the front or next to the windows. Some escorts use a numbering system and begin each touring day by announcing the **seating order.** Others rotate seating twice a day, moving in a counter-clockwise direction in the morning and after lunch, one row at a time. Members may exchange seats after that, but the rotation is still adhered to. Those in each row work out the problem of aisle or window locales. Some tour managers ask that passengers do this voluntarily, in order to avoid a structured sequence. Some leave the choice to a first-come-first-served rotation. However it is done, the important thing is that tour members feel they have some flexibility and aren't discriminated against.

Modern tour buses are generally comfortable and afford excellent visibility. On domestic tours, these vehicles are often equipped with restrooms and, sometimes, with wet bars or snack bars, even video terminals. On the typical touring bus abroad, these features would be absent, since rest and meal stops are programmed. Smoking is generally prohibited aboard the bus, although a special section in the rear may be provided, particularly if the bus is not crowded.

Tour members' luggage is loaded by the driver, since he is the expert on using space effectively. However, the tour manager should oversee this, counting the bags as they are put aboard, and making sure all are loaded. This also helps the escort to recognize bags, so that the absentee luggage can readily be identified.

Occasionally, bags may also be stored on the rear seats of motorcoaches. Carryon items are generally placed in the racks above the passengers' seats or, on occasion, on the floor, or on vacant seats. These should be taken off after each day's ride. Problems arise when tour members begin to pile up purchases and, instead of mailing some home, elect to lug around bulky sweaters, giant sculptures, sacks of books, cartons of liquor, or ornate dolls. The escort can perform a service by encouraging them to mail these acquisitions as soon as feasible, even if it means paying duty.

Along with the bus driver and/or guide, the tour manager should review the itinerary as soon as possible, checking, in particular, those items which could cause problems, like places with limited facilities or too long a stretch without a stop. Establish an understanding with the driver about flexibility on stops for rests, photos, or sightseeing. Most drivers and couriers are agreeable, within reason. Some, however, may be as schedule-conscious as train conductors and need to be eased into a slower pattern.

Bus breakdowns, while rare, are a hazard. They never occur in a convenient spot, such as close to a garage. Most tour companies prepare well for such emergencies, quickly dispatching repair trucks or new buses. The tour manager, while firmly insisting on prompt rescue, must also allay the fears of tour members and minimize their opportunity for complaint. If the delay is extensive, and the situation permits, the escort might organize a short walking tour to reduce restlessness.

Bus tours have been a fixture in this country for over fifty years, starting with New York trolleys and moving onto America's dirt roads. Not only are the roads better, but most buses are heated and air-conditioned. Some are even equipped with two-way communications, sound systems, swivel chairs, carpeting, even color television.

Trains

In the United States, **train** tours today have but a shadow of their former prominence. A decade after the Second World War, they began to decline. Today, spurred by the energy crunch, trains are trying to make a comeback and compete for part of the tourist dollar.

Even though concerns about fuel have diminished, Amtrak manages to attract its own clientele. Some are nostalgia buffs, some dislike flying, some find this form of transportation romantic and a better way to see the country. Ski trips, for example, may employ trains. There are even gourmet tours using the rails. Tourists have to have the time (although short trips are no problem), and tour members soon learn that train travel is not inexpensive.

Trains in some foreign countries have survived some of America's problems. They are often the fastest and most economical way to go. And they are frequently routed to take advantage of the most spectacular scenery. Many are super-comfortable and high-speed. However, some are old and poorly equipped, lacking clean toilet facilities, air conditioning or heating, dining cars, and other traditional amenities. The tour manager shouldn't approve a train on the basis of a romantic name alone and, if he or she knows the train ride will be a spartan one, the passengers should be warned. Remember, it *is* the tour manager's business to know!

Train seating is not as flexible as that on a bus, because the conductors ticket passengers in specific seats. However, people are normally free to move about, and to visit lounge and club cars. Encouraging a certain amount of movement is good. Group blocks of seats may be secured in advance.

Keeping track of tour members is relatively easy, but passengers can get tired and irritable. Even the smoothest train ride can seem long, and some are far from smooth. There can also be numerous border checks and other delays. If passengers disembark en route, they should be warned to stay close to the train. Most stops are only a few minutes. This may also pose a problem when a sizable group disembarks.

Few train stations in Europe have porters, meaning that passengers may be responsible for carrying their own luggage when they switch trains or head for taxis. This is another argument for traveling light.

The tour manager must also be in command of the meal situation. If the train has a diner, or if convenient stops are allowed, fine. If not, then the tour manager should tell the tourists to provide a little snack for themselves before departure. Sandwiches, fruit, beer, wine, or soft drinks can be purchased and carried aboard. Many Europeans travel this way to save money.

An occasional train ride on tour can be exciting, particularly for travelers who have rarely taken a train. The Canton-Hong Kong express, for example, offers wood-paneled walls, lace curtains, plants, and splendid service. It also features loudspeakers broadcasting news and military music—but these can be tuned out within each compartment. A few years ago, Scotland inaugurated an exciting train trip through the Highlands, with a number of optional stops.

Adventuring on the Eurail Express by Jay Brunhouse (Pelican Publishing Company, Inc., 1101 Monroe St., Gretna, LA 70053) is a highly readable, informative look at rail travel in Europe. There are maps, schedules, tips on sleeping and eating, plus numerous insights from someone who has ridden all these routes.

CHECKING INTO A FOREIGN COUNTRY

Before disembarking from the plane or ship, the leader should remind tour members once again about the routine when entering this particular country. Go over what will happen once they land. Advise passengers to have their passports and debarkation cards ready and, when they get their luggage, to have it unlocked and ready for inspection.

The tour manager should get off ahead of the group, clear through the passport check first, and then see that others get through and head for the baggage unloading area. Here both the escort and tour members must reclaim their individual luggage. Customs may require that each person take his or her baggage through for inspection, or the group baggage could be placed on carts and taken through en masse, with spot inspection.

If any bags do not arrive, the tour escort (provided other duties don't interfere) may help the deprived passenger fill out the required forms with the airline. These forms ask for a description of the bag(s) lost, a rundown on contents, an assessment of value, and a location where the passenger may be reached, ticket number, and flight number. The passenger receives a copy of this document. If everything goes well, the missing luggage will show up at the first hotel. If it doesn't ever arrive, the airlines will make a cash settlement, but this could take from six weeks to three months. If the settlement is not satisfactory, the passenger may still sue in a small claims court.

Tourists generally find (with notable exceptions) that foreign customs officers are serious and resolute. Their chief concerns are alcohol, tobacco, and drugs. Most countries permit the traveler to bring in two cartons of cigarettes, or one hundred cigars, or a pound of tobacco. One bottle of liquor, opened, is allowed. If questioned about any of these, the tour member should reply that he or she is carrying enough for "personal use only," and not as gifts. If a tour member is transporting restricted items either in or out of a country, it is that person's responsibility. The tour manager can't get involved in this and should in no way approve the breaking of any foreign or domestic regulation. Since regulations differ, the tour manager should look into the specific country's rules. These will specify everything from agricultural products and liquor to currency limits.

The tour manager should report first to the customs officials and explain that he or she has this number of tourists as part of a group. The official will then suggest either individual or group clearance. In fact, these officials have been known to wave a whole junket through the doors, saying, "Welcome to Scotland!" But don't count on it! Any talking for the group should be done by the tour manager, but only the requested information should be volunteered. Neither the tour manager nor the tour members should behave in an irritated or contentious manner with customs officials. This will only slow things up, and may result in anything from excessive baggage scrutiny to detention. Visitors are expected to cooperate.

Once customs have been cleared, or as some of the last members are clearing, the tour manager seeks out the local contact—the courier, driver, or tour operator representative. Give this person the number of tour members, the baggage count, check on the location of the bus or other transport, and then signal tour members to gather in a certain spot. Count heads and baggage once again.

The tour manager may want to allow a little time here for tour members to convert their travelers checks into local currency. This is also a good time to reconfirm flights, particularly if the stay is short. Let tour members know where the bus is located and give them a set time to conduct their affairs.

A word about changing dollars into local currency: in some countries, the airport and train station banks have identical rates with the city banks; in other places, location affects the return. Even among banks in the same general neighborhood, the rates may differ slightly. Some countries add a charge for changing money. If this is a fixed rate, it becomes expensive to complete a small transaction. A fee for changing travelers checks which are not in the local currency is common. The difference between the rates for buying and for selling a foreign currency also affects the price the American tourist pays for changing dollars. Because of the wide variance at work, the tour manager should avoid making pronouncements on the wisdom of changing money at airports, or the relative merits of using banks or bureaus of exchange. The tour manager may spell out some of the factors to be considered but should let the tour members function on their own.

As the bags are being loaded, another count should be made. There can be many a slip between the terminal and the coach. Another tour may be departing at the same time and make off with a few of your bags; or bags get picked up by airport personnel and shunted elsewhere. Perhaps this all seems overly cautious but anyone who has lost bags (and all escorts have) knows what a problem this can be. One other caution: if more than one hotel is being used for the tour group, or if more than one coach is involved, a proper separation of bags should be made so that they can be readily unloaded at the right place.

Once on board the coach, the tour manager may welcome the passengers to this country, introduce the driver and/or courier, permitting them a few words of greeting, and should then discuss the routine for the day and, perhaps, for the next day. Any procedures which need review—like the stricture about adding or subtracting luggage—should be repeated here.

Then it's off to the hotel or the ship.

❏ *CHAPTER HIGHLIGHTS*

❏ The tour manager should be the first person at the departure airport, should have travel agency help, and should greet, supervise, count, and keep track of people and luggage. The important thing is to make certain everyone arrives, meets the luggage requirements, and is on hand for departure.

❏ The tour manager should try to seat tour members according to their preferences, explaining that it may be impossible to satisfy everyone.

❏ Keeping track of people en route, and at intermediate stops, is important. Strategies for dealing with missing persons should be developed prior to departure.

❏ Besides counting heads in the international wing (for tours heading overseas), the tour manager may also handle passport, baggage, and ticket checks.

❏ Every carrier presents a different set of tour circumstances to the tour manager, from delays to turbulence to illness to complaints about cruise cabins. Keeping people healthy and happy about the train or motorcoach is also a tour manager's goal.

❏ The tour manager should know the customs regulations of the foreign country (countries) being visited, and should inform members of these rules. However, tour members have to assume responsibility for excess carryon luggage, items confiscated at Customs, and advice on the best currency exchange rate.

❏ The key concern from the moment people arrive at the domestic airport is to keep tabs on individuals, knowing where they are and how they are.

❏ *CASE PROBLEMS*

1. You are at the boarding gate with your tour group, loading everyone aboard about twenty minutes prior to departure. One tour member insists on carrying aboard an oversize parcel containing an easel and sketching equipment. You've warned him that he should not take this along, but he shows up with it and insists he can get them to take it on the plane. The agent at the gate refuses to let him through. Your tour member argues, refuses to go back to have this shipped with the regular luggage, and wants you to convince the agent to allow the package aboard. Meanwhile, the boarding is complete and the group is ready to leave. What do you do?

2. During an intermediate domestic stop, one of your tour members wanders off. As time comes to depart, she has not returned. What do you do?

3. There are certain routines which each tour member should know and certain "unlikely situations" with which they should be made familiar. The pre-trip meeting gives the tour manager a chance to review these. Make a list of the points you believe you should cover, and the way you might cover them to ensure compliance without scolding or frightening tour members.

8

THE ROUTINE ON TOUR

LEARNING OBJECTIVES

After reading this chapter you will:

- ❏ Be able to distinguish among the various tour personnel and their duties
- ❏ Understand the routine on tour, including the planning and management of various stops and the manner of informing and entertaining travelers
- ❏ Know how to check a tour in and out of hotels; how to deal with special lodging problems that arise; and appreciate the planning that goes into meals and entertainment
- ❏ Understand shopping, tipping, and the various tour options
- ❏ Know how to employ group psychology with a varied number of individuals

KEY CONCEPTS

Baggage count	Head count	Personal time
Border crossings	Hotel check-in	Photo stops
Church services	Hotel checkout	Porters
Commentary	Hotel ratings	Rail tickets
Courier	Hotel reservations	Rest stops
Cruising	Humor	Safety
Disputes/refunds	Length of trip	Seat rotation
Driver	Local guide	Shipboard routine
Entertainment	Luggage	Shopping
Games	Lunch stops	Tipping
Group psychology	Meals	Value Added Tax
Handicapped travelers	Optional tours	Youth groups

There are many titles of persons involved in touring. Some are used interchangeably, even when they have slightly different connotations.

The *tour manager* may be called the tour escort, tour leader, tour director, tour conductor, even courier. This sometimes gets confusing, because others may supplement the tour manager and bear one of the above designations.

For example, a **courier** may be assigned by the tour operator to accompany the group, so you would have a **driver,** tour manager, and courier. In certain areas, usually large cities, you might also add a **local guide,** making this a quartet. For very large tours, where several coaches could be involved, you would again multiply personnel. If two people accompany the tour from its domestic launch, one may be referred to as the tour manager and the other as the escort.

Things get even more complicated semantically when the driver also serves as courier, and may even assume some tour manager duties. Some tours also have a person called a "host" who does little managing or escorting.

It's probably easier to think of the professional personnel in terms of the jobs they perform. Someone has to drive the vehicle, handle luggage, deal with hotels and attractions, provide commentary, handle tour member problems, even amuse the travelers. Except for driving, these tasks may be shared among the staffers, depending on their individual skills and knowledge. A tour manager, for example, may merely be along to look after the tour members and to see that the tour operator performs as per the contract. However, this same tour manager, if possessed of a good singing voice, or if very familiar with the countries visited, may extend the scope of activities.

PREPARATION

It is worth repeating that detailed planning and preparation are key elements in a successful tour. The advance work makes a tour seem smooth and effortless. However, the human factor is always in play. Some of the problems encountered may be Acts of God, but most are Acts of Humans. Learning how to cope with individuals as well as situations is requisite for success as a tour manager. This means coping, not only with tour members, but with all the service and auxiliary personnel the tour manager encounters en route. Some of these individuals are intimately connected with the tour, while others exist on the periphery.

The Guide

Guides, or couriers, are often provided by the tour operator, particularly on longer journeys, and their costs have to be built into the overall cost of the tour.

These people are trained in their work, schooled in the history and culture of the country, familiar with the road system and the hotel/restaurant fraternity, and are likely to be at least semi-skilled as story tellers and entertainers. While their primary functions are educational and social, they may also share managerial responsibilities, such as the details of lodging and meals.

The tour manager remains the leader, however, and must call the shots in any dispute. Obviously, he or she would be foolish to ignore the advice of someone more familiar with the country, but there are times when the manager must listen to his or her own counsel. Couriers are not infallible. They have their own egos and their own standard procedures. They may be reluctant to venture into areas off their regular course. And they may sometimes usurp authority which belongs to the tour manager. What is needed is an understanding between these two individuals—the tour manager and the courier—and a good working relationship. This partnership can make things easier for both parties and for the tour members.

Persons who sign up for a tour often do so because of the presumed expertise of the tour manager or escort. Consequently, they expect some evidence of this on foreign shores. The tour manager can't recede into the background, relinquishing all directions, **commentary,** and diversion to the courier. This should be a joint endeavor, with the tour manager participating often enough to retain his or her reputation. Tactfully handled, this should cause no resentment from the courier but, even if it does occasionally interrupt the monologue, it should be pursued.

Once in a while, the courier may not read the group properly, and may have to be reminded of this. Some of the courier's stories could be offensive, or some of the commentary may be over-simplified, or the pace may be too strenuous. If the courier and tour manager have decent rapport, these matters can be handled with a minimum of friction.

Sometimes the courier handles all of the meal and hotel vouchers and does all of the **tipping.** The tour operator provides funds for this. If this procedure is accepted, the tour manager should check periodically and unobtrusively to see that service personnel are indeed being compensated, and that the vouchers have been properly handled. Many tour managers prefer to oversee these activities themselves, particularly if they intend to take this journey again and want to establish a personal reputation.

Normally, the courier (and driver) will be billeted in the same hotel as tour members, but crowded conditions or the whim of hotel managers may sometimes assign the courier (and driver) to nearby quarters. Since it works better to have all tour people at one location, the tour manager may make points with the courier (driver) by insisting that accommodations be found at the same place. In any event, the tour manager must know where the courier and driver are staying and how they may be most easily reached. The expenses of the driver and courier are their own responsibility, and so are their housing needs. The tour manager is involved only as a courtesy, or for convenience sake.

The Driver

Many tours operate with just a driver and tour manager, with local guides helping out in key areas. The drivers are often more than drivers; they also know a lot of history, can sing, and exchange jokes. A competent and experienced escort may prefer to travel with the driver alone. This means a heavier load of commentary for the tour manager, but it can also be more fun.

The driver's main job is to get the passengers to their various destinations safely, comfortably, and on time. Baggage transfers are also the driver's responsibility, and this person may also be involved in everything from hotel and meal arrangements to narration and entertainment. Again, it depends on the capabilities of the persons involved, and their ability to work out a good relationship.

Drivers can get sulky, especially if the tour manager keeps changing the route. The driver really has no obligation to deviate from the itinerary, and the willingness to do so depends on how this matter is approached. A cooperative driver can be terrific, happily taking tour members on little side trips, or even suggesting some sightseeing beyond the limits of the itinerary. The driver should be consulted, should be asked, and should be considered.

Occasionally, the tour manager will be stuck with a poor driver, someone who may not even know the roads, let alone the local history. One tour manager recalls a New England foliage tour where the driver was working out of a cumbersome national atlas and hadn't a clue as to the detailed network of roads in Vermont and New Hampshire. However, he was an amiable fellow, so the tour manager and he just worked out the route each night and stayed on schedule. Another tour manager recalls a dour driver in Scotland, who was supposed to provide the commentary. Whatever narration occurred was sparse, often inaccurate, and certainly colorless. This chap also got lost once the border was crossed into England. This time the tour manager had a long and serious talk with the driver, and things improved. If they hadn't, the tour manager could have requested another driver.

The driver, also, works out his own housing and expenses.

The Local Guide

Major cities and some prime tourist areas frequently supply their own guides. Even when a courier may be aboard, these specialized duties are turned over to the local guide. These people are deep into the lore of the area and can get a lot said and done in a brief time. They also know local customs, the best parking spots, and the most efficient way to process large groups through heavily-populated attractions. London is an example of a city where local guides predominate. But many American cities have their local guides as well. For some, this is a full-time occupation, but most will have other employment. Some are teachers, some actors, some students. Experience and abilities also vary. A student handling a summer job may be merely working from a memorized script whereas the veteran London guide is an encyclopedia of historical and literary knowledge.

The tour manager is fairly well locked into the itinerary of the local guide, but can make suggestions. Perhaps there is too much focus on cathedrals and shrines and not enough on other historic places. Perhaps the guide overestimates the knowledge of the tour group. Perhaps these members have some special interests, like law or agriculture, which should be satisfied. A few words with the local guide should set things right.

Fig. 8-1. Local guides are employed in major cities. (Courtesy of Bill Ramsey)

Most local guides know the drivers and couriers, and relate well with them. A few can be officious and demeaning. Since their stint is short, the tour manager can't do much about this rude behavior, but it can be noted later in the manager's report.

Either the tour manager or courier will introduce the local guide and let that person take over. There is little chance for any interplay because city tours move rapidly and pack in a great deal of information. It's the local guide's show. However, when tour managers perform this local function in their own cities, they must do sufficient research, run the route many times, keep detailed maps on hand, and observe local laws where a guide license is required. The tour manager may obtain such a license, although the effort involved may not be worth it. Some cities have a glut of guides, and the regulations governing licensing have been strengthened.

(When tour members join existing package tours, they will likely be minus the services of a tour manager, but will have a courier (or escort) along, plus the requisite local guides.)

Other Personnel

Each mode of transportation has its own specialized staff, so the tour manager may have to learn a deal with conductors, museum guides, taxi drivers, or camel drovers. The basic rules, however, remain the same. Each person must understand and respect the other's expertise and responsibilities, and each must appreciate the fact that smooth, affable teamwork makes the tour pleasant for everyone.

THE ROUTINE ON THE MOTORCOACH

A time is assigned each morning for departure on a bus tour, and this information is conveyed the previous evening and possibly posted in the hotel lobby. The escort should be up well ahead of time, making certain that wake-up calls were carried out, and checking to see that tour members arrive for breakfast. In case of absentees, calls may be placed to their rooms, since some folks go right back to sleep.

If the tour is leaving the hotel and baggage is being transferred to the coach, the tour manager checks on this, even though the porters and drivers are doing the physical work. It's a good idea to walk the corridors about the time bags are supposed to be out, noting if any are not yet out. And the manager may check again as bags are being loaded, to be certain no **luggage** has been left in the hall. Sometimes several tours will leave at the same time, so it's helpful to have someone monitoring the tags who'll note that stray bags have joined your group, or that some of your people's luggage hasn't been collected by another driver.

After getting passengers aboard, a **head count** should be made. You may count from the front, or walk up and down the aisles. Don't try to count while passengers are standing or getting settled. Wait until they're in their seats. Never leave until all members are accounted for.

It is important that passengers learn to respond to the departure schedule. While the tour shouldn't seem as precise as a missile countdown, it should try to adhere to the daily plan. Better to have time to squander later in the day than to lose it at the outset. Unfortunately, a few individuals are not team players. They behave as if they were on their own, wandering out to the bus ten or fifteen minutes late, sometimes sheepishly, sometimes defiantly, sometimes with incredible naiveté. Often the other tour members will remind this person of the lapse, by applause, or comments, or obviously displeasure. If this doesn't result in reform, the tour manager must have a chat with the offender.

En Route

Once everyone is aboard, the coach departs, and the tour manager greets the passengers, passing on any necessary information. The driver/courier may also have a few words to say, perhaps reviewing the day's itinerary. Because some travelers like to follow the trip on their maps, a few moments could be spent outlining the precise route.

This may also be the time, particularly early in the tour, to remind people about adding or subtracting luggage, about the value of foreign currency, about no smoking policies, or other matters that have arisen. This is also a good time to answer questions put by individuals, but which may interest the group as a whole. Luggage carried aboard must be properly stored, and removed each evening. When the coach is stopped, as for **meals** and sightseeing, it is usually locked and/or attended. Even so, carrying things like purses and cameras with you is a good practice. Passengers may need to be reminded of this.

Hopefully, the tour manager will soon know everyone by name, and will see that they get to know one another. Different personalities emerge, and the escort knows who can be kidded, who can come up with a rebuttal, and who needs to be drawn out. This sort of byplay helps bring a diverse group together.

The **seat rotation** was discussed earlier. This is the time for handling this chore—at the beginning of the day. Reminders about the prohibition of smoking, or about reserved areas for smoking, should be repeated here. (Smoking, incidentally, could turn out to be a minor problem. More than one escort has had to ask a tour member to refrain from chewing and spitting!)

Tour managers must always be conscious of **safety** on buses. Heavy luggage should not be stored overhead. When getting on or off, particularly at sightseeing stops, they must be extra careful. This is especially true in countries with left-hand drive. The escort should get off first and direct passengers across the road when it is clear of traffic. Although tour members are expected to stay in their seats, the escort may sometimes prowl the aisles, checking on tour members, especially those who may be having problems.

Consultation and Commentary

While the tour manager may not be as familiar with the road as the driver or courier, he or she should make every effort to project ahead. Careful scrutiny of maps, together with regular consultation with the driver, make sense. This enables the escort to help with decisions and to respond intelligently to questions.

Commentary takes experience, not only in knowing what to say but in knowing when to say it. You can't afford to ignore important landmarks, and there are also times when you'd want to make general comments about things like native music or farming habits or domestic life. Take a look in the driver's mirror, or turn around and view the passengers. Are half of them asleep? Do you want to waken them?

Some tourists will sleep through the Brenner Pass or the ruins of the Acropolis. Touring seems to induce drowsiness, and so do heavy meals and advancing age. The commentator must decide how important it is that this information be communicated at this time. If it's the right place and the right time, go ahead, regardless of nappers. But don't waste your best shots on an inattentive group.

The courier and tour manager must also know how much to say. There's no need for wall-to-wall remarks. Break the presentations up, leaving ample gaps for conversation, dozing, or personal reflection. At any one time, keep comments brief. A twenty-minute monologue is disastrous. Alternate information, songs, stories, and silence. And don't force-feed passengers with your own favorite esoteric historical theories; they can't or won't take them.

One good way to break the tedium of a bus tour is by inviting audience participation. Perhaps one or two members can sing, or tell stories. Perhaps some tour member has special knowledge of an area ahead, or relatives who came from there. Let them share. This sort of activity must be controlled, since you don't want blue material, offensive ethnic jokes, boring anecdotes, or drunken reveries. Stay in charge while involving the others.

Some tours play **games**—typical parlor games such as Charades, Twenty Questions, or other trivia. One driver brings a racing form aboard and has passengers draw numbers on which they bet a dollar or two apiece. Then he stops enroute at some convenient tavern that's carrying the race on television and lets the tour members root home their favorites. Things like this shorten the journey.

Rest Stops

Rest and meal stops are important, and must be planned. The first rest stop usually occurs a couple of hours after departure and another will take place a few hours past lunch.

When the coach makes such a stop, sufficient time should be allowed, particularly if toilet facilities are limited. This means a halt of at least twenty to thirty minutes. If this is an area where a tip is expected for use of washroom facilities, travelers should be warned beforehand. Otherwise the tour manager may end up having to rescue a bewildered traveler from an irate washroom attendant. The location of the toilets should be pointed out, along with other places, such as coffee shops and sightseeing areas that are sited nearby. **Shopping** should be discouraged on these short stops, but it can't be completely cancelled. Some people will always find a shop, even on a desert.

In some small towns there are no convenient public restrooms. This means the passengers must avail themselves of the hospitality of hotels and restaurants. In this case, the tour manager should suggest they split up and not all descend on the same place. On occasion, these rest stops also include a respite at the neighborthood tavern. Some tour manuals require that the escort never take a drink during the day. Other agencies have no such policies, and the tour manager may have one drink during the pause.

Some limited flexibility may be granted on rest stops, but schedules still must be met, so excessive leeway is taboo.

Photo Stops

Every tour has its photographers, casual or serious. They'll want opportunities to take pictures. This means some unplanned stops en route when photo possibilities appear. Since almost everything looks exciting and picturesque to the stranger, such pauses must be kept at a minimum. This is the price the photographer pays for the other benefits of a tour.

When a scenic spot is reached, the coach may halt and passengers be invited to take their shots. Warn them each time about crossing the road.

As soon as they've had a reasonable chance for a few pictures, signal them aboard. Nobody should take time to climb a nearby hill or wander off into the fields. Nonphotographers are usually tolerant of these stops, up to a point.

Fig. 8-2. Tour managers allow for periodic photo stops for those who want to capture pictorial souvenirs.

Photos taken out of a moving bus are commonly disappointing. The foreground is blurred and the composition haphazard. Suggest that photographers wait until the bus is stationary or, better still, until they can debark.

The tour manager may also want to take pictures, to bolster company files or to later share with tour members. If this is done, he or she should set an example for quick shooting and return to the bus.

One additional thought on photography. Polaroid cameras are fun to have along. While the quality of prints may not match those from better cameras, polaroids get results quickly, and offer a way to make friends with natives of a foreign country as well as with other tour members.

Lunch Stops

Unless the tour group is quite small and the touring area very civilized, the tour manager shouldn't figure on making a random decision about lunch. Before the day begins—preferably before the tour begins—luncheon stops should be mapped out. If possible, avoid remote places, but if the itinerary unavoidably places you in such a spot, then either pack a lunch or book lunch at some convenient facility. Arriving with forty people in a town that has only one small hotel is a serious mistake—unless the hotel has been forewarned.

Smaller groups have fewer meal problems. With a dozen or so travelers, the tour manager can arrange to stop, without specific reservations, in some community where there are several restaurants, hotels, and coffee shops. The group can then divide up and patronize a number of these. The escort should make sure, however, that these spots are clean, comfortable, reasonable, and that they serve decent food.

Breakfast is normally figured into the tour, and so are most dinners. Since both of these meals may be substantial, many tourists don't want to stuff themselves at a midday meal. That's a good reason to eliminate lunch from the tour price and let each person moderate his or her own noon repast. Besides, this makes it part of the adventure.

When lunch is part of the tour, the venue is undoubtedly set, and there is less concern with finding adequate facilities. Should a tour be running late, the tour manager or courier should call ahead to the planned lunch stop and alert them to this fact.

Allow a minimum of an hour for lunch under ideal circumstances; an hour and a half is more realistic. Passengers who finish eating early can shop or browse. Set a time for return to the coach.

Under the arrangement suggested above, travelers will be paying for their own lunches. If the meal is part of the tour, vouchers or travel service orders are used. In a case where no vouchers are available but you want to feed the group, discuss this with the restaurant or hotel management, identifying yourself and the tour, and arrange to pay later.

Other Stops

Passengers must be accommodated at other times: shopping, for example; brief halts for the occasional craft shop; a chance to cash traveler checks—preferably at a time when everyone exercises this opportunity.

Often the tour members will be situated in a place where **church services** are available on Saturday or Sunday. It's best to attend these before the tour leaves for the day. The tour manager checks on the hours of services and the location of the church or synagogue. Then the manager tells people how to get there, if within walking distance (and after walking the route personally), or arranges for the coach to drop people off and pick them up. Every effort should be made to find compatible services for all those on tour. Whether they wish to attend or not is their business. If several churches are involved, the coach driver works out the most efficient schedule. In some instances, alternate transportation may have to be arranged by the tour member.

On occasion the schedule may allow leaving early and stopping en route for church services. If so, the tour manager should determine beforehand the schedule and the travel time. One must also be careful not to inconvenience other passengers. Where it is truly difficult or impossible to work such services into the itinerary, passengers, including Catholics, are excused from the obligation.

Other stops may be permitted, like affording a traveler a chance to greet a friend or relative, or a pause at a drugstore, or a brief sojourn at a pub or coffee shop—if these stops don't impede the progress of the tour or inconvenience others.

Length of Daily Trip

Tour planners should consider the endurance of passengers. The age of the group will have something to do with this. So will the amount of driving the previous day, the weather, the evening activities, the meals, and the general health and morale of the group.. Don't push them.

If possible, avoid long days back-to-back. Even the most energetic, curious, and adventuresome traveler gets tired of constant movement. Schedule some shorter days, space out the free time, and arrange for multiple night stops at some hotels.

If the tour manager senses the group is getting tired, and that minor infections, like colds, are becoming common, it's time to consider slight revisions in the itinerary. A few hardy souls may be peeved, but the majority will thank you.

If you've been leaving early for several mornings in a row, schedule a later wakeup call. Green Carpet Tour managers are taught to occasionally ask for a show of hands of those who want to sleep an hour or two later—and the tour manager raises the first hand!

You must also consider company or governmental restrictions on the number of hours one driver is allowed to drive a coach. These have to be calculated as part of the travel plan.

Miscellaneous

A litter box aboard the bus helps keep things tidy and makes the driver's task easier. Good drivers police the coach every night and wash it at every convenient opportunity. This gives the tour members a feeling of being in a vehicle that is always clean and comfortable. Escorts may also check the bus for forgotten articles after passengers have exited.

Peddlers and other uninvited persons should be kept off the bus. You may occasionally bring someone you know aboard, to speak a few phrases in the native language, or sing a song, or tell a story. But otherwise only tour members and tour personnel should be aboard.

If more than one coach is used, the tour manager (particularly if this person is a feature part of the trip) should divide his or her time among them. An assistant or auxiliary escort, or a courier, might alternate with the tour manager.

HOTELS

Knowing the hotels on tour, and their *current* condition, is vital. The tour manager will have enough other problems without worrying about inadequate facilities. Select hotels that are sure to please just about everyone. Even then, there will be complaints.

There are hotels which the tour manager may find personally satisfactory. You may feel that the shortcomings are more than balanced by atmosphere and genial staff. But you must consider how fussy some folks can be. Going for a safer, higher-rated hotel may not be as colorful, but it spares you grief. Even those travelers who declare they wish to sample everything in the alien culture, and who react with delight when warned that a specific hotel is old and doesn't have private baths but does have character—these same people pout once they have to wait for a shower. Many tourists want to take America with them.

In many cases, of course, the tour manager must rely on the tour operator to **book the hotels.** Previous experience may help the tour manager to suggest accommodations, but the person on the scene will need to see what is available and how it meets scheduling and personal requirements. Larger tour operators have their own lists of hotels they frequent, so you have some idea in advance about facilities.

Ratings and Rationale

Hotel ratings go from Double A, to A, to B, to C—and out of sight. Many systems use star ratings. You're usually okay with the top two ratings, and probably okay with some of the next level (if you know the places personally), but facilities below these can often mean trouble. Tour operators are aware of this and rarely book Americans into anything but "A" accommodations. Even when tour managers are convinced that something less will be adequate, tour operators fight that notion. It may be neither flattering nor totally accurate to

Fig. 8-3. Hotels range from the picturesque manor house to the more modern versions.

characterize Americans as spoiled and picky, but experience supports the tour operator. If the tour manager does opt for a facility that doesn't appear in the top ratings, but does offer locale and quaintness, be sure the passengers are forewarned, and blend this stay with others of superior quality.

Location must always be considered. If the hotel is situated some distance from a major city, it may be more restful and scenic, but the coach may be needed to transport tour members for entertainment or shopping. If the overnight stop is a country manor, it might well schedule its own evening program for guests, or be able to direct them to diversions in the closest village. For skiers, how far is the hotel from the lifts? For swimmers, surfers and sunbathers, how far is it from the beach? These are questions the tour manager can't ignore.

Some hotels have everything going for them. They are well-sited, clean, spacious, quiet, blessed with a congenial stff, good restaurants and bars, and with ample night life nearby. Others may lack some of these features. A little mix might work—a modern structure, then a traditional hotel, then a resort-type operation with striking scenery.

Even though the tour has been booked months before, and even though you have vouchers and letters of confirmation with you, it's still smart to call ahead to each hotel, preferably the night before, reminding them that you are coming, stating an approximate arrival time, and reviewing the length of stay and the number and type of rooms booked. You may also want to be sure they have the meals straight—the ones you'll eat at the hotel and the ones you won't. Knowing the names of key hotel personnel helps.

Checking-in

If it turns out you'll be arriving earlier or later than discussed, another call to the hotel is in order. Early arrival means tour members may have to wait in the lobby until their rooms are ready; late arrival means at least a mixup in the meal schedule and possibly the dismal fact that rooms may have been given to others. Alert the tour members to these possibilities. The following procedures is recommended for **checking into** each hotel:

1. While the tour members remain on the coach (or sometimes in the hotel lobby or hospitality suite) the tour manager goes to the hotel desk and identifies himself (herself) and the name of the tour. The desk clerk produces a rooming list and the tour manager copies down the room numbers on his list (unless the hotel supplies the tour manager with a copy of their list). Make sure the singles and doubles are accurate and properly assigned, and that special requests (like rooming close to friends, or being quartered on a lower floor) are accommodated, if possible. (However,

with a large group, extensive room juggling, while it pleases some individuals, may irritate those who have not made special requests.)

2. The tour manager asks where the keys are (at the desk or in the doors of the rooms); what time meals are scheduled; where the dining room, coffee shop, bar, and other amenities are located; whether there are special opening and closing times for these facilities; whether there is any mail for tour members or messages for the tour manager; and any other questions (like location of churches and times of services, or distance to town, or shopping hours) that need answers. If you need a meeting room for a tour party or special entertainment, check on this. Some international hotels require that passports be shown at check-in time. If so, the tour manager gathers these (unless the hotel insists on this being done individually), shows them, then returns them immediately to the travelers. Some hotels (like those in China) may not have keys or locked doors. And some hotels are so large that the tour manager must secure details on how the tour members will find their rooms.

    Other variations may include the plastic keys for every guest, allowing them to open their doors electronically. This procedure may take time, since the keys may be cut while the guests are waiting.

3. In cases where the hotel refuses to honor reservations, or where there is a mixup in the number of singles, the tour manager should not argue with the reservations clerk. Ask to see the hotel manager, and politely, yet firmly, insist on the reservations being honored as booked. Proper documentation is the first step in making adequate adjustments. You must be armed with vouchers, letters, and other proof. With these in hand, try to get the problem solved then and there. Be persistent, since you are representing a group of clients much as a lawyer would insist on justice for an aggrieved party. If you are unsuccessful with the complaint, be certain you take down all the details, including names, dates, times, statements—everything. These may be required for later settlement of any claims. Any failure by any supplier to perform according to contract should be reported immediately to the nearest representative of the tour operator. Your driver/guide may assist with this, but you remain ultimately responsible. If the rooms are full, even if a culpable mistake has been made, some alternate housing is necessary. The hotel should help locate space in other comparable accommodations and should compensate the tour for any extra charges or discomfort. If alternate accommodations are in a lower class, refunds will be due the travelers. Tell them how these will be handled. All of this underscores the advisability of calling ahead.

4. Assuming all goes well, as it usually does, and the tour manager has answers for all questions, he or she returns to the group and, using the

coach microphone, communicates the details to them. Ask the tour members to jot down this information, starting with times of meals (especially the next meal), location of rooms, location of keys, and times of any other functions, including any departure instructions. Then read off the room numbers, varying the order from hotel to hotel so that the same people are not always called first. Give the room numbers of the tour manager and, perhaps, the driver/guide. Any mail on hand may be distributed at this time or the passengers may be told where to get it. Sometimes hotel brochures, available at the desk, are also distributed. Then the tour members are helped off the bus, collect their keys, and go to their rooms.

5. The luggage is unloaded, marked with the proper room numbers (usually in chalk), and delivered to the tourists. This is ordinarily a job for the porters, with the driver assisting. On rare occasions, the tour manager (if able) may pitch in if there are no porters. This could happen at remote hotels early in a season, for example.

6. After tour members have checked in, the tour manager should wait in the lobby half an hour, to field any complaints or concerns. Luggage may be misdirected or missing; toilets may be flooded; lights or TV sets may not work; heat or air conditioning may be off; or other things could be wrong with the rooms. The tour manager works with the hotel staff to rectify these problems. If a tour member is dissatisfied with a room—because of size, view, or adjacent noise, for example—the tour manager will try to effect a change, and may even offer to exchange his or her own room. (Incidentally, when seeking to change a room for a guest, the useful attributes of politeness, firmness, and persistence apply.) The compatibility and morale of the group, and honest advance discussions, will help blunt a lot of travelers' concerns. If they know what they are getting, it helps. The tour manager should be familiar with hotel variations and jargon. "Pensions" are characterized by modest facilities and relatively low cost; Spanish "paradors" are well-kept, more expensive, government-owned facilities; in many European countries a "bathroom" means the room has a tub but not necessarily a toilet (you may have to specify a "water closet"); "hostal residencias" in Spain have no restaurants. Many other specialized terms should be mastered by the tour manager. The Official Hotel and Resort Guide provides a list of common terms.

7. At the earliest convenience, probably after the bags are in the rooms and any problems have been adjusted, the tour manager should inspect the hotel, locating bars, coffee shop, hairdresser, laundry, and other amenities. This is also the time to touch base with the manager, the maitre d', and the head porter, discussing the itinerary as it affects them.

Escorted Tour

Country Pursuits/8 Days

Le Cœur de la France

This program is a perfect introduction to the French countryside for travellers on a limited schedule. **Le Cœur de la France** is designed to show you some of the country's most interesting palaces, cathedrals, châteaux and vineyards on the Ile de France, and in the Val de Loire and Burgundy.

Your journey begins in Paris, where you meet your fellow travellers at the Hôtel Lutétia-Concorde before travelling southwest to Versailles, home of Louis XIV, the celebrated Sun King, on the Ile de France. Then the pretty valley of Chevreuse leads you to the wide farmlands of La Beauce where the Cathedral of Chartres stands—in all the glory of its two soaring spires, 12th-Century stained glass windows and flying buttresses—as one of the most beautiful monuments ever built by men in praise of God.

Your next destination is the Loire Valley, known as the "Garden of France." Here hundreds of châteaux, manor houses, gentilhommières and hunting lodges stand on the banks of the River Loire and its many tributaries. After two days in this marvelous region, you can decide whether grandiose Chambord, elegant Cheverny, graceful Chenonceau, austere Amboise or uniquely sited Azay-le-Rideau—all local châteaux of great beauty—is most to your taste.

Further east the old region of Berry lies calm and secretive, a favorite of storytellers like George Sand rather than the writers of guide books. You will discover its charms for yourself with stops at the remarkable Cathedral Saint-Etienne of Bourges and the peaceful hilltop wine-town of Sancerre. At the northern edge of the Morvan National Park, the 11th-12th Century Basilica of La Madeleine in Vézelay is visible from miles around. You stop here for sightseeing and a chat with the craftsmen who bring renewed life to this ancient fortified town.

Moving south to central Burgundy, you spend two nights in a true Bourguignon Castle while exploring Dijon, near the renowned vineyards of the Côte-de-Nuits. After touring three villages where some of the greatest wines of Burgundy are produced, the Museum of Wine housed in the former residence of the region's Dukes and the famous 15th Century hospices in Beaune, you circle back toward Ile de France for a stop at the Palace of Fontainebleau, marked with the personalities of all its royal occupants. For your final night, you stay in the prettiest village imaginable: Barbizon, birthplace and namesake of a 19th Century school of painting. On your way back to Paris, a visit to Vaux-le-Vicomte shows you the jewel that inspired the jealousy of Louis XIV...and the construction of Versailles.

Day 1   Saturday
Depart Paris (Hôtel Lutétia-Concorde). See Versailles, Valley of Chevreuse and Chartres. *Château d'Esclimont*

Day 2   Sunday
Loire Valley sightseeing, including châteaux of Chambord, Cheverny and Chenonceau. *Domaine de Beauvois or Domaine des Hauts-de-Loire*

Day 3   Monday
Loire Valley châteaux of Villandry, Azay-le-Rideau and Amboise. Tours and its Cathedral. Lunch at Château d'Artigny. *Domaine de Beauvois or Domaine des Hauts-de-Loire*

Day 4   Tuesday
In northern Burgundy: Bourges Cathedral, Sancerre and wine cellar tour, Basilica of La Madeleine in Vézelay. *Château de Vault de Lugny*

Day 5   Wednesday
Semur-en-Auxois, Dijon and Route des Vins. *Château de Gilly*

Day 6   Thursday
Visit 15th Century Hospices and wine Museum in Beaune, with lunch at Hôtel de la Poste. *Château de Gilly*

Day 7   Friday
Auxerre, Sens, Fontainebleau, Barbizon. *Hôtellerie du Bas-Bréau*

Day 8   Saturday
Visit Vaux-le-Vicomte and return to Paris.

Experience has shown that clients prefer to choose their own Paris hotel. Please see our suggestions on pages 8 and 9.

LAND ARRANGEMENTS	IT9AA1CHIABK
Double occupancy—price per person	$3350.00
Single supplement	$ 380.00

Tour Dates (depart from Paris)

1990

Dep	Ret		Dep	Ret
07 May	14 May		30 Jul	06 Aug
28 May	04 Jun		03 Sep	10 Sep
09 Jul	16 Jul		08 Oct	15 Oct

AIRFARE* from New York	from $ 564.00

* airfare shown is subject to change

Your land arrangements include:
All hotel accommodations as shown in itinerary
Continental breakfasts and dinners from a restricted a la carte menu throughout except on Day 8; lunches on Days 3 and 6
All sightseeing as shown, including entrance fees
All ground transportation and porterage; local taxes
Services of a professional guide throughout your trip

Not included are personal expenses such as beverages; laundry; room service; phone calls; telexes; cables; faxes; gratuities to driver and guide; meals in Paris; any additional sightseeing or meals not included in the itinerary; any airfares.

Fig. 8-4. Up-market tours emphasize more luxurious accommodations. (Courtesy of Abercrombie & Kent)

8.   A convenient bulletin board in the lobby should be secured for the post-
ing of notices about future activities. This will save the tour manager a
spate of phone calls. Extra copies of the itinerary may be carried along
for this purpose, or daily routines may be typed or written out. If a bulletin board is not available, an easel will do as well. Tell the travelers
where these notices will be placed. Some tour managers set a daily time
for providing instructions to tour members.

Safety

Veteran travelers know enough to lock their doors when in their rooms, using
the dead bolt and chain in addition to the regular key lock. Some hotels,
however, may not have locks on their doors. This is true not only in some
foreign countries, but even in small town America. Most tourist hotels do
feature locks, and these should be used. Luggage left in the room should also be
locked. Valuables, such as jewelry, extra travelers checks, and the like should
be placed in the hotel safe. Tour managers often put the tour tickets in the safe,
particularly during longer stays.

Emergencies like fires and civil disturbances are covered in chapter 9, but
the tour manager should make an early inspection of fire exits and equipment,
note any danger spots (from balky elevators to ill-placed glass windows), and
alert tourists to these dangers. Some groups may even be walked to these exits
for practice.

This is also a time to remind people of any external perils. Some American
hotels insist that tourists stay inside the lobby while waiting for a cab, and that
they get right into the cab when it arrives. There is no loitering on the
sidewalk, and no walking through the neighborhood. Some of these dangers
also exist in other countries, so tourists must be wary.

Checkout

Always carry a travel alarm clock. Wakeup services in hotels can go awry, and
the tour manager had better be up to compensate for any failures. Some hotels
have digital alarm clocks by the beds, or as part of the beds. These instruments
may need explanation, so the travelers don't wake up and wonder how to turn
off the buzzer or kill the flashing light. This can be done at the evening meal
(after the tour manager figures it out!). After arising, go to the desk to see that
the calls are being made to the tour members' rooms, or that someone is
knocking on doors. Many a tour manager, rooming list in hand, has paced the
corridors personally, awakening his or her tour.

At least an hour and a half should be allowed for getting ready, getting
bags out for pickup, eating breakfast, and showing up at the scheduled depar-

ture time. Since some people take longer than others in getting prepared, tour members can arrange their own wakeup calls, earlier or later than the norm. However, a reminder call about an hour before departure is a good idea.

In deference to the passengers, some departure times should be later than others. Give people a chance for a few late sleeps. The schedule must be kept, of course, but make the wakeup calls as late as possible without courting scheduling disasters.

Breakfast hours on the day of departure should be arranged the previous evening, especially if this time is at variance with usual hotel procedure. This time—along with the time for bags to be put in the hall and for the coach to leave—is communicated verbally the previous day and also appears on the lobby bulletin board.

It is smart practice to have the tour members deposit their luggage outside their doors as they head for breakfast, at least forty-five minutes before departure. (If tour members are not leaving the hotel that day, but merely going on a day tour, this step is unnecessary, and an extra fifteen minutes sleep may be in order.)

At the time the wakeup calls are assigned at the desk, the tour manager should also go over the next morning's program with the head porter and restaurant manager. Shifts change, and the new people may not have been informed, so you can't check too often.

At breakfast, make a head count to see that all are up. If anyone is missing, check with this person's roommate or neighbor, or arrange to have the room called. If there is no response, check the lobby, the area outside the hotel, or knock on the door. As a final move, the **porter** may be called to open the door with a passkey.

The luggage is taken from the corridors by the porters and lined up in the lobby or by the coach. The tour manager should make a **count of the pieces** before they are loaded. After a few days, even on a sizable tour, the escort may pretty well know the bags. This is the time to catch any discrepancy. The tour manager should know where the coach is parked and may wish to schedule a brief conference each morning with the driver/courier, perhaps during or after breakfast.

After settling with the hotel, the tour manager may go to the coach. This settlement is normally in the form of a voucher. While the system varies, many tour companies make out vouchers in triplicate, keeping one for their files, sending another to the hotel in advance of arrival, and surrendering the final copy to the hotel on arrival or departure, depending on the hotel's preference.

Tour members are responsible for any extra bills they have incurred: bar bills, phone bills and the like. Once aboard the coach, the tour manager reminds tour members about any unpaid charges and asks if all keys have been turned in. Delinquent tour members should go back and settle their own accounts but the tour manager may return errant keys. The tour manager should never pay tour members' bills, nor pay for any breakage caused by tour members.

Once the luggage is tucked away, the bills paid, the staff thanked and tipped, and the passengers counted, the day's routine begins again.

MEALS

Even if you can't read a French menu without embarrassment, you must be able to distinguish among the various descriptions of meals. A *continental* breakfast means rolls or toast, perhaps juice, and tea or coffee; whereas a *full* breakfast consists of eggs, meat, toast, juice, and a hot beverage. *Table d'hote* refers to a set three-course meal at a fixed, all-inclusive price, usually minus the beverage. An *American Plan* includes meals, and a *European Plan* does not. A three-course dinner normally features soup, salad, and main course, with dessert extra. Some places, of course, may not offer salads or soups. And you may have to ask for water with the meal. The tour manager must know which meals are covered by the tour and which are not, and should be familiar with the general type of menu offered.

In addition to eliminating most lunches as part of the tour price, it makes sense to consider subtracting one or more dinners during stays in large cities. Tourists like to have at least one opportunity of choosing a restaurant in London, New York, Paris, or Hong Kong.

If certain tour members require special diets, the tour manager should mention this during the advance call to the hotels, so hotel kitchens can be prepared. Most of these requests are not complicated but some may be, so ample time should be allowed.

One of the first contacts a tour manager should make at a hotel is with the maitre d'. Introduce yourself, give the number of tour members and any diet requirements, review meal times, and ask where the tour will be seated. Sometimes tour members are free to choose their own tables but often there is an established area for them, making service and control easier. Breakfast seems to be the time when groups get confused with one another, so the tour manager may want to be on hand to help direct members to the right place. Under no circumstances should the tour manager allow members to be pushed around or discriminated against because they are members of a tour. They deserve the same attention and courtesy as shown to other guests.

Meal times vary from country to country, as do menu items and quantities. Health-conscious Americans are moving away from the ham and eggs breakfasts (although these are still popular), trying to eat lightly at noon, and making the evening meal, scheduled for six on, more substantial. In Mexico breakfast may be eaten until noon and is light; lunch begins at two or three o'clock; cocktails are served at eight and dinner at ten P.M. England's breakfasts vary, but tend toward the substantial; lunch may be the main meal, and a more modest tea replaces our dinner. Hotels catering to tourists, however, frequently adopt American standards, but British and Irish lunches are going to commence at 1:00 P.M. Things often get going much later in tropical climates.

At the first meeting with the maitre d', the tour manager may wish to extend the traditional tip, so that preferential treatment may be assured. This is particularly true when you need some special favor, like early seating, tables by the window, express service to accommodate an early curtain call, or when the group arrives late and must have special seating.

The tour escort should rotate among tables at different meals, sharing his or her companionship with everyone. If the leader pays too much attention to one or two people, even friends, others get jealous. Better to spread yourself around. Sometimes there are individuals who, because of their table manners or personalities, are fated to dine alone. Distasteful as it may be, the tour manager may have to spend a slightly greater amount of time with such persons, to temper any feeling of rejection.

The escort also shares time with cruise passengers. Ship's officers do the same, and the captain's table issues different invitations nightly. For meals ashore or afloat, tour members must be reminded to be on time. They might also be cautioned about overindulging at sea, since shipboard cuisine is usually both tempting and abundant.

Dress for meals is customarily informal, although first-class hotels and restaurants prefer to see women in dresses or dress slacks, and men in coats and ties. Even if the penalty is not ejection, the under-dressed person will feel uncomfortable. While shipboard dress is now more casual than it was, there are formal dinners, so appropriate dress should be brought along. The tour manager must set an example, and should have at least one formal outfit.

When birthdays and anniversaries occur, mealtime is an opportunity to do something special, to spend a little of the tour leader's discretionary fund. A cake is traditional and still nice, as is wine or champagne for the group. You may want to buy a card to be signed by all and, in the proper setting, a chorus of "Happy Birthday" goes over well.

Within limits, you might encourage the tour members to sample the local cuisine. There's no need to order steak and chicken everywhere. Try the rice pilaf, or escargot, or lasagna; perhaps a soup made with lake perch and local vegetable in Hangzhou, or tapioca in various forms in Fiji. Don't insist on this, however, as you may be blamed for later nausea.

Both the tour manager and the tour members should avoid street food in most locations, although many travelers cite Singapore as an exception. Some culinary treats offered by vendors look most appetizing, but it's better to be safe than sorry. Vine-ripened fruit, green leafy salads, and strong black coffee can be dangerous. Buffets are also risky, as are open food counters. Oranges and bananas are the best bet for fruits, and all fruits should be peeled. Other foods should be well-cooked.

Milk products could cause trouble, and the safest drinks are usually beer and major soft drinks. Water should be purified but make sure bottled water is opened in your presence. Forget about ice cubes if you are in an area where the water is suspect.

When asked about recommendations for restaurants on free nights, the tour manager should have some names at hand, but should not be overzealous in touting specific places, since tastes differ and what is expensive to one may not be to another. Mention and describe a few, and let the tourists make up their own minds. Obviously, the tour manager should have some first-hand experience with the restaurants suggested. On occasion the tour manager may make reservations for groups, but this is not his or her responsibility. Do not lapse into the role of servant.

Watch for ripoffs in food and drink. Take note of the brands served at the hotel bars. Are tour members being charged high prices for inferior liquor? Is the food overpriced? If so, note this in your report and pass the information along to the tour operator and your own company.

Besides the normal restaurant meals, there are also events like medieval banquets or Hawaiian luaus. At least one such meal on a tour makes an excellent change of pace.

One final food note: carry a few items like mints, gum, and cookies for distribution on the coach. Especially on long trips, where time between meals is lengthy, such goodies come in handy. When people sit for a while, they tend to get hungry, and nibbling food is appreciated.

ENTERTAINMENT

Some **entertainment** features are expected on any tour, but there's no necessity to fill every free evening. Tour members need some quiet nights, or some personal entertainment options.

When you select entertainment in advance, try to make it varied and appropriate to the tour group. Not everyone likes ballet, but one ballet during a tour could be appreciated, particularly if the company or the stars are famous. A play—one the audience understands—provides both an intellectual and recreational dimension. Folk groups are always popular. Local entertainers may be contacted via the tour operator, the country's tourist board, the hotel, or through friends. They'll sometimes appear at the hotel, sparing the group the inconvenience of traveling.

Fig. 8-5. Good tours blend entertainment with culture, providing something for everyone.

It's not always possible to be familiar with the entertainment being offered. If in doubt, check with some authority. Otherwise you may lead your charges into a theatre where the **humor** is blue, the language unintelligible, the dialogue offensive, or the music loud enough to surpass the threshold of pain. Even at the Shakespeare Theatre at Stratford-on-Avon, many American visitors have difficulty with the rapid delivery of the Bard's comic characters. A little advance explanation might help to avoid this.

In addition to knowing what fare awaits the traveler, the tour manager must also check the route for getting there. If the entertainment site is close, and you intend to have the group walk, then pace it off yourself in advance. Will the older members of the tour be able to go this distance? Are there steep hills? What is the neighborhood like? Are there obstructions, like railroad depressions, that require detours? What if it rains? If the coach is used, where will it park and how far will the tour members have to walk? After the performance, how do you find your coach, and how do you get your people headed in the right direction? Personal checking and planning is the key.

It's always a good idea to have the coach on standby, even when you plan to walk. A sudden storm could make the journey miserable. Good drivers anticipate problems and will show up at the theatre in bad weather even if not summoned. But the escort should not assume this; check it out!

Time is always a factor in scheduling entertainment. You must be sure you have time to work everything in. Sometimes hotels are unbending on meal schedules. Perhaps the dinner is set for 7:00 P.M. and the curtain goes up on the musical at 8:00 P.M. There is no comfortable way to enjoy both events. The tour manager must somehow arrange an earlier eating time.

Time also figures in the length of the performance and the resultant arrival back at the hotel. Older travelers can't take a succession of late nights, especially if followed by an early morning departure. If the entertainment is not structured, as at a nightclub or tavern, the tour manager may escort part of the group home early, leaving the serious revelers to find their own way back or to be picked up later. This means the tour manager must always be alert to the reactions of tour members. If they appear tired, bored, shocked, or uncomprehending, it's time to move on.

For entertainment scheduled at the hotel (a play reading, lecture, small musical group), the tour manager must arrange for an adequate room, which is often furnished free, and the needs of the entertainers must be coordinated with the facilities of the hotel. Don't leave any of this to chance. On occasion, particularly if the driver, courier, yourself, or some tour member has talent, you may want to stage your own brief entertainment one evening. This pulls the group together.

Be acquainted with any free entertainment: perhaps folk dancing on the green in front of Edinburgh Castle; or a Sunday evening concert at Notre Dame in Paris. Know about entertainment with reduced prices, like those available on London theater tickets; or how to get into film showings at the Cannes Festival, where you must have a badge, tickets, and, sometimes, formal dress. Tour managers are expected to know these things.

Major entertainment features—plays, concerts, river cruises—should be built into the cost of the tour. Charges for other minor attractions should be handled, if possible, out of the tour manager's discretionary fund. While the escort can't exhaust these monies on added recreation, it's silly to collect fees from members each time you visit a castle or winery. In cases where a few tour members want to do something, e.g., sailing on a lake or panning for Colorado gold, they should pay for this, even if the tour manager goes along.

In addition to varying the forms of entertainment, organized fun should also be balanced by **independent fun.** Let the tour members sample some of the area offerings on their own. This helps to diminish some of the feelings of constant chaperoning (for both the traveler *and* the escort), and permits the tourists to satisfy more personal entertainment tastes.

SHOPPING

Even though surrounded by the beauty of an evening on the Nile, some tourists are still concerned about what time the shops open in Cairo. There are travelers for whom shopping is the highlight of the trip. They want to lose themselves in the flea market, or Carnaby street, or the native bazaars. Consequently, you must allow sufficient time for them to get this out of their systems. At the same time, however, shopping time must be controlled. Other members may resent the amount of time being allotted to this activity. There must be a blend. A few stops en route, generous lunch hours, plus some full and half days to be spent as one wishes should be ample. While it's disastrous not to allow some reasonable time for people to frequent the shops, it's just as annoying to pull up to every craft or clothing sign.

Know the days and hours when stores are open. There are national holidays, bank holidays, and half holidays. Stores may close at noon and reopen later in the afternoon. They may cease business at 5:00 P.M. or remain open til 7:00 P.M. Some stores close on Monday, some on Saturday. You must check on this when making out the itinerary. If you've calculated incorrectly you had better consider some adjustment. When people are looking forward to a day's shopping in London and they find the stores are closed, you're in deep trouble. The solution may be the rescheduling of the next day's city tour, leaving that day free for the shoppers.

Some recommendations to tour members may be welcome, but the tour manager shouldn't be put in the position of touting specific shops. Neither should the escort follow slavishly the suggestions of the local guide or courier. These people may have their own shopkeeper friends and could get a cut for steering traffic their way. Consider such advice, of course, but be wary of promoting anything with which you're not familiar.

Warn tour members about possible rip-offs, or about shopping areas to shun at night. Hotel personnel and the local guides often provide such alerts. The tour manager can also aid the shoppers in other ways. Despite your lectures, however, some tour members will never get the local currency straight. Charts showing the various coins and bills are a terrific aid, but, even then, many tourists merely reach into their pickets, extract a handful of change, and say, "Here! Take what you want." Those who master the alien finance not only shop more wisely, they also get an ego boost.

The astute tour manager may also be able to convert sizes for female passengers. Size 7 shoes become 6½ in Paris, 5½ in London, and 37½ in Rome. In ready-to-wear garments, our size 10 translates into a French 42 or an Italian 44. The European OAG Travel Planner supplies this information as do brochures from many tourist bureaus.

Even more valuable is the tour manager who can spot fakes, who knows that items using endangered species may be confiscated in customs, and who has some idea of what similar goods cost elsewhere—including in the United States. This doesn't mean, however, that the tour manager is in any way responsible for purchases or for their safe arrival home. These are the buyer's risks.

In some areas, haggling is part of economic life. Merchants expect the buyer to argue about the price and to attempt to reduce it. The tourist should have some idea about how much he or she intends to pay for an article, and whether or not this is really a bargain. Then the negotiations begin. Shepherds Tours and Travel, Inc. advises its tourists to "offer 60% of what he is asking and settle for about 25% more. . . ."

Other shopping tips from experts in the field include not shopping in groups, developing a poker face when looking over merchandise, avoiding the purchase of fake items (like watches) which may be confiscated by Customs and doing a little comparison shopping before committing yourself. These veterans also caution Americans not to feel guilty about good-natured haggling, because, if the vendor can't make a profit, he won't sell. Prices inch up, so you have to be patient. Buying in quantity may be a good idea. If, for example, something costs $2 after haggling, offer $5 for three of them and use the extras for gifts.

Many escorts tell tour members to buy something they like when they see it, and not wait until later in the tour hoping to find the same thing cheaper. Freeports and duty-free shops may have some bargain items, like liquor or cigarettes, but travelers often discover they can do as well or better at shops en route. In any event, it's unwise to save all one's shopping until reaching the duty-free shop at exit time. Not only may items be higher priced or unavailable, your flight could be running late and your shopping time shortened. Remember, too, that duty-free means something was imported without duty, but you may still have duty to pay when you return to the United States, after you have used up your allowance.

RECEIPTS, TAXES, AND MAILING TIPS

Receipts should be kept for all purchases, along with the names of the stores and personnel who waited on you—especially for items that feature a hefty price tag. If goods don't make it back to the States, the purchaser has both a contact and a proof of purchase. The tour manager, even though not shopping, should note the names and addresses of major shops en route, since some tourists invariably need these details later. The tourist must remember, however, that shopping is a personal decision. Tour managers, tour operators, and travel agencies may help settle problems like lost gifts, but they have no obligation to do so.

Tourists who purchase goods in Great Britain and other European countries should be aware of the **Value Added Tax** (VAT), which is a government-imposed tax added at each stage of the production and distribution of a product or service. Many British and Irish stores will send goods abroad free of VAT, or, for over-the-counter purchases carried in hand luggage, they will issue relief forms which have to be certified by British customs in order to secure a tax refund. Tour managers should check on the details of this plan so they can advise travelers.

Finally, shoppers should be periodically reminded about the wisdom of mailing some packages home. This spares them the difficulty of carting things from hotel to hotel, and from carrying extra merchandise through customs. Gifts with a value of $50 or less may be mailed free of duty from abroad, but no more than one gift can be mailed to the same person in the same day. There is, however, no limit on the number of daily gifts which can be mailed under this provision, nor the number of days you can send individual gifts to the same person.

Visitors who have been out of the country for at least forty-eight hours can return home with $400 worth of duty free purchases, with some exceptions, as mentioned in Chapter 10.

Again, the local guide may be a big help, even if he or she does get a commission from certain stores. These are usually reputable places, since the guide and his or her company are also on the line. If the tour manager feels that the tour members have been cheated by any guide or any shop, this fact should be reported to the store management, to the tour operator, and, if necessary, to the local authorities.

THE TOUR MANAGER AT NIGHT

Some compromise must be made between the tour manager's responsibilities toward the tour members and his or her own duties and relaxation. The escort cannot ignore the group and drift off on personal business or pleasure. The manager is the group's prime contact in foreign areas and must be accessible. Even on free nights, the tour manager should be visible.

When special group entertainment is scheduled, the tour manager should always go along—well, almost always. On occasion another emergency may require the escort's attention—some serious illness, or a threatened transportation strike. In these cases, somebody else, perhaps a mature member of the tour, should be placed in charge, and the tour manager must let them know how he or she can be reached. Some tours appoint a social director anyway from among their group. This person helps organize activities for the tour like birthday celebrations or bridge foursomes. This doesn't relieve the tour manager of responsibilities, but it does provide a little backup while involving the tour members more in their own fun.

On nights when nothing is scheduled, the tour manager may socialize with tour members in the hotel bar, or may take small groups to different area attractions. Some travelers may wish to sample a special restaurant and invite the tour manager to accompany them. Others may wish to attend the races, or a play, or to pub hop, or merely to stroll through the village. The only caution here is that the tour manager dispense these hours of companionship somewhat equitably, alternating between the swingers who frequent the night life and the elderly who are afraid to venture far from the hotel.

Even though the tour manager is theoretically on call twenty-four hours a day, like an obstetrician, some personal time must be carved out. Regular nightly meetings with the driver and/or courier are essential. Here you plan the next couple of days, concentrating on the day ahead. Discuss any problems with the route, accommodations, entertainment, or passengers. Be open to suggestions for minor alterations. The escort also needs time to complete reports and records, to call ahead to hotels or theatres, or to phone friends or make business contacts for future trips. Since few telephone systems in the world are as efficient as in America, phoning can be a lengthy chore.

Tour managers are not immune from fatigue or illness. Yet they must look and act alive. This illusion must be bolstered by sufficient rest, so the tour manager must occasionally steal time for a nap, or relax with a book or television.

TIPPING

Every tour manager seems to find tipping one of the most onerous parts of the job. You don't want to look cheap, but you also don't want to overdo it. The question persists: Are you being fair or are you being taken? Although tipping is commonplace in the United States, the tour manager must still remember that the practice is optional.

The driver or tour operator courier may actually handle most tipping, with the cost of these gratuities built into the tour package price. In many ways this is a handy solution, freeing the tour manager from worrying about appropriate sums to distribute to the porters or hotel staffers. If the tour manager is representing a travel agency, however, it's a good idea to occasionally check to see that the appropriate service personnel have been tipped. You want these people to continue to think favorably of the sponsoring organization.

If the tour manager does the tipping, it's prudent to check with the driver or courier about local customs. In some places, offering money would be regarded as rude; in others, a satisfactory tip may be higher than you anticipated. Large cities fall in this latter category. Local customs in some areas may even include tipping for theater ushers.

While things like cigarettes may be used in a few places for tips, money, usually the local currency, is the customary tip. American dollars may be used as a last resort if one does not have local currency, or if the dollar is highly prized. American coins should never be used.

Tour managers employed by travel agencies may be supplied with guides for tipping, spelling out amounts that should suffice. These are based on the nature and length of service and the number of tour members. Other tour managers may want to purchase the very reasonable Tip Computer Card (Tip Computers International, 5733 La Jolla Blvd., Suite 6, San Diego, CA 92109), a credit-card-sized plastic review of how much and when to tip. A Travel Tips USA card is available at the same address.

You wouldn't normally tip airline personnel, bed and breakfast hosts, desk clerks, restaurant captain, and similar service people, but a special reason might exist for breaking this practice. You also refrain from tipping when the service is built into the cost of a meal—unless the service has been exceptional and you want to show your further gratitude. Frequently, this service charge is automatically part of the tour operator cost and, consequently, of the traveler's package price.

Keeping in mind that any currency fluctuates, you can review this list of suggested tips with Allied Travel, Inc. supplied its tours managers in Great Britain. These could vary with changes in the exchange rate.

Number of Passengers	15-29	30-45
Head water/main meal	£5.00	£6.00
Head concierge/per night	£2.00	£2.50
Special dinners	£5.00	£6.00
Driver - Airport Transfer	£3.00	
Harbor Transfer	£6.00	
Guide - Half Day	£3.00	
Full Day	£6.00	
Driver - Half Day	£3.00	
Full Day	£6.00	
Airport porterage - official rates:	15 p per case	
Hotel porterage	15 p per case	

Fig. 8-6. Tipping chart—Great Britain—suggested by Allied Travel Inc.

Tipping Varies from Place to Place

Some tipping guides go into more detail, breaking down amounts in columns for each five tour members. They also include doormen, sleeping car attendants, and personnel in nightclubs and restaurants (other than hotel). In general, the percentage of a tip for an individual service ranges between ten and fifteen percent, with a few places (like London and Rio de Janeiro) going to twenty percent.

Most tipping is part of the tour price and is handled by the agency or operator escort. Some tipping, however, is at the discretion of the tour member, who may seek advice from the tour manager. Since practices vary internationally, the escort should be up on local custom.

There are restroom and cloakroom tips (about 25¢); taxis (15 percent); hairdressers (20 percent); theater ushers (25¢); waiters when meals are not included in tour (15 percent); and numerous cruise personnel, such as stewards who deliver meals or wine to staterooms (amounts vary among cruise lines). All of these should be tipped by the tour member, unless included in the tour.

There are differences among countries. Restaurant tips, for example, vary from zero in China to 25 percent (usually added to the bill) in Buenos Aires.

Tipping of any kind in China is considered rude, and in Japan, many service people, like doormen, chambermaids, and taxi drivers, do not expect tips. Tipping in Russia and India is very minor, with 5 percent in Moscow considered acceptable. Service personnel in Rome and Paris expect visitors to be generous. so know where you are.

It is customary to tip both the tour guide and the driver, even though both are paid by their company. Some agencies suggest that this be left to the tour members, while others suggest a tip from the tour manager's expense fund, regardless of what passengers do.

Whatever the passengers elect to do should be at their discretion. The tour manager should neither encourage nor promote such a collection. Many travel agencies recommend individual tipping by tour members rather than making up a pot of money. The latter process, however, is common. In that case, the passengers elect a spokesperson who presents the purse to the courier and/or driver.

The typical formula for the tour guide (or courier) might be at least a dollar a day per person, or a minimum of $15 per person on a two-week trip with the same person. A customary tip for the driver would be half that. Where the driver also assumes duties of the courier, go with the larger amount. Remember, however, that the tour manager stays out of this, and what they wish to give (if anything) is up to the tour members.

Sometimes the tour members may also wish to make a gift to the tour manager. This should be discouraged. Any money should be refused, unless such refusal would be awkward or cause hard feelings. A small gift might be preferable, but the tour manager should tactfully let the passengers know that such rewards are neither expected nor appropriate.

A few final points:

- ❑ Always check to see if the service charge is already included on the bill.
- ❑ If visiting several countries, you might make up tip packets in the local currency for this specific purpose.
- ❑ Don't be afraid to exceed the recommended amounts, particularly when someone does you a special favor, like advancing the time of a meal.
- ❑ If confronted with surly and grasping personnel at a hotel or other stop, report this in your tour-end summary.

THE CRUISE

As with the hotel, the tour manager should try to be as familiar as possible with the ship chosen for a cruise. At the very least, the manager should review deck plans and photos, and should speak with professionals who have used this line. Much better, of course, is a personal visit to the ship, either on a familiarization trip, a previous voyage, or just prior to embarkation. This tour will familiarize the escort with the cabin arrangements and the various public areas. Sometimes the tour manager may be supplied the stateroom arrangements in advance, enabling him or her to enter these on the personal manifest and on the deck plan.

Obviously, the tour manager must be acquainted with the fundamental terms of nautical jargon. Even landlubbers know you're on a ship, not a boat, and that left and right are port and starboard. The back of the ship is aft (or the stern) while the front is forward (or the bow). There are decks, not floors, and when you descend you go below, not downstairs. The tour manager must know the names of the decks, from Sun to D, or whatever designation the ship makes. There is no need to overdo this, greeting tour members with "avast" or "ahoy," but cruising is one of those specialties, like sampling wine, which calls for its own vocabulary. Mistakes stand out.

Baggage is less of a problem than on air/bus tours. The passenger keeps his or her own baggage identification. For most tours a couple of suitcases suffice. These are brought to the dock by the tourists and carried aboard by porters. Other luggage, like steamer trunks, which may be shipped but not used en route, is tagged and handled separately.

Boarding a ship is not as fast as boarding a plane. Three of four hours may be required, and the tour manager should be on hand during this entire time. While the crew may issue stateroom assignments, the tour manager (who could be at a desk furnished by the cruise line) assists with problems, greets tour members, and helps them locate their cabins.

A tour member who wishes to move up to a better class of stateroom must pay extra for this privilege. Once aboard, changing may be difficult, since cruises are often booked solidly. If the passenger does switch, be sure you make this change on your roster.

The main meal aboard the ship is dinner. Many passengers dress formally for this occasion, and this is mandatory on some cruises. Details about dress (and other things, from passport requirements to embarkation procedures) are found in brochures supplied by each cruise line. If such brochures are not supplied, check with the travel agency and pass this information on to tour members in advance of their leaving their own hometowns.

Dress for most other meals is informal, but special events like the Captain's Dinner or the Captain's Cocktail Party call for more formal apparel. The tour manager should certainly set the tone for the group. Breakfast and lunch are likely to be open seating, and you may even order a buffet lunch by the pool, without changing from your swimsuit. The CLIA Cruise Manual provides many of these guidelines.

Meals are good occasions to check on tour members, especially on large ships, just to see how they are faring. If unable to spot a tour members at a couple of consecutive meals, the tour manager should check with others, or knock on the stateroom door.

Many ships book big name entertainers for the evening shows. They also feature movies, dances, organized games, and theme parties. In addition, sports opportunities abound: pool, shuffleboard, swimming, ping pong, deck tennis, skeet, lifting weights. The tour manager may help get tour members involved, and, health and talent permitting, join in the activities.

During entertainment in the lounge or salon, the escort will want to be present, and should circulate among tour members, buying an occasional drink for different individuals. Holding a party each week for the tour group is another nice idea and not too expensive. The advice on spending time with varied groups also applies to shore excursions. The tour manager is under no real obligation to accompany members on optional shore visits, but such a presence is helpful. Arranging for things like a group photo at the captain's table is always appreciated.

Steamboat and river cruises share some similarities with ocean trips, but the entertainment features are fewer and the shore excursions less of a problem. The atmosphere is even more informal at meals, and because the ships are considerably smaller, keeping track of people is much simpler.

Most tipping aboard ship is a passenger concern. It's customery to tip at the end of the voyage, as at the last meal for dining room personnel and the day before docking for stateroom attendants and other personnel. Bar tipping is done when drinks are bought. On seven-to-ten day cruises, the passengers usually tip once, at the end of the cruise. On longer cruises, they may tip once a week.

Bartenders, wine stewards, and deck stewards normally get 15 percent of the bill; cabin stewards are tipped $2–$3 per person per day; and waiters anywhere from $2–$4 per passenger per day. You may also want to tip the maitre d' for special services, with $5 being common.

The Cruise Lines International Association (17 Battery Place, Suite 631, New York, NY 10014) publishes a free booklet on the most often asked questions about cruises. There are several good books that rate ship lines and provide other cruising information, including a Berlitz paperback *(The Berlitz Complete Handbook to Cruising)* and *Total Traveler by Ship* by Ethel Blum.

OTHER FORMS OF TOURS

Veteran escorts will tell you the toughest kind of tour to lead is a long cross-country bus ride. Distances are great and there are often long stretches without much scenery worth commenting on. The long bus tour is a test for the tour manager, who must have exceptional patience, energy, and personality. On some tours the escort may want to nap early and then stay awake while others are sleeping, just to keep the driver company. Sufficient rest stops are also a must. More details are contained in Chapter 11.

There are many forms of tours: raft trips, two or three day trail rides, and even camel caravans. The tour manager must adapt, remembering the need to provide all the necessities for tour members, along with a good time. Heads must still be counted, illnesses attended, disputes settled, and commitments met.

MISCELLANEOUS

Optional Tours

When tour members do have free time, they may ask the tour leader for suggestions. So the tour leader should have some ideas, or even brochures. At least three options should be available. These should be side trips, events, or special places the tour manager knows about personally or from very reliable sources. Do not recommend anything about which you are uncertain. Always

Fig. 8-7. Optional tours—like this cruise to Ireland's Garinish Island—are frequently offered in addition to the regular tour package.

know which people have gone on special tours and how you can reach them. Also, check them in on return.

When in London, for example, the tour member may wish to take a cruise down the Thames to Greenwich, or spend a day visiting Windsor Castle and Oxford. A Paris vacationer could trek to the beautiful Fountainebleau Chateau; a visitor to Mexico City might opt for a bus tour of some Mayan ruins. These optional tours are at the tour members' expense, and may be recommended by the tour manager, by the hotel desk, by travel guides, by friends, or by travel magazines.

Local Tours

When taking a local tour, particularly in major cities, the tour manager should be conscious of the possibility of members getting lost. Some castles, museums, and cathedrals are jammed and it's difficult to hold a group together. A colorful hat (preferably on a tall member of the group), a pennant on an umbrella, or some other rallying symbol should be employed. If the local guide leads, the tour manager should bring up the rear, keeping folks together. If the head of the group moves too fast for the slower tourists, shout for the leaders to slow down.

Local tours may be part of the package or may be options. Many are done using the regular touring coach with the addition of the local guide. Others are walking tours—along the Royal Mile in Edinburgh, for example, or along the Roman wall in Chester, or through the Capitol Building in Washington, D.C. Travelers to Dublin could add a tour of sites made famous by James Joyce and there are similar day trips to the haunts of Sherlock Holmes in London. The United States also has these excursions, like a drive through the famous homes of Hollywood or a cruise around Manhattan.

Temporary Departures from the Tour

On occasion tour members may wish to leave the tour at some point and join it later. Perhaps they wish to visit relatives or friends, play golf, fish, or conduct some business. They may even wish to see something not on the tour. Unless this alteration appears dangerous or inconvenient, the tour manager may allow it. However, the departing member is responsible for his or her own welfare, expenses, and return. The tour manager will, as before, want to know where the person is going and who to contact in case of emergency.

Tour leaders who are very familiar with a country and who have many friends there are often able to fulfill a special request of a passenger to experience some particular thing. Perhaps a physician wants to meet another physician, or an attorney wants to visit a law court, or a farmer wants to discuss irrigation. Arranging for such meetings is a real plus for the member.

European Rail Tickets

European **rail tickets** can sometimes get complicated. Separate journeys on the same rail line may appear on a single ticket, so you must hang on to the tickets. On tours, the tour manager may carry a single ticket with the names of tour members, plus small stubs or counterfoils to be surrendered to conductors. While customs differ, the best single piece of advice is hang on to the tickets until asked to turn them in.

Border Crossings

Let the local guide or courier handle things when crossing from one country to another. Passengers should be advised to remain quiet and to cooperate with the authorities. This is no time for flippancy or belligerence. Misconduct may lead to a thorough and lengthy search of baggage, or even to detention. Sometimes the check is perfunctory and the guard may wave the coach or train right through. At other times there may be a passport or luggage check of some intensity.

Local Customs

In the same vein, passengers should be instructed to respect local customs. If the Vatican has certain restrictions on dress, they should be obeyed. If a site is considered too holy to be photographed, refrain from taking pictures. If women are not allowed in certain bars, don't make an issue of it. Go with the flow. Women tourists should also be informed of other restrictions in certain countries.

In China, hotel doors are typically left unlocked. Shorts are not worn. Sightseeing is strenuous. Tardiness is considered very rude. Evangelical literature will be confiscated. In Germany, talking with your hands in your pockets is disrespectful. And you should never squeeze a fraulein's hand too firmly in greeting. Never take chrysanthemums as a gift to a Belgian home. Those flowers are reserved for funerals. And these tips merely scratch the surface.

Taxes

In addition to knowing foreign currency, the tour manager should be aware of taxing systems in various countries. If there is a Value Added Tax, for example, explain this to the tourists. If there are departure taxes at airports (which are not included in the tour), budget for these, and determine if they must be paid in the local currency. If you stay at some American hotels with a lodging tax, note this.

Youth Groups

Most tours cater to adults, often older adults. But there are **youth tours** which, from the tour manager's viewpoint, have plus and minus aspects. You may have fewer problems with illness, and it is often more fun to be with a lively, congenial group. But accommodations will be more spartan, food less elegant, and entertainment more youth-oriented. The pre-trip briefing is especially important with students. Rules on controlled substances, curfews, and other related issues should be discussed. Consequences of improper and inappropriate behavior should be stated clearly and in writing.

Youth tour leadership requires special talents. While being able to get along with young people, the escort must also command their respect. He or she must know when to be flexible and when to be firm.

Disputes and Refunds

The policy on refunds is spelled out in the brochure and itinerary passengers receive. In general, there are no refunds once the tour starts, except in most unusual circumstances. Bills have to be paid as contracted, even if a tour member must leave for illness or is sent home because of disciplinary reasons.

Individuals who want to skip a meal, a play, or some other feature of a tour are not entitled to refunds. The food and fun are available to them; if they choose to forego them, that's their choice.

The tour manager should never engage in a dispute with a tour member over what has been paid for. If a tour member insists he's paid for some optional item on the tour, but you have no record of this, permit the individual to enjoy that item, telling him politely you'll check it all out later. Put this in your report and settle it when you return to the States. Public argument about things like this make the situation uncomfortable for all concerned.

Any damage or breakage caused by a tour member is the responsibility of that individual, as are costs incurred by things like lost passports.

SATISFYING THE CUSTOMER

No matter how hard you work at promoting friendship among tour members, you are still going to wind up with a fairly diverse set of personalities and temperaments. This is not a family; it's not a team; it's a group of distinct individuals. Each tour is different. Sometimes there is a spirit of camaraderie that pervades all activities. The people like each other and function together. This is the idea. A more likely situation is that you'll have a high percentage of nice folks and a few mavericks. Hopefully, the influence of the latter can be kept to a minimum.

The size and nature of tours has some impact on personalities. The smaller the group, the more the chance of cooperation and congeniality. Larger groups offer more opportunities for disagreeable characters. Tours into problem areas, a succession of rainy days, a multiplication of housing problems, contagious illness—these can all turn a pleasant crowd sour.

On some tours there are individuals who should never have booked this type of excursion. The place is too fast, or the accommodatons below their expectations, or the entertainment dull. All you can do in cases like this is to try to make them marginally happy, and hope they'll shape up. Your statement of "conditions and responsibilities" in your brochure should cover the worst case scenario and enable you to send home an extremely disruptive person. In fairness to tourists, it should be repeated that most of them are delightful traveling companions. You'll have the 81-year-old woman who is the life of the party; or the handicapped person who inspires others and blunts complaints; or the couple who tell you every night what a lovely day they've had. Most travelers are grateful to you and the driver/courier for all you add to their traveling pleasure.

But you do encounter problem people, and because you are destined to live closely with one another for a few weeks, these characters stand out. There are people who behave strangely, but are really harmless; and there are those who can disrupt the entire tour. The tour manager must be able to deal firmly with difficult individuals, convincing them to cease the errant behavior or be sent home.

There are people who drink too much, people who talk too much, people who complain too much. You have hypochrondriacs and introverts, tour members who are always late and others who get lost. Some members get romantically involved with the driver or courier, and still others spread rumors about everything from fellow members to potential hotel problems.

There are also squabbling roommates. If this is a married couple, the tour manager can't do much except counsel them to stop before some action is necessary. Other roommates may have been friends for years, or they may have paired up at the get-acquainted party. Now they can't stand each other, and they want you to settle things. If possible, you might pair them up with other singles. If this doesn't work, suggest single rooms (if available), for which they must pay the extra charge. If no change is possible, just tell them the arguments must cease, and they must try to get along like mature adults. They may avoid each other as much as they can, and this cuts down on public displays, at least.

If a roommate snores and the other person can't sleep, you really should arrange for another room, if not at that hotel, then somewhere nearby.

Handicapped persons represent a special challenge and there are tours that cater to them, selecting hotels that have special ramps, doors, and other items. Rambling Tours, for example, welcomes those in wheelchairs or with canes. They even have an "electric elevator" to simplify getting on and off the coach. They also assure their tour members that they know how to handle emergencies, and how to summon prompt medical assistance.

Generally, the handicapped person knows what he or she can do. Many function very well on any tour, keeping up with fellow members in any activity that doesn't demand a personally impossible physical feat—like asking a wheelchair patient to negotiate several hundred narrow castle stairs. Even then, tour managers are constantly surprised at what these special members can accomplish.

GROUP PSYCHOLOGY

There are courses, seminars, and books on **mass psychology.** These help. So do experience and common sense. While you can't know too much, regardless of the source, an astute tour manager will pick up a great deal of knowledge by just observing passengers. Put yourself in the other person's place. What would you want at this point in the tour? What would you be thinking about? That's a start.

Remember that your job is to exercise control over the group while satisfying their expectations and insuring their enjoyment. You have a captive audience. Plus, you have an advantage—they have certain fears they feel you will assuage. They don't want to strike out on their own. You know the routine, and they trust you. They may test you to see how you react to pressure, but normally they don't want your responsibility.

You should be pleasant without being saccharine, and politely firm without being dictatorial. This requires ingenuity and patience, but nobody said the job of tour manager was easy!

Here are some reminders:

❑ *Establish relationships early*   Even at the get-acquainted party, let members know you are in charge. Size them up, too, speculating on potential problems. This initial impression isn't infallible, but with a little practice you can get good at it.

❑ *Play no favorites*   Spread yourself around. Be friendly, but don't mislead anyone, and don't make others jealous.

❑ *Be respectful, but not servile*   You are a gentleman or a lady, not a servant. You don't run out for cigarettes on demand, or perform other menial tasks for travelers. Be helpful, but not docile.

❏ *Be sensitive to moods*   Pick up the signals, the comments, the body language. Know when tour members are tired, bored, anxious, afraid, hungry, thirsty, angry, suspicious, or whatever. Pace yourself and the tour to these prevailing moods.

❏ *Lead without compulsion*   Never seem to be forcing things. Make people want to go along with your suggestions because compliance promises them the most fulfillment.

❏ *Correct difficulties before they get out of hand*   If a soft answer turneth away wrath, a fast answer turneth away problems. Deal with difficulties immediately. Don't allow them to grow in the hope they'll disappear. Bite the bullet. You're the leader.

❏ *Watch for friction*   If you notice people getting on each other's nerves, try to straighten them out. Don't let this erupt and spoil the journey for others.

❏ *If you don't know something, admit it*   Don't try to fake your way through. If it's your first trip to an area, for example, confess this. Others will respect you for it.

❏ *Make people feel like individuals, even in a group*   This means addressing them by name, giving them periodic recognition, and suggesting things for them personally—a book they should buy or a person they should meet.

❏ *Learn how to use the microphone and other equipment*   Don't stumble around trying to find the mike switch. Know how close to hold it to your mouth and how high to keep the volume. If you have cassettes aboard to play, know how to work with them. This goes for any equipment you have, short of driving the coach.

❏ *Encourage members to participate*   Draw them out. Spend some time with them, and introduce them to others. Try to get them into small groups for events on their own. Ask them to do things, from singing to assisting you with small chores.

❏ *Do not provide what people should have brought*   Don't surrender your raincoat, razor, umbrella, or alarm clock. Do not loan people any money.

❏ *Keep a sharp eye on elderly or ill tour members*   Other passengers may be too busy or too embarrassed to note or report such things. The person who is not feeling well may keep quiet in order not to spoil the fun of others. That means you have to be on top of the tourists' physical conditions.

❏ *Always know where tour members are*   Get them in the habit of making reports. Get addresses and phone numbers.

❏ *Have a few surprises*   Games, pools, awards, impromptu entertainment, drinks on the house—these are ways to keep people happy and the tour lively.

❏ *You are the host*   So act like one!

THE TOUR MANAGER AS HOST

Talents differ among tour managers. Some are indifferent story tellers but are good on history and customs. Others are more efficient than eloquent. You do the best with what you have, but possessing some show business skills can enliven a group. Some tour managers are amateur magicians and demonstrate their art. Others have a stockpile of sure-fire jokes. Still others know hundreds of songs and can get the tour members singing. One tour manager keeps a small library of books in the back of the coach, all related to the area being visited, and travelers can consult these volumes for information. Another leader runs an occasional bingo game aboard the bus. Some put on an impromptu talent show, using tour members.

A sense of humor helps. There will be hotel mixups, confused dinner reservations, a play people don't understand, foul weather. Displaying an upbeat spirit (while still attending to the resolution of the difficulty) makes everyone a bit more relaxed. Keep in mind that these little hitches provide the story material for tour members once they get home.

Never discuss problems in front of others. That's why the tour manager needs a private room. This is the spot for the tour manager to go over matters with the driver or courier. It is also the place to talk to tour members. Public chastisement is uncomfortable for everyone. Pick an appropriate time and place, and handle all confrontations tactfully.

Never discuss personal problems with tour members, like your failing marriage or your financial straits. Never bad rap your tour operator or your own agency. These are family matters.

Like Caesar's wife, the tour manager must be above suspicion. Don't let your personal flaws erode your authority. Stay away from the bottle, the men or the women, and the race tracks, unless you can handle all of these. Keep your temper in check. Stay out of situations that could lead to problems.

In the final analysis, people on tour aren't any different than people anywhere. It's just that they are somewhat forced into unity, and the tour manager has to make this artificial situation work.

❏ *CHAPTER HIGHLIGHTS*

❏ Because titles of professional personnel on tours are sometimes used interchangeably, it may be best to separate them by duties rather than names. Someone supervises, someone comments, someone drives. Where there is a tour manager, this person is in charge overall. In package tours for which tour members join up overseas, the courier is in charge of things.

❏ Local guides are required in many locales, and they are an asset, trained to cover a lot of material in a brief time.

❏ The tour manager constantly counts heads, counts baggage (unless that duty is assigned elsewhere), and generally looks after the well-being of the tour members. The tour manager may also do commentary.

❏ Everything should be planned, from rest stops and photo stops, to lunch stops and shopping.

❏ The tour manager checks with the hotel desk for keys, mail, meal times, departure times, and other matters. Any hotel problems are also settled by the tour manager.

❏ Entertainment should be selected carefully and scheduled properly. Shopping hours and venues should be known to the tour manager. Even though the tour manager is always on duty, it is possible—and wise—to find some quiet time for compiling reports, preparing for the next day, or just relaxing.

❏ Even when tipping is primarily the responsibility of the driver or courier, the tour manager should be familiar with the general range of tips and should also know the proper amounts to tip driver, tour operator, courier, and other personnel.

❏ In many ways, the cruise tour is easier to manage, but the tour manager should remain in evidence, should be alert for any passenger difficulties, should know the shipboard routine, and should be able to advise on tipping, if asked.

❏ Many other bits of information are important for the tour manager to have, from the availability of optional tours to the explanation of local customs and taxes.

❏ Group psychology is helpful in handling a diverse tour group. The tour manager remains calm, remains in charge, solves problems while making certain the tour members are enjoying themselves.

❏ CASE PROBLEMS

1. One of your tour members is making a return trip to the region you are covering. Even though he knows the place only superficially, he is spoiling the trip for others by commenting loudly on certain attractions the tour manager is also trying to describe. Furthermore, he's continually making comparisons regarding hotels, meals, and entertainment, always to the detriment of the present tour. This not only irritates you personally, but, as tour manager, you can see it disturbs other people who are wondering what you are going to do about it. So, what do you do? Be specific.

2. As is your custom as tour manager, you call ahead the evening before you are due at a hotel in Paris. The manager tells you that he wired your office two days earlier to inform you his hotel had a serious fire and it is now closed for repairs. The telegram never reached you because you were on the road. You have the manager on the phone, and, of course, you do have confirmation for the space for which you have paid. What do you ask the manager? Tell the manager? What else might you do?

9

SPECIAL PROBLEMS AND SITUATIONS

LEARNING OBJECTIVES

After reading this chapter you will:

- ❑ Understand the procedures to be followed when luggage is lost, people are lost, or when items like passports and credit cards are lost
- ❑ Know how to conduct yourself in the event of illness or death of a tour member, and how to acquaint yourself with foreign laws and customs
- ❑ Be aware of actions to be taken in case of political unrest or natural disasters
- ❑ Have a grasp of travelers' rights

KEY CONCEPTS

Acts of God	Delays	Political crises
Advisories	Drug laws	Reimbursement
Airline tickets	Fire	Seasickness
Bumping	Illness on tour	Surcharge
Cancellations	Laws, in foreign countries	Travel rights
Consulate assistance	Liability concerns	Unclaimed baggage
Credit cards	Lost luggage	U.S. government
Crime prevention	Lost passport	publications
Cultural differences	Natural disasters	Vouchers
Death on tour	Overbooking	

Some tour problems are beyond the control of even the most cautious tour manager. Most, however, can be anticipated and avoided. A strong argument can be made for keeping a checklist, and for having a set of detailed rules and instructions. Think about difficulties that might arise, and do a dry run on your strategy to meet them. Keep a list of local contacts in every region you visit, and know where you can turn for help.

Besides experience and careful planning, tact and common sense are valuable assets, especially when the unexpected occurs. Above all, don't panic. Too much depends on you. Maintain a calm demeanor, even if the whole tour starts to collapse about you. Getting excited is not only demoralizing to others, but also prevents you from thinking clearly and logically.

Some of the common problems a tour manager might face are covered in previous chapters. This chapter focuses on a few of these in more depth, or explores other less common happenings.

Keep in mind, however, that this list of problems is not exhaustive. Olson Travelworld, the exclusive distributor of Winter Olympic tickets in 1988, discovered that the Calgary Olympics organizers not only provided them with the event tickets they requested, but also loaded them down with four times as many tickets as they wanted, including many non-premium event tickets. The **surcharge** for these tickets had to be passed along, in part, to those buying the Olympics package, so there were complaints all the way down the line from participating travel agencies to clients who had already paid for their tour package.

The tour manager may have a minimum of direct control over situations like strikes or bankruptcies, but these and other actions eventually affect the tour. Strikes may paralyze carriers, interrupt local traffic, close down hotels, disrupt food service, create unacceptable increases in cost, or, at the very least, turn a vacation into a nightmare.

Bankruptcies are also becoming more common. Travel trade journals feature a story in almost every issue of the closing of a travel agency, the demise of a tour operator, or the financial woes of an airline. When any of these things occurs and disrupts a tour already scheduled, planners may have to scurry around for alternate suppliers in order to avoid tour members scrambling for the return of their deposits.

In situations like this, the tour manager is often caught unawares and may take some heat from tour members—especially if the tour is sold on the basis of this individual's popularity—without having much access to remedies for the problem.

The most common airline complaints include flight cancellations and delays, **lost or damaged luggage, overbooked flights,** poor service, ticketing and boarding problems, and the confusion over differing fares. All of these difficulties can become major or minor, depending on the scope and length of the situation.

LOST AND FOUND

Luggage

Bags are one of a tour's major headaches. You can't check them too often, because they disappear at airports, between trains, and between hotels. People leave something behind, grab the wrong bag, or put their suitcase with another tour's baggage. Travelers frequently fail to heed the warning about adding and subtracting luggage. So the count is made, and it is correct, but that's because somebody added a bag. That means someone else's luggage may be left behind. It's often the innocent who suffer. They are minus toilet articles or underwear or jackets until the lost items catch up. They may have to replace things in order to cope, or depend on the sympathy and generosity of fellow tour members.

When luggage is lost at the airport, notify the carrier and help fill out any requisite forms. The airlines will contact agents at the departure point and the next stop (in case the bags were routed ahead). The baggage claim area, of course, would have been searched thoroughly by the tour manager, driver/ courier, and the individual whose bags were missing. If there were other tours departing the airport at about the same time, check on their destinations, then get in touch with them to see if they have the errant luggage. If they do, have the bags delivered to the next feasible hotel.

When you are on the move, make certain you allow sufficient time for the bags to make it to the proper hotel. Don't cut the time too close, and try to pick a hotel when you're staying more than one night. You could have the luggage following you all over Europe.

If you don't notice the loss until you get into the hotel, notify the desk clerk, bell captain, or porter. They'll search the hotel—the lobby, elevators, basement. Meanwhile, the driver may be checking the coach. Tour members must be asked if they have any extra bags in their rooms. Sometimes all guests in smaller hotels may be called in an attempt to locate the cases. If these methods turn up nothing, then check out the airlines, other concurrent tours, and the last hotel.

Should luggage other than your own show up in your count, notify the hotel porter or bellman. If you've just arrived via air, contact the airlines (or the ship, if you just docked), telling them the flight you came on, and helping them identify the luggage.

On cruises, scour the dock area first for lost bags, then report the loss to the purser, perhaps after you have queried all your other tour members.

Most luggage is found within a few days. Some airlines may search as long as three weeks before declaring the bags lost. Passengers have up to forty-five days to file claims for luggage lost on domestic lines, but need to check individual foreign lines for their policies.

By law, the domestic airline liability is limited to a total of $1,250.00; international limitations are generally fixed at $9.07 per pound for checked bags and $400.00 for carryon items. These amounts can be increased if the passenger pays a surcharge, which may be one hundred percent of your fare on international flights.

Luggage Insurance A more sensible alternative is the purchase of baggage insurance (unless your own homeowner's policy covers items lost away from home), which may run as little as $5 for $500 worth of coverage for a few days, to ten times that amount for $1,000 worth of coverage for a couple of weeks. Obviously there are higher premiums for even more protection.

It is also sensible planning to leave expensive items like jewelry in a safe place at home. Tourists should take only what is needed. They should identify their bags inside and out, keep a list of items being carried, and mark their luggage with something distinctive, so that it won't be picked up by mistake. Many bags look the same, and airport rules about showing baggage tags may vary.

What happens with **unclaimed items?** Most of them end up in the Unclaimed Baggage Center in Scottsboro, Alabama (or other Alabama towns) and are sold to anyone who walks in. A high percentage of the lost items are clothing, with men's shorts selling for as little as 50¢, and trenchcoats up to $20. There are cameras, wet suits, skis, toiletry kits, portable radios, jewelry, and, of course, a wide assortment of luggage.

When bags are lost and the overseas passenger finds himself/herself without clothing, the airline may have a policy of granting an allowance (e.g., $50–$75 a day) to purchase necessary items. The passenger buys the items, keeps the sales slips, then submits a claim for **reimbursement.**

Missing Tour Members

Suppose you are checking people in at the point of departure, and one or two persons have failed to arrive. Check first with the airline agent, just in case the people slipped by and went directly to the counter or gate. If the agent's records also show these people as absent, call the missing person's home.

No answer? Perhaps these folks are on their way. Do they have any friends who are already here? Can they tell you how the absentees planned to get to the airport? Have you looked into restaurants, bars, and rest rooms?

Now you are up against it. The plane has been called for boarding, the missing tour members still have not arrived, and you haven't been able to get in touch with them. If a representative from your travel agency is with you, turn the problem over to this person. If not, call the agency, explain the problem, have them continue to try to reach these absent members, and make arrangements for them on a later flight. If there are any additional charges, of course, the passengers must pay them.

In cases where a passenger is missing from an intermediate flight and you must leave, deposit an explanatory note with the appropriate airline ticket counter, and have this airline agent help get the tardy person to the next tour stop.

Remember that *your first responsibility is to the tour as a whole*. This means you'd ordinarily depart without the missing person(s). Exceptions to this rule would be if you happen to have this person's passport and he can't leave the country without it, or his tickets (although these may be left at the airline counter); or if the individual is elderly and you have no idea where he or she is. You can't merely abandon people. In these extreme cases, you would turn the group over temporarily to some responsible tour members and join them as soon as you can. The driver/courier at the destination should be told what has happened and he or she will take over until the tour manager gets there. It should be stressed that the situation must be a real emergency, and, even then, there may be reasons why you have to go.

Sometimes a tour picks up passengers at different locations in the United States. Say that, at one of these stops, a passenger doesn't make the connection. Have this person paged at the airport. If there is no response, call the person's home, or, if known, the hotel where he or she spent the previous night. If you still come up dry, notify your agency, the tour operator, and the airline. They will try to find a way to enable the missing party to catch up with you.

If tour members become lost en route, check the hotel, fellow passengers, likely area locales and, as a last resort, notify police. Before you move on, you must know what happened to them. Perhaps some local agent or hotel staff member will take over and get the passenger routed on. Perhaps you may have to delay departure until you know the whereabouts of the missing person.

Aboard ship, the obvious place to check is the cabin, then with others who know the person, and then in the ship's public places. Enlist the aid of the purser.

If a cruise passenger who is flying to the port city fails to show up at the dock, check the airport. If time permits, and the distance is not great, you might even take a cab out there and look around. But don't endanger your own sailing. The paging system can, of course, be used with advantage both at the airport and aboard ship.

The drill is, in summary, to check the area, check with friends, check the last destination, check with authorities, and then decide whether you can leave or not. Circumstances usually dictate that you must depart. In this case, always leave some instructions to enable the lost person to join you.

Loss of a Passport

This is a most important document and should be kept on one's person at all times. There could be routine checks by authorities, or a need for identification when financing purchases, or a requirement when cashing checks in a foreign bank. Warn tour members not to leave their passports in rest rooms, hotel rooms, or on the airplanes or coaches.

Should a passport be lost, go over all the places where it might have been mislaid. If nothing turns up, contact the nearest American embassy. They will require proof that it is really lost, like a statement from the police, plus the witness of a person with a valid passport, perhaps yourself. Getting the new passport takes time—at least half a day. Tour managers should carry a list of tour member passport numbers, plus date and place of issue.

One tour manager mentions spending his only free day in London helping a tour member get a new passport, and this person lost it again at the very next stop. Fortunately, it was located aboard the plane.

"If I had lost my passport," said the tour manager, "I think I'd have taped it to my body for the rest of the journey."

Loss of a passport is always a serious matter, but it may be far more serious in some countries than others. **Consulates** are normally closed on weekends and at night, so a message should be left about the lost passport, with a request for assistance and a phone number where you may be reached. Cautious travelers also keep their passport number in several places and may also have an extra passport photo handy.

Loss of Funds and Tickets

Loss of these items is the responsibility of the individual, but the tour manager should know how to advise the passenger.

It's nearly impossible to recover stolen cash, unless the money is found by a scrupulous person who has the time to seek you out. If lost in a carrier, a hotel, or restaurant, you would have the tourists report this to these places. They could get lucky. But the best solution is to carry very little cash.

Everyone who watches television should know how to handle lost travelers checks. Report the loss, with the number of the checks to the nearest office of the issuing company. If reported on weekends or holidays, repayment may be delayed but, on weekdays, most companies will speed up refunds. American Express has an emergency service that provides everything from cash to payment of hotel bills and airline tickets. Be sure to keep the number of your travelers checks in several different places, so you can retrieve them when detailing the loss.

There are a number of different **credit cards,** and they have their own rules. Some credit card companies and banks limit **liability** of the owner of a stolen credit card to a certain sum, like $50, $100, or nothing. The loss must be reported immediately, so that credit may be curtailed and the thief apprehended. Tour members may also provide themselves with inexpensive insurance to cover any credit card losses.

If tour members end up without any funds because of a theft, they may phone relatives and have them send an International Money Order overseas or a postal money order in the United States. Up to $2,000 may also be wired to individuals in the states by relatives with Master Cards or Visa Cards. American Express has its own plan.

Tickets   As mentioned earlier, airline agents sometimes inadvertently pull too many tickets from a folder, leaving a few individuals short on the next leg of the journey. That's why the tour manager should be on hand when the tickets are removed, and why the ticket envelopes should be checked again before the tour manager leaves the counter.

If tickets are lost, either by you or by a passenger, the loss should be reported immediately to the carrier and to your own agency, as well as to the operator handling that portion of the tour. Substitute tickets will be provided and any difference settled by you at a later date.

Many tour managers keep all the tickets themselves. While this does place a burden on one individual, it lowers the possibility of someone in the group mislaying his or her own tickets. When tickets are lodged in the hotel safe, the tour manager should be certain the safe will be open prior to the scheduled departure.

Many travel guidebooks recommend paying for tickets with credit cards as added protection against loss. They also counsel carrying some identification, like a driver's license, in the event ownership of the ticket is questioned.

Other Losses

If the tour manager loses the travel **vouchers,** work through the driver or courier, or through the closest agent of the tour operator, to secure substitutes. Hotels may be willing to take your word (or your signed statement) and expect the vouchers later. If the driver/courier handles the vouchers, your resposibility diminishes.

Should tour members lose their health or vaccination cards, they could be detained in a foreign country. Even though these cards are used on entry into the United States, nations whose conditions require certain shots will check tourists on exit. American customs officials recommend treating this loss like a passport loss and contacting the United States embassy or consulate.

Tour members can misplace all sorts of items: false teeth, jewelry, hats, coats, glasses, cameras, and gifts. While these losses are problems for the traveler and not the tour manager, it is difficult not to get involved. Tour members expect their leader to help.

One tour director, leading his first tour recently, was accosted by a female tour member who said, in anger, "It will be your fault if I'm pregnant!" While he was puzzling out this remark, she told him she was holding him personally responsible for her loss of her handbag, which contained her birth control pills.

It must be confessed that tour buses get lost, too. No one is perfect. Drivers and guides may be unfamiliar with a certain stretch of road, or a detour may throw them off. The tour manager should see that the coach gets back on course as quickly and quietly as possible. That's what maps and signposts are for!

ILLNESS

Passengers are expected to provide for their own medical needs, including adequate insurance. This means bringing along their own drugs, prescriptions, and diets, and making their own arrangements for any checkups or hospital stays.

The tour manager, however, will probably carry items like aspirin, cough drops, nosedrops, bandaids, and remedies for upset stomachs. Yet one must be careful about dispensing these, since resulting problems could be laid on your doorstep. A knowledge of first aid, including CPR and artificial respiration, is a handy skill. You may never need them, but people will look to you for assistance in any emergency, including illness.

Colds, headaches, nausea, and diarrhea are common ailments. At home they may be minor irritations but when traveling with a group they become serious maladies. Colds and respiratory infections spread rapidly. Try to get any sick person to a doctor as soon as possible for that person's good, as well as the health of the tour.

The person who is ill should make contact with the physician, rather than the tour manager selecting a doctor. However, if the tour member is too sick to do this, the tour manager may ask the hotel clerk or other person in authority to secure a physician. Hotels often have their own doctors, or someone they can call in an emergency. Aboard ship there is the ship's doctor and usually a small hospital or sick bay. The senior steward is the person to notify on an airplane and, if a passenger becomes ill on the coach, head for the nearest hospital or doctor's office.

Seasickness is something a tour member may prefer to handle alone, remaining in bed and shunning meals. Up to a point, this is fine, but, in the event of a prolonged illness, the tour manager should insist the person see the ship's doctor.

The list of possible medical problems is endless. Diners get food poisoning. Drinkers have hangovers. Some tourists develop allergies. Skiers get broken limbs and may need anything from an ambulance to a rescue helicopter. In addition to assuming responsibility for the securing of medical treatment, the passenger must also assume any financial obligation incurred by the visits to doctor, hospital, or pharmacist.

A tour director bringing home a group of weekend skiers had one young woman aboard with a severe case of sunburn. He treated it by breaking some vitamin E tablets and applying them to the burn areas. These entered her bloodstream and the coach had to make an emergency stop at a hospital en route. The tour manager was lucky he wasn't sued.

Here are some random comments by escorts regarding illnesses:

❏ "I've run into everything from helping a diabetic with insulin shots aboard a train to taking a passenger to a hospital where she had a kidney transplant."

❏ "One client, after flying over Greenland, told me she was pregnant, thereby nullifying her insurance. In Heidelberg she miscarried and was hospitalized, ruining that day for everyone. I got her to Milan and aboard a plane for the States—which she had to pay for."

❏ "Some foreign physicians are very cooperative. A couple of my people had sore throats. I phoned a physician and he ordered a pharmacist to stay open until I got there. This was in Austria, about a dozen years ago. And I remember I paid only ninety-five cents for the prescription."

❏ "An older woman on my tour kept fainting. The doctor said she shouldn't continue with us. I telephoned the States and had her son meet us in London and accompany her home. She was sick for several months. One added problem was that her grandson was with her. He was a nice kid, about twelve, and several of the other tourists wanted to take him with them, to finish the tour. But I said 'no' and sent him home. Had I allowed that, I'm sure the volunteer would have been back in a few days complaining about the inconvenience."

Tour Manager's Responsibilities and Education

If possible, a sick person should be accompanied to the hospital by the tour manager, just to see that everything is settled. Relatives should always be notified. On occasion, the tour manager may even have to remain behind temporarily to make sure that the tour member is okay. Another tour member may also remain with the patient until both can rejoin the group.

When a person must be sent home, relatives should be phoned and asked for instructions. The tour manager then makes the arrangements and probably stays with the person until the flight departs. The local agent or hotel may then take over. Costs are the responsibility of the tour member or his/her relatives.

Prevention is always the best remedy. Travelers should have a pretour exam, and should get the shots and other medicines recommended for that particular journey. IAMAT (International Association for Medical Assistance to Travelers) and the International Health Care Service provide publications giving information on weather, sanitary conditions, required clothing, and other matters affecting health in diverse countries across the world.

International SOS Assistance provides medical help around the globe, and HOME (Help in Overseas Medical Emergencies), which has a modest membership fee, handles such things as local burial or return of the deceased to the United States, medical service or evacuation, and the repatriation of minors.

Also valuable for traveler and tour manager are the annual booklet, *Health Information for International Travel* (Superintendent of Documents, **Government Printing Office,** Washington, D.C. 20402); updated weekly "blue sheets" on localized disease situations (Office of the Chief, Sanitation and Vector Control Activity, Quarantine Division, Room 107, 1015 North American Way, Miami FL 33132); plus other publications available from the government or from various health agencies and associations.

Tour managers can attend seminars on all aspects of medical attention. These courses cover emergency care, immunizations, diet, locating a physician abroad (there is a directory of foreign physicians, by specialty), health requirements for re-entry into this country, and even how to deal with jet lag.

Although their concern is for the tour members, tour managers may also become ill. This gets particularly sticky, since the success of the tour depends to a great extent on their staying healthy. Tour managers who are under the weather should seek immediate medical attention, sneaking in rest when they can, eating and drinking sensibly. They may also have to "play while hurt," like professional athletes. If the tour manager is unable to continue with the tour, he or she should phone the agency or operator and a substitute will normally be provided.

Common Sense Should be Used

Both the tour manager and tourist should exhibit a little common sense in terms of health. If warned not to drink the water, don't do so. If the tour calls for some extra precautions because of an extensive amount of walking, travel at very high altitudes, or primitive living conditions, the tour members and their leaders should be forewarned.

When you consider that about one out of every thirty travelers abroad will be hospitalized for sickness or accident (and another twelve thousand will die) each year, this emphasizes how common sickness may be. These statistics do not include those who don't feel well but blunder ahead anyhow.

Handicapped travelers may encounter difficulties of their own, although there are tours catering to them, and both carriers and accommodations are becoming more sensitive to the special needs of these tourists. AMTRAK has unique facilities for the handicapped, including wider doors, specially-designed seats in the dining cars, and other innovative equipment. Bus stations are ordinarily on one level, and restrooms take the handicapped person into account. A growing number of hotels have tailored their architecture to the needs of handicapped citizens, installing ramps and other aids, like grab bars in the tub and toilet areas.

Airlines should be contacted in advance about any requirements for handicapped persons. This means notifying them of requests for things like wheelchairs or permission to board a seeing-eye dog.

It is difficult for tour managers to know everything about tour members in advance, but the more they know, the better they may advise. They can help with adjustments for the handicapped, and they may even warn persons with recent operations, including dental surgery, or with ear infections, or anemia, or advanced pregnancy, about the discomfort and possible danger of air travel.

The tour manager may also remind travelers before they start that any who have medical problems, allergies, rare blood types, and other health considerations, might want to enroll in Medic Alert (P.O. Box 1009, Turlock, CA 95381) for $15. This secures a wallet card or bracelet with specific information on one's personal needs, plus a phone number that can be reached by a foreign physician who may need to obtain data.

Though this isn't a tour manager's concern, it's worth mentioning that travel agencies often protect themselves from costly lawsuits resulting from illness or other problems (like misinformation, bad advice, and delays) by taking out liability insurance.

DEATH

If sickness and lost luggage are traumatic for the tour manager, even more terrifying is the thought of a group member **dying.** Although the prospect of someone expiring on a tour is remote (less than one out of every twenty-five hundred travelers dies each year), the chance is always there, and the consequences invariably difficult.

There is no uniform procedure for dealing with the death of a tour member. Every country seems to have slightly different rules. Airlines and cruise ships are reluctant to broadcast their special routines for managing such tragedies. For the tour manager, getting specific and comprehensive information is impossible. However, there are some constants.

Should someone die overseas, the first contact should be made with the closest American embassy or consulate. The U.S. officials will then mediate with foreign officials regarding death certificates, embalming, the notifying of relatives, and other matters.

Here are a few things to consider:

❏ In some countries you need permission from authorities in each separate geographical division through which the body passes.
❏ Most nations require that bodies be disposed of within twenty-four hours. This makes speed essential in getting instructions from the next-of-kin.
❏ If the next-of-kin opt for burial in the foreign country and later disinterment, they'd better be familiar with that nation's laws. The body may not be allowed to be moved for six months or more.
❏ Getting a body back to the United States can be expensive, perhaps costing several thousand dollars.
❏ If a body is shipped back by air, the airlines need a signed death certificate, plus a statement from the mortician or embalmer, and assurance that the coffin has been hermetically sealed. Countries like Israel and various Moslem nations prohibit embalming, so the pledge about the sealing has to suffice.

When death occurs, the tour manager should call a physician, perhaps an ambulance, and check in with the American consul or ambassador. Either the State Department official or the tour manager may then help with other arrangements, like discussing disposition of the body with relatives, or attending to burial services. If death occurs in some remote place, the burdens of the escort become even heavier.

When the next-of-kin request that the body be shipped back to the United States, they will be charged according to distance and the weight of the coffin. Deceased persons have freight priority, and that adds to the expense incurred. This payment must be made before the body leaves foreign soil. Relatives can arrange such payment via the State Department in Washington, which will transfer the funds to their foreign consulate. In some cases, shipment may be delayed until the local government is satisfied that the deceased left no unpaid bills.

(One thing the tour manager might do in the pretour meeting is tactfully suggest that each passenger leave written instructions about what should be done in case of death overseas. This might be part of the person's will.)

When a person dies on an airplane, the crew will usually cover the body with a blanket but not move it. The pilot then calls ahead to the nearest airport, relaying a message to authorities there (either in the country or abroad), setting in motion the things mentioned above, like clearing local regulations and contacting next-of-kin. Other passengers are generally disembarked before the ambulance takes the body from the plane.

When death occurs on a cruise, there are three ways this is handled. Burial at sea remains a possibility, but more common are transfer of the body to an airplane at the next port for the flight home, or the keeping of the body in the ship's cold storage until the cruise is complete. While, at first blush, it seems a trifle bizarre for a widow or widower to continue the vacation with a spouse lying below, this is often done. Among other things, it saves considerable expense and red tape. Ships like the QE II have their own mortuaries and can handle all emergencies aboard.

Through all of these grim arrangements, the tour manager must not only remain calm, but must also prevent the atmosphere from turning into one large funeral procession. A Canadian tour manager did this so well, only the dead person's roommate on a three-day British Columbia tour knew about the death. This happened on the first day and the other members did not yet know their fellow passengers. The death was handled with quiet and dispatch.

CRIME

Social critics used to observe that the only place in the world where citizens were not safe on the street was in America. That has changed. Other cities across the globe now have higher **crime rates** and represent dangers to travelers. Whether you are conducting a tour of Americans or visitors through our country, or taking Americans elsewhere, caution is the byword.

This means locking hotel doors securely, knowing where the key to your room is (preferably at the desk), maintaining a watchful eye on your purse or wallet. Purses should be in your lap in a public place and not in the seat next to you: firmly in your hands when touring museums or playing the slot machines. For men, inside pockets are best and the wallet material that makes removal difficult is an added safeguard. Some law officers instruct tourists to walk against the traffic flow if you think you're being trailed by a car, to drop your wallet or purse in a mailbox if closely pursued, and to head for a police station, fire station, hospital or hotel.

There are a lot of other protective actions one might take. For men, pinning the travelers checks packet inside a suit jacket pocket is a safeguard. Some people hang valuables in a bag inside their shirts, with the drawstring around their necks.

Travelers have to be alert when jostled. Spin around; confront the person who pushed you, keeping your hands at your side. Women should hold on to their purses and keep them on an inside shoulder. One dodge is for cyclists to speed past, ripping a bag from an outside shoulder.

Valuables should be left in the hotel safe, even if you are staying but a single night. Some hotels provide lock boxes. If so, you then have to make certain your key isn't stolen!

Tour managers must confer with local guides about safe and unsafe areas and warn their charges about such dangers. All crimes, like thefts and as-

GLOBUS · GATEWAY

REGIONAL DISCOVERY

Russia Yesterday and Today

Moscow, Vladimir, Suzdal and Leningrad

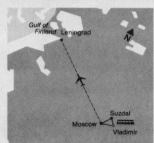

Tour **RR** - 9 days
from $1168 to $1398 plus air fare

ALL THIS IS INCLUDED

- Airport transfers in Moscow and Leningrad for tour members whose flights are reserved as explained on page 19
- Services of a professional Globus-Gateway tour director in addition to your Intourist guide
- Twin-bedded rooms with private bath or shower in first-class or best available hotels as listed on page 15
- 7 continental breakfasts (B), 6 lunches (L), and 7 three-course dinners (D) including the special dinners described in the itinerary
- Private deluxe motorcoaches
- Aeroflot flight Moscow-Leningrad

- Complete unabridged sightseeing program including all the special highlights listed in the day-by-day itinerary
- Inside visits as shown **in bold** in the tour description, including admission charges
- Theater or folklore performance in Moscow
- Leningrad theater evening
- Tips for baggage handling and to hotel personnel
- All local taxes
- Globus-Gateway travel bag and portfolio of travel documents

Day 1   DEPART USA. Overnight transatlantic flight.

Day 2   ARRIVAL IN MOSCOW, USSR. Capital of the Soviet Union, Moscow began as a wooden fortress on the Moscow River in 1147. The fortress developed into the Kremlin as we know it today, and the town gradually spread into a modern metropolis with a population of over 8 million. Meet your traveling companions at dinner tonight. **D**

Day 3   MOSCOW. Red Square is the center of this 800-year-old city. At its core is the Lenin Mausoleum, Ivan the Terrible's St. Basil's Cathedral, and the famous **GUM department store.** Walk across the square to the **Kremlin,** a city-within-a-city adorned with medieval towers.

▼ *Moscow. The Kremlin Palace*

cathedrals and palaces filled with art treasures reflecting almost ten centuries of Russian history. A particular highlight is the visit to the **Armory,** oldest of the Kremlin's museums. Recently reopened after extensive renovations, its exhibits include Ivan the Terrible's throne veneered with carved ivory, Peter the Great's sword and throne, and the famed Fabergé eggs. Sightseeing continues through the city's historical center as well as its new residential areas and parks. See the Bolshoi Theater, drive along Gorky Street to Garden Ring and on to Kalinin and Kutuzov Prospects; then visit the **Novodevichy Convent** and enjoy the sweeping panoramic view from the Lenin Hills. Ride the opulent **Moscow Metro** and shop for souvenirs in the "Beryozka" shops. Tonight attend an unforgettable theater or folklore performance. **B,L,D**

Day 4   MOSCOW. At the **Pushkin Museum of Fine Arts** admire Babylonian, Egyptian, Greek and Roman art treasures, as well as a rich collection of European paintings from the 18th to 20th century. On to the **Kolomenskoye Estate** for a look at its ornate Church of the Ascension of Christ, early Russian wooden structures, and a precious treasure of tiles and 17th-century icons. Learn more about contemporary Russia as you stroll through some of the 90 pavilions of the **Exhibition of Economic Achievements,** a spacious park with fountains, boating facilities, cafés and restaurants. **B,L,D**

Day 5   MOSCOW-VLADIMIR-SUZDAL. 100 miles east, to ancient Vladimir. The western approach of the fortress city on the River Klyazma is guarded by the 12th-century **Golden Gate.** Visit this impressive two-storey ceremonial gateway built as part of a massive system of fortifications. Then into the city itself, once the capital of Russia. Its beautifully restored medieval **Cathedral of the Assumption** is one of many remnants of a glorious past. Later today savor vistas of typical Russian villages and landscapes as you motor to Suzdal, where you are awaited at the **Pokrovsky Monastery** for an evening feast of Russian cuisine. **B,L,D**

Day 6   SUZDAL-MOSCOW-LENINGRAD. Founded around the turn of the millennium like Vladimir, Suzdal has remained much smaller and quainter. Its carefully preserved historic buildings illustrate the styles and ways of life from the dark middle ages to the present day. Stroll through cobblestone streets, past lovely gardens and orchards in the old residential areas to the 11th-century **Kremlin.** Visit the five-domed **Cathedral of the Nativity of the Holy Virgin** with its famous golden gates, as well as the highly interesting 13th-century **Rizpolozhensky Monastery.** Afterwards return to Moscow for an early evening flight to Leningrad. **B,L,D**

Day 7   LENINGRAD. Very few cities in the world match the grace of Leningrad, founded by Peter the Great and originally named St. Petersburg. Construction began in 1703 with the Peter and Paul Fortress and Cathedral and the city eventually spread over 100 islands linked by 700 bridges. Leningrad suffered severe damage during the revolutions of February and October 1917 and later during World War II when a cruel 900-day siege claimed more than half a million victims. See today how the city has been restored to its former splendor. Drive along Nevsky Prospect, Leningrad's elegant thoroughfare lined with shops and baroque buildings. Visit **Kazan Cathedral,** its interior aglow with malachite and other precious stones. Also on the list is spectacular **St. Isaac's,** Leningrad's largest cathedral. Finally the Winter Palace complex, formerly the residence of the Czars and now home of the world-famous **Hermitage Museum.** Among the exhibits are celebrated works by Rembrandt, Leonardo da Vinci and the major French impressionists. Tonight enjoy a visit to the theater. **B,L,D**

Day 8   LENINGRAD. Excursion to either **Petrodvorets** or **Pushkin** and Pavlovsk. Petrodvorets was Peter the Great's summer palace, built to rival Versailles with its formal gardens, fountains, gilded domes and statues. **Pushkin** was the home of Russia's last Czar and Czarina, Nicholas and Alexandra. If this excursion is on the programme, you'll visit the magnificent **Catherine Palace** and later tour the lovely gardens of **Pavlovsk.** Tonight a gala farewell dinner — Russian style — with vodka, champagne, caviar, music and dancing. **B,L,D**

Day 9   RETURN TO USA. Jet back home, arriving the same day. **B**

All arrangements in the Soviet Union are under the management of the official Government Tourist Organization Intourist. Slight changes to the day-by-day itinerary cannot be excluded.

130 US

Fig. 9-1. For destinations like Russia, Intourist guides routinely accompany the tour manager, and group travel is the norm. (Courtesy of Globus-Gateway)

saults, must be communicated to local authorities, and must be included in the tour manager's report.

If it seems necessary in certain locales, members may be alerted to prostitution and solicitation. Some nations have severe penalties for engaging in sex for hire, and the traveler will find this is not just another lark in a convention city. For that and other reasons, it's best to keep moving if propositioned.

LOCAL CUSTOMS

If there are other customs and laws which may be different, the tour member must be warned, especially about what they do during free time. Perhaps no one is allowed to roam without an assigned guide; perhaps certain areas are off limits to photographers; perhaps there are dress codes or religious regulations with penalties for disobedience. There may also be temptations to engage in black market activities for goods or money. All of these are taboo.

Traffic laws could also come into play, especially if tour members elect to hire an automobile on free days. Be sure they know things like legal speed limits, the meaning of road signs (which are becoming more universal), parking restrictions, insurance limitations, and, in a few countries, the existence of portside driving.

Even pedestrians have to be wary. Many come from cities where jay-walking is tolerated because it's the only way to make it across busy streets. In some nations (and in some American cities) this behavior could result in a fine.

Here are some specific things to be aware of in certain countries:

- ❏ Uganda frowns on mini-skirts, hot pants, and skirts slit above the knee. Wearers may be arrested and detained until suitable clothing can be found.
- ❏ In Thailand, it's forbidden to touch someone's head.
- ❏ In 1987, drug arrests of Americans went up 22 percent, and occurred in fifty-nine different countries. Even carrying prescription drugs containing narcotics has resulted in arrest when tourists couldn't produce a physician's certificate. Most drug arrests of Americans occur in Mexico. Tourists should remember that, in some countries, penalties for possession are severe, including execution.
- ❏ Even a minute amount of alcohol in the blood can result in a driver's arrest in Norway, with a stiff fine, perhaps three weeks in jail. Speeding exacts similar retribution.
- ❏ Some words and gestures which mean one thing in English may be considered obscene in other countries.
- ❏ Muslim fundamentalists object to having their photographs taken, and many airports and military installations are off limits to photographers.

Violators may be arrested or, at the very least, will have their film and/ or camera confiscated.

❑ Some shrines require the visitor to remove his or her shoes; others separate the sexes.

❑ Exchanging currency with natives of many countries is taboo. So is the selling of personal items, like an extra pair of jeans.

❑ Some countries, like Italy, have no drinking age limit, while others have age limits ranging from sixteen (The Netherlands) to twenty (Norway) and older.

❑ Taking antiques out of Turkey without authorization may result in severe penalties.

❑ Bringing more than two pounds of coffee into Yugoslavia is illegal.

There are thousands of additional legal considerations and **local customs** the tour manager should know. Some U.S. Government publications provide current information, and so do some national travel services. Pan Am puts out an "Immigration Guide" for a number of countries. Travel magazines are a source of tips on a variety of nations. *Travel/Holiday,* for example, spotlights different countries in each issue, providing tips on weather, health, hotels, restaurants, and sources of further information. Some guidebooks go into detail on customs and taboos. Travelers will also be enlightened by *The Travelers' Guide to European Customs & Manners* and *The Travelers' Guide to Asian Customs & Manners,* both of which are issued by Meadowbrook Press, 18318 Minnetonka Blvd., Deephaven, MN 55391. Included for each country are sections on conversation, public manners, dress, hotels, eating out, tipping, staying in private homes, transportation, holidays, legal matters, safety, and other topics. There's even a brief vocabulary of common phrases for each language.

For Americans who may get arrested in a foreign country (for fraud; drug possession; immigration or customs violations; currency, alcohol, or motor vehicle crimes; even debt charges, like writing bad checks), the help the U.S. consulate can provide is limited. Consular officers can visit the prisoner, provide some forms of services (like checking on personal belongings taken or conveying money), attend the trial, and keep the Department of State apprised as to the conduct of the case. Beyond that, their powers are constrained. They certainly can't barge in and demand the immediate release of a jailed American in a foreign country.

There are also books which cover this subject, including: *Going International* by Copeland and Griggs, *The Hassle of Your Life* by Atkins and Pisani, and *The Practical Traveler* by Grimes.

The U.S. Department of State (Bureau of Consular Affairs, Citizen Consular Services, Washington, D.C. 20520) provides information on travel to dangerous countries. The International Legal Defense Counsel (111 S. 15th St.,

Philadelphia, PA 19116) provides legal assistance for Americans living or traveling abroad.

The best advice, however, is to know the laws of the countries you visit (or to which you bring tourists), to obey these laws, and to stay out of trouble. If the police say they don't want you taking photos of a bank transfer, don't take the photos. If the rules call for a certain standard of dress, play it safe.

POLITICAL PROBLEMS

Never isolate yourself from local happenings. If you know you are entering a **troubled area,** call ahead to the hotel or to the embassy and get a reading on the current situation. Many guides suggest talking with porters rather than hotel management, since the latter tend to be more sanguine. If things look too volatile, you should cancel reservations in that locale and secure accommodations elsewhere.

If you do find yourself in an area where there is unrest, political or otherwise, caution tour members to avoid rallies and demonstrations and, in fact, to return quickly to the hotel if anything seems to be happening. No tourists should participate in marches, picket lines, assemblies, or even informal debates. Play it cool.

Should armed conflict arise while the tour is in a specific locality, call the embassy or consulate for instructions. They may suggest removal to a rural area or evacuation. While waiting for these changes, the group must stay together and out of danger.

Bob English of Peter Travel, was caught in Cairo in 1973 when a joint Egyptian-Syrian attack was made on Israel. A high percentage of English's tour members were Jewish. He called his group together, contacted the American embassy, and succeeded in having the tour evacuated by ship.

Another tour under the direction of twenty-four year veteran Charles Kissane was in Angkor Wat, Cambodia, when all borders were suddenly closed and all transportation frozen. Kissane managed to secure vehicles to get his group out by road. It took a stiff bribe for the border officials.

Incidentally, most brochures and itineraries make it clear that political upheavals, armed conflicts, and **acts of God** are not the responsibility of the tour operators. Any expenses involved in getting out of these tight situations must be borne by the tour members themselves.

Common sense should guide tour operators who plan visits to certain areas. Trips to Beirut would not only be unwise, they would also attract few tourists. But some of the concerns are relative. Americans, with a shaky grasp of geography, often wonder if it is safe to travel to Ireland, not realizing any unrest is confined to a small portion of that island.

The problem is that violence or the threat of violence can erupt anywhere. Who would have thought that idyllic Fiji would lose its tourist trade in the wake of a 1987 coup? American travel alone fell off 20 percent, even though the bloodshed associated with such strife never materialized.

From 1984 to 1988, American tourism to South Africa was cut in half. Some major tour operators stopped circulating their brochures.

In 1986, following the American bombing of Libya, fear of terrorists cut travel to Europe drastically. Great Britain initiated all sorts of programs to lure travelers overseas, ranging from free **airline tickets** to lottery prizes. Travel to that country alone fell 40 percent. American travel agents were concerned about booking trips abroad, fearing that lawsuits might result if any travelers were killed or injured.

Other countries fared even worse. Travel to Greece was down almost two-thirds, and just about every European nation saw a decline of at least 30 percent. Of course, some countries, like Canada, prospered, and even Russia was advertising that their terrorism rate was extremely low.

Periodically, the Department of State issues advisories to American citizens, recommending against all but essential travel to certain hot spots—like Libya, Bolivia, Iraq, Iran, Chad, El Salvador, and other destinations. The State Department's Citizen Emergency Center in Washington can be phoned (202-632-5225) during weekday working hours for the latest information on a volatile situation.

Actual military action is not the sole worry. Tour managers and tourists should also be concerned about paralyzing strikes, food shortages, seriously overcrowded hotels, demonstrations, or even an open hostility that makes vacationers uncomfortable.

Fear of death or injury is only one factor in the decision to travel to a risky destination. Tour members have paid money for this trip. They want to enjoy themselves. Can the tour operator fulfill this promise? Does the tour manager want to be saddled with this responsibility?

ACTS OF GOD

First of all, tours should shun areas where some natural disturbance is imminent. There's no sense in continuing on to the Florida Keys if hurricane warnings have been posted, or trekking to some South Seas paradise during a period of volcanic activity. However, if you find yourself on the spot when calamity strikes, you usually employ for the group the same precautions you would take as an individual.

You find appropriate shelter from hurricanes and tornadoes, locating a spot, preferably underground, with strong walls and overhead protection.

Earthquakes also require shelter, trying to stay clear of structures that may collapse and injure you. In all cases, get the group swiftly to safety, keep them together, and maintain calm. Once the danger is past, summon aid.

When a flood threatens, get the tour membes to higher ground. Be firm and serious, and allow no procrastination.

Genevieve Smith of Green Carpet Tours recalls:

"Several years ago on one of our Alaska tours, the group overnighted at Fireside Inn, Milepost 543, British Columbia. During the night a flash flood damaged two bridges leaving the group stranded out in the middle of nowhere, as there were no alternate roads. The telephone was out of service, so the escort could not advise Portland of this situation. He explained to the group that he had been advised by a highway crew the bridges should be repaired in approximately twenty-four hours. At his request they said they would advise via their radio communication system the onward hotels about the situation. After receiving the message, one of the hotel managers called Portland to advise us of the situation. In the meantime, the group was playing bingo, bridge, and eating too often, thanks to the escort who had skillfully implanted the thought 'enjoy this unique adventure.' And this is what they did! Although they were detained thirty hours they completed the tour without further mishap. On the final day of the tour the escort received a sizable gratuity and we received no complaints."

Caribbean BOUNCES BACK...

The start of the Caribbean's winter tourism season marks a return to relative normalcy for the areas hit in September by the wrath of Hurricane Hugo.

Hugo, which killed as many as 26 people and left 50,000 homeless, did little real damage to the Caribbean's tourism industry, with the exception of the U.S. Virgin Islands. Power, water and communication on these islands and on Dominica and Monserrat are still trouble-ridden.

Perhaps the biggest problem for tourists was the lack of air service, which grounded thousands of travelers for as long as a week. But, thanks to

Many Escape Hugo's Wrath

Reprinted with approval from Travel Weekly.

emergency preparations, no travelers were killed and few were injured.

See the beauties of the

Caribbean for yourself. Contact your Travel and Transport consultant for details.

Fig. 9-2. Following any disaster, tourist officials are anxious to reassure prospective travelers. (Courtesy of Travel & Transport)

Hurricane Hugo tested the facilities and ingenuity of hotels, tour operators, and tour managers. A Club Med group was transferred to a safer island. Tourists staying at a hotel along the southeast coast were directed to shelter within the hotels. Some hotels affected by the San Francisco quake served their guests a cold buffet by candlelight.

There are some good tips for tour members (and managers) during **natural disasters:**

1. Stay at the hotel as long as possible. They have food, emergency generators, perhaps even communication equipment. Unless the structure is unsound, it's best to stay put.
2. Check the back of your hotel door for evacuation information, and the room desk or bureau for additional details, or for candles.
3. Do not leave your tour group. Tour coaches have two-way communication and may be your link to help. Tour buses headed for San Francisco during the 1989 earthquake were warned away by radio. The tour group also provides support and identification.
4. Tour managers should contact the sponsoring tour operator or agency as soon as possible. Alternate travel arrangements may be made there rather quickly, and relatives could be notified.
5. When traveling overseas, contact the nearest U.S. embassy or consulate as soon as possible for a realistic evaluation of the threatening situation.
6. Tour managers should know that airlines have contingency plans for emergencies, diverting planes away from trouble areas, sometimes scheduling extra flights to evacuate stranded passengers. Even though not obliged to do so, airlines may also provide meals and hotels for their passengers. Airlines and cruise ships may also offer reduced fares or a free trip to travelers who have had their vacations ruined by storms or other emergencies. Some airlines refunded or exchanged tickets to Caribbean destinations cancelled out by Hugo. Some travel insurance policies cover out-of-pocket costs resulting from natural disasters.

FIRE

Fire is always a concern, especially when staying in strange hotels. There are numerous booklets available on what to do in case of fire. The tour manager should secure one and master it.

When the tour enters any hotel, and after check-in has been accomplished, review the alarm system with the desk clerk. Is it a siren, bell, or what? Locate fire escapes and stairwells and suggest that tour members do the same. If there are fire alarms or other fire fighting equipment, note locations. Tell tour members to count the number of doors between their rooms and the stairwells or fire escapes. They could be caught in heavy smoke and have to feel their way to safety.

Tourists should also check around their own rooms, noting whether or not there is a ledge, how the windows open, and where they are in relationship to adjacent buildings. All of this must be accomplished without frightening the guests unnecessarily.

Hotel room keys should be left in the same spot each night, so they can be picked up in the dark. If you have to leave the room because of fire, don't waste time packing clothes. Put on your shoes (which should also be handy) in case you must walk through broken glass. A small flashlight would also be a sensible thing to pack for occasions like this. Guests who leave their rooms during fire should take their keys with them. The stairwells could be blocked by smoke or flames, and the person may have to come back to the room.

Manuals instruct persons caught in fires to do the following:

❏ Phone the desk and see what is happening. You could be the first to detect the presence of smoke.

❏ Feel the door to see if it's hot. If it is, don't open it. Stay inside awaiting rescue. If the door is cool, open and close it rapidly (to prevent suction and to keep smoke from getting at belongings left behind). Move toward the predetermined fire exits, turning on any alarms you encounter en route. Walk or crawl, depending on the amount of smoke. Keep low and close to the wall. Never take the elevator.

❏ Your aim is to get below the fire (since heat and smoke rise), but, if you can't get down, go to the roof—a secondary safety area.

❏ Once the fire is underway, you may be better off staying in your room, with wet towels wedged into the door cracks. Fill the bathtub with water in case the water pressure goes off. You'll need the water to wet more towels. Air conditioning and heating systems should be turned off, and windows may be opened slightly. Use the drapes (which are a hazard anyway) to signal location, then lie down (to escape carbon monoxide gas) and await rescue. As a last resort, the windows may be broken if this offers a chance of escape.

❏ Some tour managers agree on a place to meet after evacuating the building. This makes it easier to count heads and check on who is safely out. Neither the tour manager nor other members should re-enter the burning building to find someone. Leave that to the professionals.

❏ Remind tour members to check all these things themselves, and to avoid foolish behavior, like smoking in bed.

❏ Aboard ships and airplanes, the crew handles demonstrations and drills which will be employed in case of fire or other disaster.

According to the American Hotel & Motel Association, better than 95 percent of American hotels, both chain and independent units, have all guest rooms equipped with smoke detectors; but less than half the independent hotels and only about two-thirds of the chain hotels have sprinklers in the rooms. Sprinklers in hotel public and service areas are more common.

There is also growing concern about fires which have erupted on cruise ships. Post-fire investigations reveal crews unfamiliar with fire-fighting equipment and controls, smoke alarms that failed to go off, lack of fire fighting training and drills, and ignorance of safety requirements by ship's officers.

A major problem is that, although 90 percent of the world's cruise traffic originates in the United States, this country has little control over the safety precautions of the vast majority of ships, which are built overseas and fly foreign flags. America does have a voice in the International Maritime Organization (IMO) which is supposed to set standards, but many feel the higher standards set by the U.S. are impossible to impose on foreign countries, even though the preponderance of passengers are Americans.

DELAYS

Transportation can be delayed for a variety of reasons, from weather to strikes, from equipment malfunctions to road conditions. This happens to airplanes, ships, trains, coaches, even taxicabs, despite their precautions to guard against such failures. When such **delays** occur, try to determine how long they will be, and then use your ingenuity to make the wait as comfortable as possible for your passengers. Level with your tour members about the situation and don't lie about the delay time.

If a coach breaks down, the driver will summon a mechanic or a replacement. If feasible, the passengers can wait in a nearby town or hotel, or they may have to stay aboard the bus. Some latitude may be allowed for strolling around the vicinity of the breakdown, but don't let passengers wander off, and keep them out of danger areas.

With train delays, there is usually little you can do, unless the train remains in the station and you can disembark people. With ships, the situation is generally eased. Since the ship is really a floating hotel, tour members can be more comfortable and also find things to do. Of course, in both situations problems could multiply with heat or air-conditioning off and electricity not working.

Airline delays seem to cause most concern. Whole itineraries may have to be rescheduled; accommodations could be lost or replaced; food must be provided; other carriers and suppliers need to be reached. It can be a mess. Stateside, even though inconvenienced, airline delays are rarely as big a headache as overseas hangups.

Fig. 9-3. Always a travel headache, airline delays can cause myriad problems for the tour manager.

Tour manager Charles Kissane was once stranded with his group in a remote area of Afghanistan after their chartered aircraft broke down. "We were there for two days. I had to arrange for sleeping in a large barn, and I think I got every egg in the village. We subsisted on bread and eggs. Because of the delay we missed our international flight from Kabul to Teheran, and had to make alternate arrangements on a line that had very few flights. In Teheran the hotel had cancelled our rooms because we hadn't shown up. The hotel was now full, so I had to call all over town to get one or two rooms in a dozen different places."

Barbara Leonard of Discovery Tours found herself stranded with her group when a ferry service wasn't operating and couldn't take them to their hotel across the water. While the courier took tour members to a museum, the tour manager worked on both the ferry service and alternate accommodations. Finally she contacted the ferry authorities and got her group across.

"That's when the company's emergency allowance is used," she adds.

When Dick Linde, a minister with considerable tour experience, found himself in Tokyo's airport with five hours to kill, he knew there wasn't sufficient time to get into town and back, but he didn't want to spend these hours cooped up in a small lounge. So he rented a room in a nearby hotel and tossed a party for the tour members.

Situations vary. Groups have been caught on the runway and forced to remain aboard for several warm and boring hours. Here's a real test for the tour manager, who should circulate among the tourists, radiating as much good will as can be mustered, assuming you are allowed out of your seat.

Since ultimate responsibility rests with tour managers, these individuals must insist that carriers live up to agreements to provide adequate substitutes.

David Davidowitz of Vagabond Tours for the Deaf hit a snag on his first escorted tour in 1966. With thirty-four deaf tour members, he reached London airport to find thousands of Americans sleeping all over the place. His tour's airline was the only carrier not on strike but, when they tried to board the plane, they were turned back. Their seats had been sold.

"An airlines official offered us one more day in London. I refused. These deaf people had to get back to their jobs. I told the airline agent to get my seats back. The flight was held up for four hours. Four airline officials pleaded with me about babies and the elderly. Finally I told him if he wanted to pay a million dollars because of loss of jobs, that was his worry."

Then they offered Davidowitz a bribe, which he turned down, leading to the airline capitulating. The deaf group got their seats, infuriating the other passengers.

Davidowitz said, "We came over with them, and we're going home with them."

His clients witnessed the entire scenario. The tale of his standing up for them "spread across the U.S.A.," he says.

MISCELLANEOUS

There are numerous other things which can go wrong. Some are serious; some are humorous. Your American tour operator may promise one thing, but the foreign representative has a different impression and this leads to confusion. Lack of communication with suppliers at all levels can cause difficulty.

Loretta Cutler of Travel & Transport arrived at her German hotel the evening of America's moon walk. The town was filled with German citizens who came to see the historic occasion in the local hotels. The hotel manager said he couldn't supply the single rooms they'd promised, but offered enough rooms for people to share. All but one refused to share. After a couple of hours of fruitless protesting, Ms. Cutler had to find other rooms in the city.

When traveling between countries on a multination trip, passage through customs can sometimes be difficult. You may get caught up in a concentrated drug search, or arrive the day after a bombing or riot and be subject to extensive scrutiny. Relax, and think and act sensibly. Keep tour members from irritating local customs officers.

"One of my passengers refused to let Russian officials open her handbag," said one tour manager, "and they got a little rough with her. She had some film in there which really wasn't any problem, but she just insisted on her rights. They arrested her and I had to get her out. It was a bad scene, and we missed our plane. The other tourists could have killed her."

On a more humorous note, a tour leader writes:

"Once our rooms were not ready when the tour arrived, so I bought everyone a drink in the hotel bar. The delay continued, so I suggested that the people roam around for about an hour while I watched their carryon items in the bar. After everyone had returned and claimed their belongings, one item remained—a man's coat with several pairs of women's panties stuffed in the pockets."

Believe it or not, an award has been established for the most horrendous travel complaint. Charles E. Reilly, president of a Philadelphia management development firm, solicits the worst travel experiences for individuals who seek to qualify for Reilly's Frankenstein Travel Award. He started the award in 1984 and has received hundreds of entries annually, from people sharing staterooms with mentally unbalanced roommates to tourists being delayed for as long as a week.

The foul-ups are legion, and range from murder to food poisoning. But tourists are not without their recourse.

TRAVEL RIGHTS

Knowing your **travel rights** was mentioned earlier in this text. It might be wise to review some of them in more detail.

1. Airline schedules are not guaranteed and can be delayed by such circumstances as weather, mechanical failure, or traffic delays. Policies as to what is done in these circumstances vary from airline to airline, ranging from booking on the next available flight to the rare occasion of monetary compensation.
2. When overbooking results in a passenger being **"bumped,"** the airline is supposed to place the affected passenger aboard the next available flight, after asking for volunteers who might be willing to change their flight plans for some form of remuneration. The "bumped" passenger is supposed to arrive at his/her destination within an hour of the original flight. If this timetable is not honored, payments equal to the price of a one-way ticket (minimum $200) must be offered for delays of up to two hours, and compensation up to a maximum of $400 for delays longer than two hours.

3. Reimbursement for lost luggage was covered earlier in this chapter, but damaged luggage is supposed to be repaired by the airline or an equitable, depreciated, replacement cost provided.
4. Tour members who lose their tickets (if they are carrying them personally), may be required to buy another ticket, then file for reimbursement (which could take several months). A refund fee from $25 to $50 may be charged.
5. Congress periodically introduces, debates, modifies, passes, or rejects legislation focusing on consumer rights. Some of the principles mentioned above were enunciated in a comprehensive bill introduced in 1987. Other considerations centered on the required publication by the Department of Transportation of statistics like late arrivals, **canceled flights,** lost luggage, missed connections, bumping, and even the total number of complaints filed with DOT for each specific carrier. Anyone who requests a copy of this data would be entitled to it. Restrictions on advertising of fares, notice of bankruptcy, and even the specific fines to be levied for violations were spelled out in this legislation.
6. The overriding concern of government intervention in consumer affairs is that the client gets what he or she pays for. In addition to the legislation enforced by the Department of Transportation, there are other laws under the jurisdiction of agencies like the Federal Trade Commission (which watches for improper marketing practices), the United States Postal Service (which ferrets out mail fraud), and the Treasury Department's Secret Service Division (which has jurisdiction over credit card fraud). State agencies, local consumer protection offices, the Better Business Bureau, and some travel associations (like ASTA) may also be helpful.
7. Brochures like ASTA's *Avoiding Travel Problems* and the Federal Government's inexpensive booklets on *Your Trip Abroad* and *A Safe Trip Abroad* are wise investments for the tour manager.

CONSULAR ASSISTANCE

A review of what the American embassy or consulate can do may also be in order here, since their actions, as mentioned earlier, are limited. The consulate can provide a ninety-day passport replacement, supply a list of English-speaking physicians or other professionals (without recommending any specific person), monitor absentee voting, warn travelers about war and other disorders, locate missing family members, extend a repatriation loan for direct return to the United States, and they may even offer the service of a notary public. The consulate, however, won't make loans, cash personal checks, hold or forward mail, or make hotel reservations.

TO PUT THINGS IN PERSPECTIVE

With all this discussion of disasters, delays, and fraud, it's only fair to put things in perspective.

Airlines in the United States carry approximately one million passengers daily on some fifteen thousand flights. Although there have been a couple of spectacular disasters in recent years, the overall record is outstanding. Out of more than four million flights annually, the fatalities can normally be counted on one hand.

The same holds true for tourist dangers abroad. When tourists are killed or injured, that's rare enough to make news. Consider Northern Ireland, an area Americans seemed terrified to visit. As one commentator put it, "Your chances of dying a violent death are at least ten times greater in a dozen major American cities than they are in Belfast."

Tour managers should be cautious and sensible, but they should also be realistic and should not overreact to unwarranted public fears.

❏ *CHAPTER HIGHLIGHTS*

❏ Common traveler complaints include flight cancellation, delays, lost or damaged luggage, overbooking, poor service, ticketing and boarding problems, and confusing information.

❏ The tour manager should be familiar with the routine for tracing lost luggage and for helping pasengers reclaim their belongings or file for reimbursement.

❏ Tourists can also become lost, so keeping track of tour members is a prime duty for the tour manager. Travelers should also be warned about retaining possession of passports, credit cards, and money. The tour manager may assist in providing information on replacement.

❏ In cases of illness, the tour manager might be prepared to handle first aid emergencies, but should be cautious about recommending medicines or treatment. A physician should be involved immediately for any serious ailments. The tour manager is helpful, but leaves treatment to the professionals.

❏ Before departing for certain areas—especially those with vastly different cultures and customs—the tour manager should become familiar with routines to be followed in the event of tour member death.

❏ The tour manager must be personally careful about documents and monies he or she is carrying. He/she should warn tour members about high crime areas, pickpockets, and other dangers. They may also advise travelers on ways to safeguard their property and person.

❏ Tour managers should educate themselves on specific customs and practices of countries they will visit, especially where violating these rules may result in embarrassment, arrest, fines, or even death.

❏ Political problems can affect tours, so the tour manager should stay current on volatile situations, taking advantage of U.S. government bulletins, as well as trustworthy local advice. Danger areas should be avoided.

❏ When natural disasters occur, the tour manager has the responsibility of keeping the group calm and dealing with matters as swiftly and intelligently as possible. The tour manager is expected to know what to do in the event of trouble; to know the sources of help and information; and to know the procedures for handling things before, during, and after a crisis. The authority of the tour manager may be limited, and must be exercised with restraint and under the direction of local authority.

❏ Delays are often a nuisance and may require the tour manager to move quickly to an alternate plan.

❏ Tour managers should be familiar with the travel rights of passengers, ranging from lost luggage to being bumped from a confirmed flight.

❏ Consular assistance is limited and subject to the rules of the host country.

❏ Considering the volume of tour traffic managed by American airlines—and by foreign hotels, airlines, and cruise ships—the positive experiences far outweigh the negative.

❏ *CASE PROBLEMS*

1. You arrive in Paris early one morning with a tour group of twenty-eight persons. None of the luggage accompanies this flight, and you are told that it won't arrive until the next morning at the earliest. Your group is scheduled to attend a welcoming cocktail party that evening at your hotel, and almost all tour members have no good clothes to change into, not even socks and underwear. What actions can you take with the airline? What suggestions can you make to your tour members? What follow-up actions will you anticipate?

2. As tour leader for an American group traveling through Spain, you are located in Toledo, but are scheduled to spend the next two days and nights in Madrid. Watching television that night in your Toledo hotel, you learn that there are massive anti-American demonstrations taking place in Madrid, protesting United States policies in Central America. What do you do, if anything?

10

THE RETURN TRIP AND AFTERWARDS

LEARNING OBJECTIVES

After reading this chapter you will:

- ❑ Know how to prepare for the return flight, check luggage and tour members into the foreign airport, and see that all members safely enplane
- ❑ Realize the exemptions and limitations which apply to tour members heading through American Customs
- ❑ Appreciate the numerous follow-up chores required of the tour manager, from thank-you notes to reports
- ❑ Learn how to schedule and organize a reunion party for tour members

KEY CONCEPTS

Customs
Department of
   Agriculture
Duty
Evaluation cards
Exemption allowance

Expense forms
Farewell party
Foreign airport
   check-in
Hotel/restaurant
   critique

Reconfirmation of air
Reunion
Thank-you notes
Tour manager's report

As the time to return home nears, the tour manager must start thinking about re-entry into the United States, or, if the tour is enjoying this nation's hospitality, about sending our guests home. In either case, **reconfirm airline space** at least seventy-two hours before departure. Also check on flight and sailing times, on type of equipment being used, on meals aloft or afloat, and on any connecting flights that must be met. Also confer on times the group should be at the airport or pier, and discuss any special regulations affecting the homeward journey.

If members wish to extend their tour, this is, of course, at their own expense and direction. The tour manager or tour operator may assist in making these additional arrangements, which should be concluded well in advance of the departure date.

Tour members may wish to complete last minute shopping, so it's smart to allow for some blocks of free time in the final days. It's also wise to book a hotel not too distant from the airport or docks. You don't want to spend hours trying to get to the point of departure, particularly if you have an early flight or sailing.

Another intelligent move is to schedule some event, like a dinner (or cabaret or play), the evening prior to departure. This adds a pleasant punctuation mark to the trip, and also allows you to see that all tour members are accounted for. Don't make this a late night; just something to top off the excursion. On the coach going back to the hotel (or sometime before the tour members retire for the night), go over the next day's itinerary, reminding people not to pack their passports (or health cards), but to have them handy for inspection, counseling them on what they can expect en route and at customs, and repeating the instructions about rising and departing.

CHECKING-IN

Allow plenty of time to get to the airport, and sufficient time to handle matters once you get there. Arriving two hours ahead of departure is advisable. Sometimes you may ease your burdens by arranging check-in procedures at the time you re-confirm your group's departure.

Bring the passengers into the terminal and locate them in one area in the lounge. Ask them to wait there until you **check all of them in.** The driver and porters will be unloading the luggage and transferring it to the airline counter. Tour members should not leave their carryon luggage unattended at this time, but should request that another member watch it if they go to the rest rooms. This may be the occasion for farewells to the driver and/or courier. They'll want to move the coach. Usually these individuals visit the waiting tour members to say their goodbyes.

The airlines may or may not weigh baggage. If they do weigh it, they may accept a total figure divided by the number of tour members. Anyone in violation of the weight or number rules must pay any difference personally, and even though your experience tells you such changes are infrequently made, don't assure the tour members that excesses will be no problem.

When you go the airline counter, you'll be carrying the tickets and the passports you've just collected from tour members. The agent there will match passport to ticket, perhaps examine health cards, pull tickets, weigh and tag luggage, make out boarding passes and then return to you the ticket envelopes, boarding passes, passports, and baggage claim checks. The passports and boarding passes go to tour members; you retain the ticket envelopes, especially if some tickets remain for domestic connections, and the claim checks. If someone wants the ticket folder later as a souvenir, fine, and you may want to give baggage checks to any individuals who are leaving the tour in the United States before you reach the final destination.

As before, make certain that the agent hasn't pulled too many tickets, and be sure that the bags are tagged for the proper destinations in the States. Regardless of final routing, the bags will come off at **customs** and will then be returned to the ongoing airline. If you have persons going to different American cities, double check their baggage tags.

If there are any final instructions to be given, like changes in flight times, the departure gate number, the type of aircraft being used, the sailing time and cabin arrangements, the meal schedule, and the like, do this now. If some free time remains, let tour members visit shops, restaurants, or bars in the vicinity, but schedule an early time for them to be back in this spot so you can lead them to the gate.

Should this airport or pier feature duty free goods, the carrier usually allows ample time for passengers to shop. Travelers from Dublin to New York, for example, will deplane at Shannon Airport for an hour in its huge duty-free shop.

If airline officials permit early boarding for tour groups, take advantage of this. Try to make amends now for any inferior seats on the way over; give these people the choice seats, again trying to keep spouses and friends together. Board last yourself, counting everyone aboard, and counting them again as soon as you are settled.

RETURN JOURNEY

The trip back is much like the trip over, except that the group will be both more tired and more stimulated. When you can, visit with each of the people, gathering their impressions, and sharing their experiences. This might also be your last opportunity to treat them to a drink.

Some tour members may need help with the debarkation or custom declaration cards. Assist them in filling these out. Be sure you know the proper responses to questions about customs. For example:

❑ Each traveler is allowed an **exemption on goods purchased** out of the country. This amount ($400) is figured on the fair market value of those

goods in that country. Tourists coming from certain American possessions, like the Virgin Islands, may be permitted double that amount.
Families traveling together may pool their purchases and exemptions. A
husband and wife with two children, for example, could bring home
goods worth $1,600 without paying tax or **duty.** After the $400 per person exemption, the next $1,000 in goods is subject to a straight 10
percent levy. After that, the money due the government depends on the
article being brought in.

❑ Exempt from duty are items at least one hundred years old and original
works of art, although there could be exceptions. Also allowed in duty-
free are a carton of cigarettes, one hundred cigars, and up to a quart of
alcohol . . . for persons over the age of twenty-one.

❑ If you wish to take more than $5,000 in foreign currency into the United
States, you have to file a special report. This rule also applies to other
monetary instruments, like cashier's checks. The tour manager should
advise tour members to get rid of foreign coins before leaving that country, since they aren't of much use in America, except as souvenirs.

❑ To qualify for the $400 per person exemption, you must have been out-
side the United States for at least forty-eight hours, and you cannot
claim twice within the space of thirty days.

❑ To merit an exemption, the articles must be with you. Those shipped
home are subject to duty. Items of clothing and jewelry which you may
have used during the tour are still subject to the legal limit.

❑ Generally speaking, unless you have special permission (and few tourists
do), you are forbidden to bring into the country any fruits, vegetables,
plants, seeds, flowers, meats, or pets. This is to prevent the spread of diseases potentially harmful to crops, animals, or humans. This is serious
business. Authorities believe the Mediterranean fruit fly blight was the
result of a person coming back to America with infected fruit. This crop
disease took three years and $100 million to control. Travelers taking
farm tours may have their shoes inspected and disinfected. There are
also special low energy X-ray machines designed to detect meats and
fruits, and beagles are utilized at some airports to sniff out contraband.
At least twelve hundred violations a month are discovered by officers of
the **US Department of Agriculture.**

❑ Tour managers should keep abreast of new regulations. The United
States Customs service publishes an informative brochure titled *Know
Before You Go.* The USDA (6505 Belcrest Rd., Hyattsville, MD 20782) is
a source of information on the importing of everything from plant shoots
to big game trophies.

The exceptions get complicated. You can bring in soups and soup
mixes, but not if they contain meat. You can import straw hats and bas-

kets, but not items stuffed with straw. Fully cured cheeses are allowed, but cottage cheese is not. Rocks and shells are okay—if you remove all traces of soil. Breads, cookies and bakery items are generally okay, as are canned fruit and vegetables, and some commercially canned meats.

❏   If the tour member does not have goods in excess of $400, there is no need to itemize.

Never advise any one to do anything illegal, and do not condone such practices if suggested. True, people do get by with some illegalities, but you never want to be in a position of countenancing such behavior.

CLEARING CUSTOMS

Passage through customs is always something of a problem. Tourists are tired and frightened, even when they have no reason to be nervous. You must remind them they are on their own when clearing customs, and that you can't really assist them. Somehow these frail, elderly folks, laden down with packages, make it through.

If you can, get off first, clear the initial passport check, and head for the customs hall. You may be able to round up carts for the rest of your group and assist them in loading their gear as it comes off the conveyors. Again, try to get through quickly yourself (if your luggage cooperates), and then arrange for a place to meet, and for porters to handle the luggage and transfer it to the proper airline.

You can't hurry or hassle the customs officers. Let them do their job. Sometimes they open everything; other times the search is more cursory. But the options are theirs, not yours. Once everyone has cleared customs, paid any duty owed, and assembled outside the area, keep them together as you secure ground transportation. If the domestic terminal is close, you may decide to walk it, but a bus is more likely. Pay any porters and also pay for the ground transport service.

This may be the place where some members separate and head off to other cities. Take time for a proper farewell, and agree to contact them about any plans for a **reunion** of tour members.

Once you have reached the domestic terminal, count heads again, and check your passengers in. If there is a long wait between flights, allow travelers time off, arranging to meet well ahead of departure. If time is short, take them right to the gate. They can now put away their passports and, if you wish, you can hand them their ticket envelopes. All they really need at this point are their boarding passes.

People leaving the tour at this point will, of course, be handed their own tickets.

Since mixups are possible at any time during the tour, including this final day, the tour manager must stay in charge. An ongoing flight could be overbooked or delayed by weather. Some tour members' names could be left off the manifest. The tour manager deals with these problems as they arise.

HOME

When you reach your final destination disembark first and help others off. Go to the baggage claim area, checking the carousel number in advance.

Travel agency representatives should be on hand to help greet passengers, and you may want to make a short, oral report to them on the trip. Your duties are not really over until all baggage has been claimed and the last tour member has left the terminal. If luggage is lost, help the tour member fill out the proper form. If all goes well, say your goodbyes and head home yourself.

FOLLOW-UP

Some cleanup chores remain.

❑ Some travel agencies and tour operators send **evaluation cards** to tour members, asking for their impressions of the tour and the personnel in charge. They may mail these back, with or without a signature. Sometimes these may be circulated during the return flight or voyage, or before members leave the baggage claim area. It works better to mail them.

❑ The tour manager may send a short note to tour members shortly after coming home, thanking them for their cooperation, and discussing any future gatherings. Responses of tour members sometimes provide excellent copy for future brochures, but don't force this; let it be spontaneous.

❑ Add the names and addresses of tour members to the agency mailing list, and also gather any other names they care to supply.

❑ Complete your **expense forms,** retaining a copy for your own files, and return any unused funds.

❑ Fill out the **tour manager's report,** including highlights of the journey and any untoward events, such as illness, breakdowns, delays, itinerary changes, or tour member dismissals.

❑ Include a **critique of the hotels and restaurants,** the entertainment, the carriers, the tour operator, and the performance of the various personnel. Be specific, since generalities don't help much, and don't focus on the negative only. Positive suggestions also aid in planning future trips.

❏   As soon as possible, dispatch **thank-you letters** to suppliers, hotels, tour operator personnel. and others. You may also want to drop a longer letter to tour members, including names and addresses of people they may have met, and addresses of shops and the like. This may be the place to establish a date for the tour members' reunion.

❏   Even though you've just returned from a trip, this is the time to start preparing for the next tour, and to prepare clients for this future excursion.

MANAGER'S REPORT

Some travel agencies and tour operators have their own special forms to be filled out; others leave that to the tour manager. It makes little difference, as long as the essential information is there.

There are three essential elements in this report:

1.   A diary-like list of events, particularly those things which are unusual, like a departure from the itinerary, special local problems, illness and other things.

Example:

MAY 16:   Arrived late to Florence and had to pass up half of musuem tour. Bus breakdown delayed us three hours. Also had to find a physician for Ms. Holly who had been bothered by dizzy spells. Group was good about the changes. Ms. Holly was able to continue with the tour.

2.   A critique of hotels, restaurants, and services. These will be helpful for future trips, and also provide information for other agency personnel.

Example:

MAY 22:   Das Kaserne Hotel is small but very clean, and the staff is friendly and accommodating. Meals here are superb, the best of the trip. The west side of the hotel is near the Autobahn and that makes sleeping difficult. I'd always ask for rooms on the east or north. The hotel is also located quite a distance from the main Berlin shopping area.

3.   A complete rundown on all expenses. It helps to carry a small notebook to record expenses as they are committed. These may be transferred to other forms that evening. Record expenses in the local currency, with conversion rates, and all the figures can later be translated into dollars.

Example:

MAY 14: Lunch in Lyons	28 francs
Phone calls	7 francs
Wine for Douglas anniversary	172 francs
Admissions to winery	30 francs
Dinner at hotel	105 francs
	342 francs

The tour manager may want to report separately on the tour operator and this operator's personnel. And there could be other items which require more space and more details. There is flexibility for this.

Most travel agencies and tour operators require that the tour manager retain receipts for expenses, both as a way to settle accounts intelligently and as a method of recording costs for tax purposes.

Although you don't want to make a major literary work of this report, it does help when you are thorough. Even if your superiors don't read every word, the information is there. It may be valuable to you in future years to be reminded of the difficult time you had getting transportation after the theater in London, or the problem of pickpockets in some port of call.

REUNION

Getting together at least once again after the trip is a nice idea. Some tour groups meet annually, and some members take several tours together after this initial shared experience.

First, set a convenient date for the reunion, avoiding any important conflicts, and staying clear of normal vacation times.

Then select a locale. This could be the home of one of the tour members, or your home, or the home of an agency VIP. It could be the recreation center of an apartment complex where a tour member lives, or the hall of some company that provides the facilities free for local groups. Be certain that this hall has no restrictions against things like liquor. The site must also be large enough, convenient, and at least marginally attractive. Invitations should be issued at least two weeks ahead of the event, and preferably a month. Spouses should be included.

Try to come up with a theme that matches the geography of the tour. This may mean national colors, pennants, maps, posters, even native costumes. The food, too, can take on the national character—pasta, gyros sandwiches, rice pilaf, trifle, Irish coffee. Have some records or tapes playing appropriate music to set the mood.

(2)   June 1 (Inverness)

Cookies for bus	$1.92
Kingussie Museum (fees)	61.20
Lunch	9.36
Jean	6.32
Books	6.32
Mt. Royal Laundry	17.51
Books/Maps	10.48
Books/Records — 7.60	17.60
Culloden Fees	36.00

166.71 — 20.24

June 2 (Ballachulish)

Loch Ness Museum Fees	64.00
Gifts	**33.44**
Lunch	16.00
Tip to Singer (Hotel)	8.00
Skye Ferry	88.00
Necklace for Adaline (tour member)	9.59
Bumper Sticker	16.00
Drinks (Double Room people)	10.96

245.99 — 49.44

June 3 (Ayr)

Lunch (J, E, self)	17.36
Books — 16.00	**29.92**
Drinks	9.12
Church	1.60

58.00 — 16.00

June 4 (Windermere)

Jean	40.00
Gretna Green fees	16.80
Gretna Green pic	3.20
Lunch	8.80
Gifts (Group)	4.80
Drinks	5.12
Cruise Fees (Lake)	83.20
Tape & Book (Tour)	12.80

174.72 — 40.00

Fig. 10-1. The tour manager may record expenses in a small notebook, then transfer them to a larger notebook, ledger, or report form in the evening. These informal figures will later be typed up for the final report. In this case, personal (non-tour) expenses have been underlined.

June 2 (Ballachulish)

Loch Ness Museum (fees)	64.00	
Gifts	33.44	
Lunch	16.00	
Tip to singer at hotel	8.00	
Skye Ferry	88.00	
Necklace for Adl.(tour member)	9.59	
Bumper Stickers	16.00	
Drinks for double bed tour members	10.96	245.99

June 3 (Ayr)

Lunch (Jean/Eileen)	17.36	
Books (tour)	13.92	
Books (bob)	16.00	
Drinks	9.12	
Church	1.60	58.00

June 4 (Windermere)

Jean	40.00	
Gretna Green (fees)	16.80	
Gretna Green Pic	3.20	
Lunch	8.80	
Gifts for group	4.80	
Drinks	5.12	
Lake cruise (fees)	83.20	
Tape & book (tour)	12.80	174.72

June 5 (Windermere)

Lunch	7.36	
Parking for coach	3.20	
Drinks	4.80	
Crisps	.64	
Book (Jennifer)	15.92	
Book for tour	12.72	
Laundry	13.92	58.56

June 6 (Chester)

Lunch	8.88	
Phone	2.16	
Tip	1.60	
Gift(tour)	1.67	
Books (Bob)	2.88	
Tea	1.76	
Gifts for Group	4.80	
Abbey donation	2.40	
Drinks	6.40	32.55

Fig. 10-2. The final, typed report (cross reference 10-1)

EXPENSE FORM

NAME:	BRANCH:	REPORTING PERIOD:

DATE	FROM - TO AND BUSINESS DAYS AWAY	Air, Bus Rail, etc. Fare	AUTO EXPENSES		Lodging	BUSINESS MEALS			Other Allowable Expenses		TOTAL EXPENSES	Client # Expense # Tour #	Date	Place & Type of Expense Incurred Name of Club, Restaurant, type of entertainment.
			# of Miles	Amt.		Brk.	Lunch	Dinner	Description	Amt.				

SUBMITTED BY:_____

APPROVED BY:_____

TT-AG-14

NOTE: This form should be used for a maximum of 2 weeks only.

Fig. 10-3. Some agencies and operators require tour managers to use a regular expense form, such as this form used for all business-related expenses. (Courtesy of Travel & Transport)

The program somewhat runs itself. People will be happy to see one another and they'll be exchanging stories. Have them bring their photos or slides. These should be circulated and you might run a contest to judge the best pictures in several categories. Be sure you have the right projectors on hand, with extension cords, empty trays, an extra bulb, and a screen.

Occasionally, the courier from overseas may be able to join you. Some of them make promotional tours through the United States and you could schedule your reunion around their visit.

Tour members who are unable to come, primarily because they live out of town, might be phoned and given an opportunity to chat with some of their old friends. Ultimately, you wrap it up, but keep these people posted on future trips, and on other local events that may extend the experience they enjoyed.

There is no need to make this a major expense item for the tour manager, agency, or operator. Often, the tour members bring food or drink, and the sponsors may supply a few door prizes along with awards for best photos.

❏ *CHAPTER HIGHLIGHTS*

❏ The tour manager should reconfirm space at least forty-eight hours before departure, and should check on other details of the return trip.

❏ A farewell gathering the night before departure is a good idea, both as a method of seeing that all members are on hand and okay, and as a way to end the tour on a high note.

❏ The tour manager checks passengers in about two hours before departure, and gives them a time and place to reassemble for enplaning.

❏ Familiarity with American customs regulations is vital, realizing the exemption amounts and items, along with the taboo imports.

❏ Getting through Customs can be smooth or hectic, and the tour manager can't do a great deal about this. The officials are in charge. The tour manager does do everything possible to prepare tour members and to escort them to the ongoing flight, while seeing that the luggage is also handled.

❏ There are many tasks left to the tour manager, even after the tour members have departed for their own homes. Expense forms, reports, thank-you notes, letters to tour members, evaluation cards—all of these must be completed and, where appropriate, delivered or mailed.

❏ Reunions of tour members, where feasible, are good for client relations. They need not cost a lot of money, and some of the food and drink items can be supplied by tour members themselves.

❏ *CASE PROBLEMS*

1. As you are waiting in the lounge for the return flight to the United States, a tour member takes you, the tour manager, aside, and requests that you carry aboard a plastic bag of dirt taken from a piece of land in Tunisia, where his grandparents were born. "You're the tour director," he says, "and they won't bother you." What should you do?

What should you do if another tour member asks you to bring through Customs an extra carton of cigarettes for him? He already has a carton to declare, and you have none.

2. You are allowed an adequate amount for meals on your expense account, but you also have several meals bought for you by tour members, the tour operator courier, and the hotel or restaurant managers. Perhaps a third of your meals are covered this way. Now you are trying to decide whether you should list these meals as part of your expenses. Your rationale is that you probably had other expenses you can't remember, that the money was there for you to use, and that this is a fairly common practice. How will you resolve this?

DOMESTIC MOTORCOACH TOURS

LEARNING OBJECTIVES

After you've read this chapter you will:

❏ Understand more about the scope of domestic motorcoach tours
❏ Appreciate the duties expected of both driver and tour escort
❏ Know how to ensure better relations between driver and escort
❏ Have a grasp of the routine on tour, from passenger indoctrination and regimen, to hotel check in and checkout
❏ Realize the amount of preparation necessary for the tour escort in order to present intelligent narration

KEY CONCEPTS

Coach	Motorcoach tour operators	Rest stops
Coach driver	Name badges	Seat rotation
Exiting coach	Naps	Smoking
Farewell gathering	Narration	Tour escort
Frequent rider benefits	National Motorcoach Network	Upscale tours
Games	National Tour Association	Wakeup calls
Indoctrination session	Researching narration	

Despite the images of tourists exiting from airplanes or sunning themselves on cruise decks, there remains a vast domestic market for tourists, both American and foreign. Well over 200 million charter and tour passengers take to the roads each year, using the services, not only of the industry giant, Greyhound, but also employing one of the more than thirty-six hundred **motorcoach tour operators** available in this country.

In 1988, twenty-eight independent operators, operating a thousand **coaches** and carrying over three million passengers annually, merged to form the **National Motorcoach Network.** This is merely one of the innovative measures adopted by this form of carrier. Motorcoach travel clubs have been created, promotional funds expanded, and the coaches themselves equipped for the demands of the modern traveler. Many tour operators work on air/coach combinations, enabling them to concentrate their trips into fewer days, a trend applauded by customers.

Some tours, like the New England Fall Foliage Tour, have a long and successful track record. So do trips to American landmarks, from heritage circuits on the east coast to Disneyland and California excursions. But there are many more. Presley Tours promotes a "Country Christmas" tour through Nashville; there are "Color Country" trips through the Southwest; Frontier Tours began a special "grandparents" tour, encouraging the seniors to take along the grandchildren. The business is competitive, so operators seek a niche where they can corral a market segment. Competition means going head-to-head with other firms on the cost of a tour, meaning that it becomes harder to spread these costs over a smaller number of passengers. Achieving a peak coach load is the key to marketing success. This means determining how many passengers' fares are required to make the trip profitable, and then meeting or exceeding this goal regularly.

ASSETS AND CONCERNS

What tourists seem to like about motorcoach tours are the relative value of the tour ticket, the freedom from driving and the hassles of driving, the opportunity to see country more intimately, a certain flexibility in route and schedule, and the opportunity to share the experience with others.

While there are tours of two weeks, even longer, many motorcoach tours are considerably shorter. Gray Line of New York, for example, not only transports visitors to the Big Apple sites and sights, the company also offers day trips to places like West Point, Atlantic City, or Woodstock.

Perhaps a more typical tour would be this seven day tour of New England which begins in Boston and spends two nights in this city. It includes day tours to Concord and Lexington, a circuit of the Freedom Trail, visits to Bunker Hill and the warship "Old Ironsides." After Boston this excursion heads for Bar Harbor, Maine, exploring natural wonders like Mount Desert Island, Acadia National Park, Northeast Harbor, and other sites, including museums and old country inns. On the fourth day the touring coach swings through the White Mountains of New Hampshire, visiting Franconia Notch and riding an aerial tramway forty-two hundred feet to the summit of Mount Cannon. Days five and six are spent in Vermont and along the shores of Lake Champlain. A scenic

Fig. 11-1. Some domestic tour companies make a specialty of certain popular trips. (Courtesy of Mayflower Tours)

drive through the Adirondacks follows and, on the final day, a cruise on Lake George before returning to the point of origin.

One complaint common to motorcoach tour operators is that travel agents are always more interested in selling a tour that involves air—since their commission on the air is a major profit item. All-motorcoach trips do not have the same sort of appeal. Perhaps many travel agents see these tours as lacking a certain glamor.

If that's the case, they might consider some of the **luxury tours,** which include not only very modern vehicles (semi-reclining seats, larger windows, even an extra step for disembarking), but also prime hotel space, top restaurants, and talented tour directors. Prospects for these upscale tours are generally a little older, probably retired or semi-retired, and with better-than-average incomes.

And, for the motorcoach afficianado, there is even the opportunity for **"frequent rider" discounts** on future trips.

Amid all this modernizing, the tour manager, guide, escort, and driver (on some tours, one person wears all these hats) still make or break the trip. On longer journeys, like a nine-day California Holiday trip, a sociable, well-informed, efficient tour director is a must.

Laurence Stevens fulfills this role for Mayflower Tours, Inc., which operates out of a Chicago suburb. Formerly an executive with American Express and later a publisher of travel-related books, Stevens, a native of England, began escorting after his retirement from publishing. Here are his thoughts on the role and duties of a motorcoach tour manager.

The Coach

The touring vehicle is not a bus, but a *coach*. A bus is something used for school or urban transportation. A coach is more luxurious, with special suspension for a smooth ride, soundproofing, tinted windows, air conditioning, upholstered seats with footrests, overhead racks, restroom, individual reading lights, cassette player, two-way base communcation, and a microphone for the tour escort. Some newer models have VCRs and television monitors, so passengers can enjoy movies or travelogues while traveling.

Coach Restroom

The restroom is really for emergency use, since heavy normal use will overload the system and create a strong sewage odor. The toilet system on a coach consists of a holding tank and a chemical to break down sewage and odors. Most drivers dump and flush the tank every couple of days or so, depending on usage. Only toilet paper can be discarded in the coach toilet. Anything else, including

Fig. 11-2. In major tourist areas, ample parking is usually provided for coaches.

paper towels, will cause the chemical to be ineffective, resulting in a smell that permeates the coach.

Checking the Coach Prior to the Tour

Before boarding any passengers, the tour manager (escort) should inspect the vehicle. Is the coach and its upholstery clean? Have the windows been washed? Is there chemical in the restroom toilet system (checked by pushing the flushing button)? Has the driver equipped the restroom with paper towels and/or moist towelettes? Is there running water in the restroom sink? Most important: Does the microphone work? "It's practically impossible to run a quality tour if one has to shout down the coach all the time. If the microphone is not working, the escort must insist that it be fixed as soon as possible after the tour departs—or, better still, insist on another coach with a working microphone." Does the driver have maps and supplies? The tour company should have furnished the coach company with an itinerary several days before the tour is due to start, so that the driver knows just where he is going. It is the driver's job to drive the coach and follow itinerary instructions. The escort should not have to engage in navigating on a regular basis—although the escort should help the driver in difficult situations—especially if an itinerary and/or routing is new to the driver.

Escort/Driver Relationship

"Some **coach drivers,**" says Stevens, "are easy to get along with; others behave as if they are next to God and are extremely difficult for the escort to work with." The driver is responsible for the safe operation of the coach, making sure there is adequate fuel on board at all times, for cleaning the interior of the coach each night or first thing in the morning before the coach departs, dumping and flushing the restroom holding tank when necessary, loading and unloading the luggage, helping people on and off the coach, and following the itinerary as supplied by the tour operator.

Unless the driver is playing a dual role, he or she should not be on the microphone, except for explaining the operation of the coach on the first day and helping to greet people each morning. Some drivers may try to compete for the mike, supplying their own jokes, anecdotes and commentary. If escorts are to remain in control, this sort of competition must be discouraged.

Some drivers resent being told what to do by the tour escort. This escort must remember that the driver may have years of experience and several million miles of accident-free driving, and therefore resents being treated as an underling. Things usually run more smoothly if the escort treats the driver as an equal and discusses things as with an equal. The driver should be made to feel part of the tour. Laurence Stevens suggests inviting the driver for a drink after dinner the first night, just to break the ice.

"There *are* problem drivers, people who have no personality, who can't follow directions and keep getting lost, who resent the escort, who hog the microphone, who come between the passengers and the escort, who compete with the escort for acceptability, or who are just plain difficult to work with."

Most tour companies keep a list of unacceptable drivers and may request that the coach company not assign these drivers to any of their tours.

If a tour manager happens to be along in addition to the driver and escort, that sets up a whole new set of relationships. The tour manager is then the supervisor of the itinerary, in terms of the package being fulfilled. This person also treats the others as peers, and tries to make a team of the trio of players.

First Day Check-In

In addition to checking passengers aboard the first day, the motorcoach **tour manager or escort** checks baggage and records the number, much the same as the tour manager does when boarding a plane. The routine is also similar to the counting procedures explained in Chapters 7 and 8. Lost baggage is a headache, and leaving a bag behind because someone changed the count may mean that this bag never makes it back before tour's end. It's the driver's responsibility to count the baggage each time the tour departs, and to inform the escort if a bag is missing.

Although rules vary among tour companies, most operators limit the tour member to a single piece of luggage, plus a carryon bag.

Passenger Indoctrination

As soon as possible on the first day, the escort introduces him/herself and the driver, explains all policies (no smoking, seat rotation, baggage, hotel and wakeup routines, and the like), and may toss in a few jokes, just to warm up the passengers.

Many tours hand out **name badges** on the first morning.

"One way to break the ice," says Stevens, "is to pass a bag full of name badges around the coach with the request that if a passenger gets his or her own badge it should be put back. Everyone will then have a name badge with someone else's name on it. When the coach arrives at the first rest stop, people are asked to get off, find the person to whom the badge belongs, and introduce themselves."

If the group has a get-together the first evening, in their own dining room or meeting room, each person can also be asked to stand, give his or her name, and tell a little about himself or herself.

Counting Passengers

The tour escort's nightmare is leaving someone behind at a rest, lunch, or sightseeing stop. So a count must be made every time the coach starts off again—and *before* it pulls away. If all seats are filled, it's easy to spot a missing person. When the tour has twenty-five to thirty people in a forty-four-seat coach, however, you have to physically count heads. With people standing or milling around, this can be difficult. If someone is stranded, the coach company will have to pay to get that person to the next hotel. This is expensive, but, more importantly, it causes the tour team to lose face.

Seat Rotation

This, too, was discussed earlier as a way to reduce grumbling about certain seat locations. Virtually all domestic tour companies engage in regular **seat rotation,** probably moving two rows in a clockwise direction twice a day. A person sitting in the front seat on the step (or door) side in the morning will move back two rows after lunch and another two rows the next morning, and so on. Some coach companies rotate one row instead of two. The length of the tour also makes a difference in terms of rotation policy.

If the coach is not full, the back seat may remain empty, since it vibrates most, is the noisiest spot, and is located next to the restroom.

Smoking on the Coach

Nearly all tour companies have a **no-smoking policy** on their coaches, including the restroom. An exception may be made by some companies for the driver, who could be a heavy smoker and might get nervous after a few hours without a cigarette. If the driver does smoke, the window to the left is left open, venting out the smoke. If this smoking proves offensive to passengers, however, the escort will enforce the no smoking rule, even with the driver.

Researching the Tour and Narration

Well before the tour leaves, the tour escort must become familiar with the itinerary, hotels, meals, sightseeing arrangements, places of interest en route, plus interesting anecdotes or trivia that can be shared. While one must avoid boring the passengers, the escort still has to provide information on the area they're traversing, like the name of the large river they just crossed. This often means substantial research time, which is part of the escort's job.

Because of the vastness of the United States and Canada, it's not always possible to hold the knowledge in one's head, so this means exhaustive research and a method of compiling the details for future reference. Laurence Stevens enters all of his research on a computer and can print out any information he needs for a particular tour.

Apart from the history of the various states traveled through, the escort **narrates** the history of towns and settlements, plus interesting anecdotes about specific areas. For example, when Stevens takes a Washington, D.C. tour, the coach passes through Frederick in Maryland, the home of the legendary Barbara Frietchie who supposedly defied the Confederate Army under Stonewall Jackson by defiantly flying the Union flag. Stevens reads tour members the John Greenleaf Whittier poem commemorating this determined woman. At Mount Vernon, Stevens can call on his knowledge of English history to trace back to our first president's British forebears. When he heads west, Stevens bones up on Indian lore, tidbits about the Gold Rush, tales of the untamed frontier. Every trip requires hours of research in order to bring the area alive for travelers.

Escorts recommend that a plentiful supply of state and city maps be on hand, along with materials available from state tourism offices, from libraries, and from organizations like AAA. Stevens collects and files away materials picked up en route at tourism offices, hotels, and attraction sites.

En Route

As mentioned in Chapter 8, the routine on tour should be varied enough to keep people interested while allowing them their own personal time. Laurence Ste-

TRAVELING THROUGH MAYFLOWER COUNTRY

WHO TAKES A MAYFLOWER TOUR
People who enjoy having a good time and a wonderful vacation. Everyone is welcome, especially travelers who are particular about how they travel and prefer the benefits of an escorted vacation. Each tour is planned with you in mind. Mayflower Tours combines the value and convenience you want, with the companionship and security you deserve.

GREATEST VALUE
Before you make any decision on your travel plans, we want you to compare our tour price, feature by feature, with any other insured and bonded tour operator. We are proud to say that our tours combine the greatest value with a very affordable price!

FULLY ESCORTED
One of our greatest sources of pride is the number of complimentary letters and calls we receive about our Tour Directors. They are Mayflower's prized treasure. Their informative commentaries and service add to the enjoyment of traveling in Mayflower Country.

AIRPORT TO HOTEL ROUND TRIP TRANSFERS INCLUDED
You may relax with the knowledge that Mayflower Tours provides round trip transfers from the airport to your hotel. Transfer coupons will be provided in your documents along with information on meeting your Tour Director.

INCLUDED MEALS
Your tour includes some meals. We have also given you the opportunity to dine on your own. The included meals are usually dinners, however, we occasionally include breakfast or lunch when there is a very special place we would like you to experience.

STAY AT TOP HOTELS
Mayflower uses only the best in travel-oriented hotels and inns. We list our hotels in the itinerary so you know the accommodations and quality you are getting before making your reservation.

LUXURY MOTORCOACHES
You always travel on deluxe, temperature-controlled motor-coaches, with a professional driver. The coaches feature reclining seats, lavatories (on tours within the continental U.S.), overhead storage racks and glareproof windows.

GUARANTEED SHARE FOR SINGLE TRAVELERS
Many of our tour members travel alone and would like to share a room for cost and companionship. If you call us more than 45 days before a tour departs, we will arrange a roommate for you. If we can't find one, we guarantee that you will travel at the twin rate.

LUGGAGE
You may bring one large suitcase, as well as a small carrying case, on all of our tours. Your Tour Director and bellmen will take care of the suitcase, and we ask that you keep the carrying case with you.

MAYFLOWER MONEY
We want to "Thank you" for traveling on a Mayflower Tour. At the end of your vacation, you will recieve MAYFLOWER MONEY. This is a certificate entitling you to a $5 per day reduction on a future Mayflower tour. Another great reason to travel with Mayflower!

THOUGHTS ON TIPPING
When someone has gone out of their way to do their best, we know that many people like to personally reward a job well done. Gratuities for luggage handling and meals that are listed as part of your tour are included in your original payment. Tips for services of a personal nature, as well as your Motorcoach Driver and Tour Director are not included in the tour cost.

WE LOVE GROUPS
Taking a Mayflower Tour is an ideal experience for any type of group, whether it's a club, organization or church. Traveling together is a wonderful way to meet new friends and share experiences with old ones. If you are interested in taking a group to Mayflower Country, please contact your professional travel agent for more information.

For information about reservations, cancellations and refunds, please see our back cover.

Fig. 11-3. Tips for tourists (Courtesy of Mayflower Tours)

vens suggests these activities: 1) *narration time,* when the escort provides information and humor: 2) *games time,* featuring both team games like bingo, and personal games, like crossword puzzles: 3) *quiet time,* a period for travelers to just kick back, study the landscape, and listen to cassette music; 4) *nap time,* when tour members can sleep, often right after leaving the hotel in the morning and then right after lunch.

"A good escort will observe and recognize the mood of the passengers and not try to play games when the people would prefer to sleep. Games should also be avoided when the coach is passing through scenic areas, since this is one reason the tour members came along in the first place."

Rest and Lunch Stops

Virtually all domestic motorcoach tour operators schedule **rest stops** every two to three hours. If the tour leaves the hotel at 7:30 A.M., a rest stop should be set for 10:00 or 10:30, depending on what is available. Lunch stops are normally scheduled between 12:00 and 1:00 P.M. and last about an hour. A midafternoon rest stop is usually part of the program, too.

For some rest stops, the major fast food restaurants suffice, but some tours show more ingenuity and select places where passengers can sit down and not feel rushed. Stevens recommends some of the *76 Truck Stops* because they have ample parking, can handle large numbers, and often have gift shops. Tollway rest stops in the east are also popular.

Exiting the Coach

The routine for distributing hotel keys has been covered and varies little on domestic tours. Some keys are at the desk, some in the doors, and some are distributed by the tour escort, either as people leave the coach or while they are still in their seats.

Most tours **exit the coach by sides,** with the front row the first to exit, followed by the next row, until one side is out or nearly out. Then the other side starts from the rear and peels off toward the front. The next time they get off, the process will be reversed, so the last become first.

Wakeup Calls and Departure

Stevens favors the idea of having each person arrange his or her own **wakeup call.** He also follows the regimen described in Chapter 8 for having the bags outside the room in ample time to facilitate pickup. Meanwhile, the tour manager or escort settles the account with the hotel, except for personal bills run up by individual travelers.

"Departure day can often be one of the most frustrating for the escort. Very often the bill isn't ready, or if it is, it's wrong. For example, most hotels provide a complimentary room for the escort—but the front desk neglects to take this into consideration. Baggage charges are often incorrect. Or the hotel has charged a passenger's personal phone call to the master account. Or the front desk is charging a higher rate than was contracted for by the tour company. And so it goes.

"The delay problem can be solved by the escort calling the front desk and requesting the bill be ready by a specific time, so there's no long wait. Many other problems can be solved if the escort carries along a copy of the original contract between the hotel and the tour company."

End of the Tour

If the tour has "come together well," passengers will be sorry to see it end. It's important to leave the passengers in a good frame of mind, so that they'll return to the same tour company for another trip. If there is a **farewell dinner,** some tour escorts ask tour members to recount the most memorable experience for them. It could be a special meal, or some scenic treasure, or something patriotic like the Military Tattoo at Williamsburg, or the peace and serenity of Arlington Cemetery, or the power of the Vietnam Memorial Wall, or the pageantry of Mass in Montreal's Basilica of Notre Dame. Relieving these times helps reinforce the pleasures of the journey.

As with any other tour, the escort or tour manager must file reports, usually according to the rules established by that particular tour operator.

Tour reunions would be unlikely, since the group is likely to be a mix of people from a number of geographical regions. However, some groups do manage to have a little gathering after the tour. The tour escort—if not already on the road again—might be in attendance.

An umbrella organization that serves many tour operators in the United States is the National Tour Association, based in Lexington, Kentucky, and boasting a membership in excess of three thousand. In addition to playing the same watchdog role as other associations in terms of legislation, NTA also provides promotional materials, sponsors a marketplace to serve suppliers and operators, and conducts educational seminars to acquaint members with pertinent topics.

❑ *CHAPTER HIGHLIGHTS*

❑ More than thirty-six hundred motorcoach tour operators handle over 200 million passengers annually. Tours vary in length, type, destination, quality, and price range.

❏ Today's touring coach provides a smoother, quieter ride, along with restrooms, reclining seats, taped music, even VCRs and television.

❏ Although the coach driver has responsibility for the condition of the coach, the baggage count, the cleanliness of the restroom, and the safe operation of the coach, the escort or tour manager must oversee these duties, making certain the itinerary is adhered to, and that the baggage is properly handled.

❏ Conflicts between driver and escort are possible, but can be eased by making the driver feel part of the team.

❏ The escort takes the passenger count, handles the briefing of tour members, and provides commentary on the trip. For this latter duty, the escort must do considerable research and develop a handy system to retain the information. This tour manager/escort also enforces any rules, like the no smoking regulation or mandatory seat rotation.

❏ Time sent on the coach should be intelligently divided among times for narration time for games, time for sleep, and quiet times for sightseeing. Adequate rest and meal stops should be sensibly planned.

❏ First and last days on a tour are important, so the tour escort tries to have members leave feeling good about the trip. A farewell gathering while passengers exchange their views on the most memorable experience helps plant a positive image.

❏ CASE PROBLEMS

1. When you reach your hotel in Phoenix, you realize that one of your tour members, a woman traveling alone, is not with you. The last time anyone recalls seeing her was when the coach stopped for a three-hour visit in Old Tucson, some 120 miles away. What do you do?

2. As tour escort on a New England Fall Foliage tour, you're accompanied by a driver who continually reaches for the mike. As soon as you put it down, he picks it up, telling stories, making comments on the area, and sometimes contradicting what you've just told the people. It also gets back to you that, at rest and meal stops, he is making derogatory remarks about how you are conducting the tour. Typically, he has a segment of the group that has warmed to this approach, but others are unhappy about the obvious dissension. What actions do you take?

3. Your coach driver is a heavy smoker and lights up while driving. Since his air vent takes care of most of his smoke, there are no complaints from passengers about secondary smoke. However, one of your tour members, also a heavy smoker, complains that tour rules prohibit him from smoking, even though he paid almost a thousand dollars for this trip. He wants to know why he can't smoke if the driver is allowed to smoke. How do you respond?

MANAGING INBOUND TOURISM

LEARNING OBJECTIVES

After reading this chapter, you will:

- ❑ Understand more about the scope and impact of tourism to the United States and throughout the United States
- ❑ Have a better idea of how states and cities promote tourism and how much they spend
- ❑ Know what sort of functions a local tourism bureau performs

KEY CONCEPTS

American Hotel & Motel Association	Local tourism	Travel writers
Attractions	Mystery tour	U.S. Travel & Tourism Administration
Customized itineraries	Receptions	Walk-in services
Group tour guide	Send off events	Welcoming parties
Inbound tourism	Shopping tours	
	State tourism	

Although we have concentrated on the role of the tour manager in conducting groups abroad or through the United States, including along-the-way materials on hotels, carriers and other segments of the travel and hospitality industry, we shouldn't neglect the vast efforts of public and private sectors to attract tourists to this country, or to particular states or cities.

Every nation with a story to tell promotes tourism. For some countries, tourism is one of the two or three most profitable enterprises. America, a relative latecomer to the field of inbound **tourism,** is more interested than ever in generating income to offset the trade imbalance. More than twenty-two million foreign visitors troop to our shores annually, adding more than $15 billion to our coffers, and supporting some 300 thousand jobs. In addition,

Americans, a very mobile citizenry, travel all over this country, favoring locales like New York and Disneyland, but also peopling the Colorado mountains, the New Orleans Latin Quarter, the sunny Southwest, or the ski slopes of New England. Some states spend upwards of $20 million a year to lure travelers, while even some small cities have tourism budgets surpassing a million dollars.

A 1988 *U.S. News & World Report* graphic showed Los Angeles as the prime tourist target, with nearly fifty million visitors. Nearby Orange County, with Anaheim and Disneyland, adds another thirty-five million. San Diego, Atlantic City, Washington, D.C., New York, Las Vegas, San Francisco, Atlanta, and Dallas round out the top ten travel destinations. Minnesota's Twin Cities follow, and then a pair of attractions, Orlando (Disneyworld) and Niagara Falls. Boston, Chicago, Philadelphia, Miami, St. Louis, and New Orleans are part of the next ten locales.

INCREASE IN FOREIGN VISITORS

While travel by Americans to Europe continues to grow moderately each year, the increase in **visitors to our shores** is far more impressive. The attraction for Europeans is the decline in the dollar, making the United States a real bargain. Some French, for example, can holiday cheaper in Florida than on the Riviera. But America must still be promoted, because there is competition from places like Mexico and South America, where foreign currency also goes a long way. To help bolster its share of this market, the **U.S. Travel and Tourism Administration** has been more aggressive in establishing overseas offices, with **walk-in services,** and in expanding their media campaign abroad. Hotel chains have also been active, sponsoring European seminars to familiarize travel agents and tourism directors with the variety of lodging options available in this country. The **American Hotel & Motel Association** has teamed with the U.S. Travel & Tourism Administration (a division of the Department of Commerce) in providing these workshops and in staffing the overseas offices. A print and television advertising campaign ("America—Catch the Spirit") ran in nine major European markets in 1988, as well as in South America.

A significant number of foreign visitors are repeaters. They've seen one part of the United States and want to see more. So more tour operators in this country are dreaming up ways to get a piece of this business, organizing trips that will appeal to the more sophisticated traveler.

At the same time, there is also an emphasis on luring Americans to their own scenic attractions. Advertising campaigns sell the virtues of various states and cities as vacation destinations. Travel agencies and tour operators also pick up on services which can be supplied to visiting groups—like meeting and

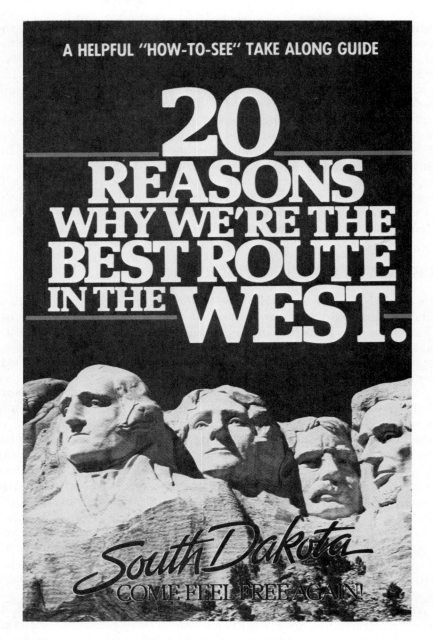

Fig. 12-1. Every state makes its case for tourism. (Courtesy of South Dakota Tourism)

greeting, setting up spouse programs, conducting local tours and sightseeing, providing packages, accommodations, or car rental. A new wrinkle in recent years has been the development of **shopping tours,** either as an independent appeal or as one offered to visiting groups. A San Francisco tour operator runs a "Shop Till You Drop" package before the holiday season, and a New Jersey firm takes shoppers to suburban malls, factory outlets, to Amish country in Pennsylvania, and even through east coast wine regions.

STATE TOURISM

State tourism, which was once fairly amateurish and under-funded, has grown professionally and budgets nearly $300 million for promotion. New York and Illinois led recent spending lists, averaging over $20 million each. The expenditures seem worth it. Tax revenues alone amount to nearly $12 billion for the fifty states, and jobs related to tourism and hospitality exceed five million. For its $21 million plus commitment, New York gets a return of about fifty-six million visitors annually who spend more than $17 billion.

What does all this promotional money buy? Printed materials (ranging from city brochures to current event calendars), advertising, videos, the hosting of **travel writers** and tourism officials, the cost of correspondence and phone responses, travel, seminars, staffing, office costs, and many other budget items. Along with printed guides, many states also supply human guides, located at rest stops along the Interstate system perhaps, or at key attractions. Tourism bureaus work with local and regional tour operators to transport visitors around city and state, following an itinerary as complete as the more expansive foreign itineraries.

LOCAL TOURISM PROMOTION

Cities also get in their bids for the tourist dollar. All large cities and many small ones, have tourism bureaus plugging their virtues, which may be nightlife or outdoor recreation, romance or inexpensive prices. Palm Springs sometimes focuses on summer hotel bargains. Massachusetts exploits its colonial heritage. New York City and New Jersey put together a package marketing stopover visits for travelers en route elsewhere. Cody, Wyoming features its Old West atmosphere and ties to Buffalo Bill. For Honolulu, it's sunshine and an exotic setting; for Omaha, Nebraska, it's "big city spice at a small town price."

Rebekah Vohoska serves as director of tourism for the Raleigh, North Carolina Convention and Visitors Bureau, one of the more than 950 bureaus in

Fig. 12-2. A series of brochures explore Raleigh's attractions and events. (Courtesy of the Raleigh Convention and Visitors Bureau)

the United States. These are the services and resources she sees the tourism offices supplying:

❑ **Group tour guide.** This printed piece includes information on the history of the area, attractions (with group rates, dates and hours, minimum time needed for a visit, parking, handicapped access, and complimentary policies), accommodations (group rates, complimentary policies, baggage handling charges, number of rooms, facilities, services), restaurants (seating capacity, sample menus for groups, complimentary policies), recommended tour itineraries, sightseeing and guide services, slides or photos of major **attractions,** shopping facilities, detailed maps, fuel locations for motorcoaches, coach washing and dumping stations, parking restrictions and provisions for parking in congested areas. ("Complimentary policies" refers to the granting of free accommodations, meals, or entry fees to persons such as the driver and escort.)

❏ Tourism bureaus may help groups *select hotels* that meet their needs, either by having the hotels contact the group directly or by serving as a clearing house and forwarding the details. This "one-stop-shopping" saves the tour planner a lot of time and money.

❏ **Customized itineraries** may be organized by **local tourism** bureaus. Shopping tours, educational tours, visits to historical sites—all of these can be created, if they don't already exist. One recent innovation is the **"mystery tour,"** where people sign up, not knowing exactly where they will end up. Tourism bureaus help fashion these.

❏ Tourism bureaus also work at *educating* community hotels, restaurants, and attractions about the importance of group tour business. Complaints about accommodations, meals, or other tour aspects may be funneled through the tourism bureau for corrective measures. The bureau works daily with all facets of the hospitality industry, trying to make their community "tourist friendly."

❏ *Emergency help* can be provided by the tourism bureau. Details on where to go to get a coach repaired, or how to locate specialized medical information, or when local hotels are likely to be booked solid—this sort of specific data is available through the bureau.

❏ *Hosting travel writers* is often a function of city tourism bureaus, taking these journalists to key attractions, letting them sample the food and hospitality, supplying them with materials and information. The result of these activities may be favorable commentary in newspapers or magazines.

❏ Many bureaus are sponsoring **receptions, welcoming parties or send-off events** for tour groups that spend at least a night in the city. "In Raleigh," says Ms. Vohoska, "a character costumed as Sir Walter Raleigh bids groups farewell after a night in a Raleigh hotel, giving them a brief overview of the city and supplying each person with a small souvenir of the city." Other cities may host a celebration for the group upon arrival.

❏ *Familiarization tours* are a province of the tourism bureau. These are designed to acquaint tour operators with the services and facilities of the

Raleigh

Raleigh Convention and Visitors Bureau   January 1990

CONVENTION BUSINESS HAS STRONG START IN '90

The Raleigh Convention and Visitors Bureau began the decade with a renewed sales thrust, and, along with that commitment, the announcement that the North Carolina Vocational Education Summer Workshops confirmed a decision to meet in Raleigh in 1991 and 1992.

With this major booking and the U. S. Volleyball Association's Championships in May, the Bureau expects convention business to play a major role in the city's economy in the '90s.

VOCATIONAL EDUCATION

After winning the bid for the 1989 and 1990 N. C. Vocational Education Summer Workshops, the Bureau announced that the meetings have committed to meet in Raleigh *again* in '91 and '92, for a total of four years.

About 3,500 delegates will attend each year, using 4,300 room nights in nine Raleigh hotels. The estimated annual economic impact is $2.73 million.

According to June Atkinson, Chief Consultant for the Division of Voc.

Councilman Barlow Herget, Mayor Avery Upchurch and Councilman Ralph Campbell enjoyed the inaugural ride of the Raleigh Trolley Dec. 6. People attending the ribbon-cutting ceremony cheered as the trolley left City Market to begin its lunchtime route.

The Bureau's Advisory Council, led by board chairman Leigh Wilson, had its first meeting Nov. 2 at the Capital City Club. Business and civic leaders learned more about RCVB and community issues that affect the hospitality industry in Raleigh. "

Ed. Services, Raleigh was selected again due to the proximity of hotels in the area, and competitive room rates.

Atkinson speaks favorably of the meetings held in Raleigh in August 1989: "They went smoothly, hotel staff was cooperative with our staff and we found the Visitors Bureau to be very cooperative and helpful."

VOLLEYBALL CHAMPIONSHIPS

After months of negotiations, plans for the U. S. Volleyball Association's (USVBA) National Open Championships and Annual Meetings have been finalized. It was announced in February of 1989 that USVBA selected Raleigh, and through cooperative efforts of the USVBA Carolina Region, N. C. State University, N. C. Amateur Sports and the RCVB, Raleigh is prepared to host this major event.

Over 2,500 athletes, coaches and officials will meet in Raleigh May 10-19, using more than 600 hotel rooms each night. The event is expected to have an economic impact of $2.75 million during the 10-day period.

N. C. State University will be the site of the championships, with 150 teams competing in Carmichael Gymnasium and Reynolds Coliseum.

RECENT BOOKINGS

Some other conventions recently confirmed for Raleigh include the Southeastern Society of Social Psychologists, Southeastern Conference on English in the Two-Year College and the 1st Annual Exposition for Environmental Research in the Sunbelt. State groups that selected Raleigh include the N. C. Writers Network, N. C. School Counselors and the N. C. Guild of Professional Chimney Sweeps.

CONVENTIONS BOOKED BY RCVB

October: 9 Bookings
Economic Impact: $1,078,500
November: 5 Bookings
Economic Impact: $ 302,875

Total:
14 Definite Bookings
Economic Impact: $ 1,381,375

Fig. 12-3. Tourism newsletters are mailed to a number of different audiences, for a number of different reasons. (Courtesy of the Raleigh Convention and Visitors Bureau)

area. These are often a cooperative effort with destination marketing organizations and the state travel office. Hotels, services, attractions, transportation access, and other items are showcased. Experience demonstrates that tour planners are more likely to bring a group to a place they have visited personally.

❏ There are numerous *miscellaneous services* a tourism bureau supplies, from answering queries by letter or phone, to locating special facilities for a handicapped tour or an athletic team that needs space to work out. They offer brochures, photographs, slides, videos, escort notes, and other marketing tools. Many bureaus feature toll free numbers and facsimile machines to speed information to tourists and tour operators.

The National Tour Association issues a spiral-bound book to members entitled *Partners in Profit: An Introduction to Group Travel Marketing*. This eighty-four-page document is full of specific ideas for attracting and servicing groups. One section covers all the considerations a tour operator and tour supplier should weigh while the visitors are in the area. For example, this checklist is supplied as a guide to activities prior to the group's arrival:

Tour member list	Motorcoach servicing area
Arrival and departure times	Unloading and loading area
Meal times	Evening entertainment
Payment arrangements	Complimentary policy
Rate agreements	Reservations and cancellation policy

The copy goes on to provide suggestions for attractions, hotels, and restaurants, along with bus companies and the public sector.

PACKAGING THE INBOUND TOUR

Before soliciting tourist business from other locales, each state or community has to take an inventory of its assets. Some areas may boast of beaches and mountains, while others focus on history and glitter. South Dakota exhibits Mount Rushmore; Missouri heralds Mark Twain; and Philadelphia pictures the Liberty Bell. Communities may take advantage of a centennial, a sporting event, or some current travel fad.

These qualities can't be merely captured in an ad. First, the area has to organize tours, hotels, and attractions into a format that appeals to potential visitors.

New Orleans, for example, builds local tours around jazz, Creole cuisine, visits to the French Quarter, steamboat rides on the Mississippi, motorcoach

ATTRACTIONS

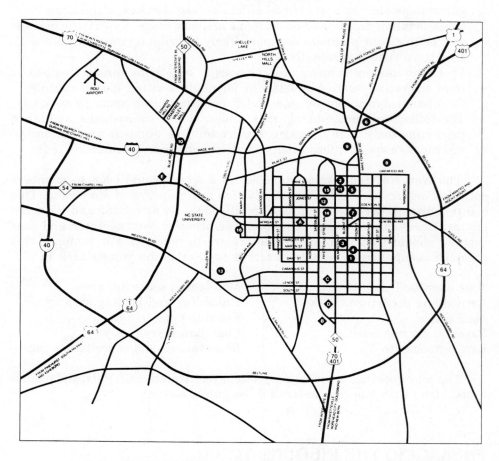

Discover old and new Raleigh by visiting the attractions listed and located on the map.

A. Raleigh Convention and Visitors Bureau
B. Greater Raleigh Chamber of Commerce
C. Raleigh Civic and Convention Center
D. Memorial Auditorium
E. State Fairgrounds

1. Artspace, Inc.
2. Capital Area Visitor Center
3. City Gallery of Contemporary Art
4. City Market
5. Executive Mansion
6. Farmers Market
7. Haywood Hall Museum
8. Historic Oakwood
9. Mordecai Historic Park

10. North Carolina Museum of Art
11. North Carolina Museum of History
12. North Carolina Museum of Natural
    Sciences
13. Pullen Park
14. State Capitol
15. State Legislative Building
16. Wakefield/Joel Lane House

See the Raleigh Convention and Visitors Bureau's Visitors Guide for a comprehensive listing of all Raleigh attractions.

Fig. 12-4. A group tour guide published by the city's convention and visitors bureau contains a map of attractive locations. (Courtesy of the Raleigh Convention and Visitors Bureau)

stops at historic plantations, Civil War battlefield drives, and even a Louisiana swamp tour. Seasonal attractions are Mardi Gras and the Sugar Bowl.

The massive state of Texas lets visitors choose from among dozens of tours, from a circuit of bustling Dallas to a stop at San Antonio's fabled Alamo. Cowboy culture is headlined along with the arts, and the video lure of the familiar Ewing ranch site is paired with an across-the-border glimpse of Hispanic food and customs. There is Padre Island and the appeal of Four Flags Over Texas.

Minneapolis markets its theatrical prominence, its array of urban attractions, and its full slate of professional sports. Florida wants you to know about Fort Lauderdale and Disney World. Colorado Springs sells its year-round activities, while Asheville, North Carolina focuses on its "cool, green" summer image. Rome, Georgia is into "mystery tours." North Dakota writes about its wide open spaces and outdoor opportunities.

All of these promotions take effort, staff, and money. Some states—like Illinois and New York—may spend between ten and twenty million dollars to bring outsiders to their locales, while other states must be satisfied with budgets under a quarter of a million dollars. Both levels of promotional activity may be abetted by corporate or travel industry money, justified on the basis of benefit to each community.

The Travel Agency

Just how active a role the travel agency plays locally depends primarily on demand and on the potential for profit. In areas where inbound tourism is heavy, like New York and California, many agencies will be anxious to participate in bookings, or could even schedule their own packages.

One consideration in dealing with inbound groups or with local tour operators is the fact that profit margins may be slimmer. The agency would not normally get any commissions from the air, and may not benefit from numbers the way it would with its own tours.

Agencies may provide service to walk-in clients who want to tour the region, or they may market operator packages, or they could display their own tailor-made tours. The motive may be profit, or it may be competitive service, but it should be analyzed carefully as a contributor to overall agency goals.

Reaching Foreign Visitors

Some cities and states may not worry much about foreign visitors. If they show up, they show up. Their concentration is more domestic, and perhaps even within a limited geographical range.

Other locales go after tourists from Europe and the Far East, from Canada and Mexico. This may mean some advertising in foreign markets, plus attendance at trade and travel fairs, and, certainly, providing a reference book of service, called a "tariff," to prospects and those who promote the locale's offerings.

Besides the normal itinerary suggestions, this material may include hotel information, a list of attractions, and a rundown on services offered, from airport pickup and car rental to escort and translation possibilities.

Inbound Tourism Considerations

For some agencies, an incoming tour department makes sense as a method of diversification, as an additional source of revenue, or as a means of balancing out some slack periods.

However, some additional staff expertise is required, as well as commitment of time and dollars. As mentioned before, the potential for profit is complicated by the lack of air commissions and the fact that the incoming group operator is also interested in profit.

Several travel agencies may bid for the business, and this is like any other competition. Bidders want to be successful, but they don't want to bid so low that they get the account but lose money. Any bid must be realistic.

Dealing with distant groups is fraught with problems, including delays in communication, misunderstandings in terms of language, difficulties in obtaining visas, lack of professionalism, a volatile political climate which may affect bookings, and perhaps even a balky or confused group of tourists who may not understand the planned routine or may not want to follow it.

Some Contacts

Besides aid from tourism bureaus and embassies, the tour operator or travel agent may also want to consider staying in touch with airlines, with stateside representatives of international travel suppliers, with certain hotel chains, and with regional counterparts of large groups which have overseas contingents.

The United States Travel and Tourism Administration (USTTA) has offices in half a dozen foreign countries, but the main domestic office is located within the Department of Commerce at 14th and Constitution Avenue NW, Washington, DC 20230.

The Travel Industry Association of America (TIAA) also assists those seeking to develop an inbound market. Their address is also in Washington, at 1889 L Street NW, in the zip code area 20036.

ASTA (The American Society of Travel Agents) also maintains an Inbound Services Committee.

Tour Manager/Tour Escort

Inbound tour groups may have their own director, a person who may or may not be familiar with the territory. In the latter case, local guides or local tour operators can fill this gap.

In large cities, guides may have fulltime work, at least during the peak tourist season, but smaller communities may have guides on call for special occasions. These could be retirees, teachers, students, Chamber of Commerce personnel, or others with the time and knowledge to devote to this pursuit. For special groups, like travel writers, tourism bureau staff members may serve as guides.

❏ *CHAPTER HIGHLIGHTS*

❏ Tourism is a major source of revenue for many countries, including the United States. Consequently, considerable money and effort is expended on promoting and servicing this industry.

❏ State and local tourism is also highly developed, with total expenditures in excess of $300 million in advertising and promotion annually.

❏ Local tourism bureaus provide printed materials, customized itineraries, videos, familiarization tours, welcoming functions, query responses, marketing tools, and other items, along with cooperative programs involving attractions and the hospitality industry.

❏ Tour operators and travel agencies must be realistic in considering plus and minus factors of inbound tourism.

❏ Tour managers and escorts perform the usual supervisory and narrative functions for city and regional tours, but may be employed either part or full time.

❏ *CASE PROBLEMS*

1. You are director of tourism for a city of 500 thousand located in the southeastern United States. The largest local hotel, a member of a national chain, enjoys an above average occupancy rate and considers this to be largely the result of reputation and national advertising. They complain constantly about the rooming tax they pay to the city to support tourism, and are uncooperative when it comes to activities that involve local tourism. You really need their participation. What can you do to bring this hotel around?

2. You receive a request from a farm organization from Spain to visit your farm belt area. You are the state tourism director and want to make a good impression on the visitors. At stake are not only the potential for grain and equipment sales, but also the strong possibility of regular tours by farm groups, as well as spinoff excursions by other Spaniards. Home base in your state will be the capital city, with a population of nearly a million, but most of the time will be spent visiting agricultural sites, equipment manufacturers, and food processors. List some of the things you must consider as you plan for these twenty-five visitors in the initial group. At this point, just make these general considerations, but add in any specifics that occur to you as things that will make the visit memorable.

AFTERWORD

To some degree, a tour manager's duties are defined by the nature of the assignment. Serving as a local guide normally requires only the ability to educate and entertain visitors. There are no baggage or head counting responsibilities. The other end of the spectrum is the driver/guide who handles the coach, the baggage, the hotels, the attractions, the money, and the commentary.

Most tours are able to share some of these duties, as described in earlier chapters. As many as three individuals may be aboard—driving, narrating, directing. The more typical complement, however, would be the driver and the escort (who could have another title), except for the tour groups that arrive with their own tour manager along. It breaks down to people getting tour members to their destination, transporting them around, handling their needs, and providing them with information and entertainment.

The more skill and experience the professional brings to the job, the better the chance of a memorable tourist experience.

GLOSSARY

Act of God A natural event—usually weather-related—which alters (tour) plans, and which is normally neither anticipated nor preventable.

advertising Any paid form of nonpersonal presentation and promotion of ideas, goods, and services by an identified sponsor, and using forms of the media.

advisory In this context, a published notice, by government agencies, of conditions in some foreign country. the term may be used generically to cover other forms of travel counsel.

affinity tour A tour whose membership is composed of individuals sharing some common affiliation, like membership in a club or organization, or association with an educational institution or church.

AH&MA American Hotel & Motel Association, a lodging industry trade association.

all-inclusive tour Or all-expense tour—a tour that includes all or most of the costs for a unit price.

ARTA Association of Retail Travel Agents, an American trade association.

ASTA American Society of Travel Agents, a United States trade association of travel agents and tour operators, which also offers foreign membership affiliation.

baby-sitter card Jargon for an information sheet supplied to travelers for purposes of informing relations and friends left behind as to where they may be reached.

brochure Printed sales tool used in the travel industry and elsewhere.

bumping Displacement of a traveler because of some real or perceived priority.

cancellation insurance A policy designed to cover monies which might be lost in the event of sudden cancellation of a planned tour by an individual tour member.

carrier Transportation firm which carries passengers or freight.

carryon luggage   Baggage retained by the traveler and not checked through the carrier.

charter   One of a varied number of contract arrangements with a tour troup and a carrier for exclusive use of its services.

confirmation   Acknowledgement, written or oral, that a hotel, carrier, restaurant, or other travel entity has received and approved a reservation.

consulate   The headquarters of a government official, a consul, charged with representing fellow citizens abroad.

costing   The process of analyzing the varied elements of a tour in terms of cost, in order to arrive at a tour price.

courier   May be used interchangeably to denote tour manager, but could also be a European guide or escort who accompanies the tour manager.

CTC   Certified Travel Counselor, an individual who, because of experience and successful passage of an examination, is entitled to certification.

customized itinerary   An itinerary specifically designed for an individual or small group.

customs   Procedure for checking individuals and baggage entering a country, with the possible assessment of tax or duty involved. This term could also refer to the cultural behavior of a people which should be understood by the traveler.

deregulation   Refers to the Airline Deregulation Act of 1978 which ended Civil Aeronautics Board regulating authority and opened up airline relationships with nontravel agents—among other things.

dummy   A page-by-page layout for a printed piece like a brochure, newsletter, magazine, or book.

entry fees   Charges assessed for admission to certain sites and attractions.

escort   Another term sometimes interchanged with tour manager, signifying the duties of accompanying a tour group and handling the travel details.

Eurailpass   A railroad ticket for specified lengths of time providing unlimited travel throughout fourteen countries of Western Europe.

evaluation cards   These may be cards used on familiarization tours to rate hotels, restaurants, attractions, and carriers; may also be cards used by tour members to critique a particular tour.

FAA   Federal Aviation Administration, part of the Department of Transportation, with responsibilities that include airports, pilots, routes, and equipment.

FAM trip   Free or reduced fare tours offered to travel agents and travel writers to familiarize them with carriers, accommodations, travel areas, and other tour amenities.

FIT Foreign Independent Tour, a travel itinerary arranged for and paid for in advance by an individual.

frequent flyer A program to promote travel by allowing airline passengers to earn trips or reduced rates on travel services for the miles they fly with participating airlines. Coach tours may also promote "frequent rider" packages.

GIT Group Inclusive Tour, a prepaid tour package requiring the tour members travel together in order to earn the group price.

head count The process of keeping track of tour members, counting them every time you change locations.

health card A card listing shots and other health information required when traveling to and from certain locales.

hotel ratings Various guidebooks, indexes, and individuals rate hotels according to both objective and subjective evidence, awarding letters, stars, or other designations to symbolize their assessments.

IAMAT International Association for Medical Assistance to Travelers, a non-profit association that studies health conditions worldwide and publishes information on its findings to members.

IATM International Association of Tour Managers, a professional organization for this job category.

ICTA Institute of Certified Travel Agents, the organization that oversees the testing for certification of travel agents.

incentive tour A trip organized to reward employee performance, especially in the sales area.

IT number Code number assigned to a qualifying tour by the International Air Transport Association, allowing the sponsoring travel agency to earn an additional commission on the air.

itinerary A day-by-day schedule of travel plans and arrangements on a specific tour.

jet lag A popular term for the sense of disorientation that accompanies east/west (and vice versa) travel through a number of time zones.

land costs The cost of the land portion of a tour, exclusive of en route transportation charges.

leisure travel Vacation travel, as distinct from business travel.

local guide A person, typically in large cities, who conducts tour members through the locale's attractions.

luggage insurance   A policy protecting travelers against financial loss when baggage is lost or stolen.

media   A collective name for the various channels of communication, principally print, broadcast, outdoor, and direct mail.

motorcoach   Bus designed for tour groups, with added facilities and additional comfort features.

National Tour Association (NTA)   An organization composed of tour operators and tour suppliers.

net rate   Wholesale rate for varied travel services and accommodations that may then be marked up by the travel agency (or tour operator) for resale to the tour member or traveler.

news release   A form of communication to the media generated by those seeking publicity.

off-season rates   Reduced costs of travel services and accommodations during periods when travel to these locales is normally lightest; varies from place to place; the "high" season is the opposite.

optional tour   An additional side trip which may be elected by the traveler in addition to the regular tour package. This would not be covered in the overall tour price.

overbooking   The practice of booking more space or rooms than you can accommodate in order to protect against those individuals who do not show up.

override   Extra commission paid by carriers, hotels, and other suppliers as an incentive to people like travel agents to sell this particular firm's service.

page proofs   As a final step before a long printed piece—like a book—is readied for publication, the publisher/printer prepares and circulates unbound printed sheets in the size they will later appear as part of the completed work. These are proofed for any errors.

paper stock   Sheets of varying weight, color, and texture which may be imprinted.

passport   Official identifying document used for travel abroad and return.

porterage   Baggage handling service, or the cost of such service.

print advertising   Advertising that relies on the printed word, as distinct from advertising that is broadcast. Newspapers, magazines, and direct mail are prime examples.

publicity   Promotional material that possesses news value and is distributed to the media.

room list   A sheet maintained by the tour manager (and hotel) listing tour members and their assigned rooms.

seat rotation   The technique of having coach passengers move routinely from time to time to allow others a choice of seats.

shell   A partially imprinted brochure which can be used by a travel agency or tour operator to add printed information in the marketing of a trip.

telemarketing   Primarily, the use of the telephone to solicit sales; but television and other telecommunication devices may also be used, and direct sales may not always be the object.

Tourism Bureau   An office at the national, regional, statewide, or local level staffed by individuals whose job is to promote tourism in that area.

tour manager   Although the duties may vary from situation to situation, this person is usually defined as the one with overall responsibility for the conduct of a tour.

tour operator   A firm that packages tours and then markets them to others, such as travel agents.

tour package   All of the services a tour member purchases when paying for a tour. Typically, this includes accommodations, some meals, sightseeing, some entertainment, porterage, an escort, and other items. Air may or may not be included.

trade journal   A publication directed to a readership composed of persons in a certain profession or occupation.

travel agent   A person or firm that markets travel services to the public.

travel rights   The legal rights possessed by travelers. Tour managers should be familiar with these.

up-market tours   Tours directed to a more affluent target audience and featuring things like more luxurious accommodations.

USTTA   Established in 1981, the United States Travel and Tourism Administration has overall responsibility for the promotion of tourism in this country.

VAT   Value Added Tax, a government-imposed tax based on the value added at each stage of the production and marketing of a product or service.

videocassette   A self-contained tape which may be played through a television set, using a Video Cassette Recorder. Widely used for travel programs.

visa   An authorization added to the passport of a person entering certain foreign countries; may contain restrictions as to length of stay or other travel limitations. Also the name of a credit card.

voucher   A coupon or other document supplied travelers by tour operators to exchange for things like prepaid accommodations or meals.

wholesaler   Tour operator who packages the elements of a tour and then sells this package to someone like a travel agent for ultimate sale to a consumer traveler.

INDEX